Not What My Hands
Have Done

Not what my hands have done can save my guilty soul.
Not what my toiling flesh has borne can make my spirit whole.
Not what I feel or do can give me peace with God.
Not all my prayers and sighs and tears can bear my awful load.

Thy work alone, O Christ, can ease this weight of sin.
Thy blood alone, O Lamb of God, can give me peace within.
Thy love to me, O God, not mine, O Lord, to Thee
Can rid me of this dark unrest and set my spirit free.

Thy grace alone, O God, to me can pardon speak.
Thy power alone, O Son of God, can this sore bondage break.
No other work, save thine, no other blood will do.
No strength save that which is divine can bear me safely through.

I bless the Christ of God; I rest on love divine.
And with unfaltering lip and heart, I call this Savior mine.
His cross dispels each doubt; I bury in his tomb
Each thought of unbelief and fear, each lingering shade of gloom.

I praise the God of grace; I trust his truth and might.
He calls me his; I call him mine, My God, my joy, my light.
'Tis he who saveth me, and freely pardon gives;
I love because he loveth me; I live because he lives.

– Horatius Bonar (1808-1889)

Not What My Hands Have Done

Horatius Bonar *&*
Charles Hodge

The Trinity Foundation

Contents

The Everlasting Righteousness

Horatius Bonar

Foreword

I T HAS been nearly 2,000 years since the Apostle Paul wrote his letters explaining the Gospel of justification by faith alone to the saints in Asia and Europe, and the light of the Gospel shone brilliantly in the spiritual, intellectual, and moral darkness of ancient Rome. But Antichrist, already at work in the first century, soon sat in the temple of God, expelling and persecuting the saints and suppressing the Gospel of Christ for a millennium. His dominion ended when God raised another witness to his truth in the sixteenth century.

It has been nearly 500 years since Martin Luther recovered the Gospel in Europe. Once again, in the sixteenth century, the light of justification by faith alone dispelled the spiritual, intellectual, and moral darkness of medieval Rome. The resulting civilization owed its salient features to the Gospel of Jesus Christ – to the first Christians and the Reformers – but for the past century the proclamation of that Gospel – and civilization – has been waning.

Now, nearly every day brings news of some new Roman resurgence; Antichrist is again in the ascendancy. Churches, once heirs of the Reformation, reach détente with Rome. The Roman Church-State, ruled by the most absolute monarch on Earth – a monarch who claims to speak for God himself – maintains diplomatic relations with most nations on the planet. Protestants have forgotten what their forefathers protested and the truths for which they were murdered by Rome.

Protestants have forgotten what their forefathers protested and the truths for which they were murdered by Rome. Charismatics and evangelicals eagerly embrace the theology of Rome. The Roman religion is on the march again.

9

Charismatics and evangelicals eagerly embrace the theology of Rome. The Roman religion is on the march again.

How has this happened? How did the heirs of the Reformation lose the Gospel?

Deception is the chief work of the devil, for we are told that he is a liar and the father of lies. Christ said that the devil appears as an angel of light, as a good shepherd and protector of the sheep. The puerile portrayals of the devil on television and in the movies lead many to suppose that he is easily recognizable, but they have been easily fooled. Millions have been deceived by his false gospels, all of which replace the Gospel – the life, death, and everlasting righteousness of Jesus Christ – with something else. Those false gospels are usually not irreligious – atheism has its place in the devil's arsenal, but religion is far more useful. The road to Hell is paved with religious beliefs and observances.

False gospels are usually not irreligious – atheism has its place in the devil's arsenal, but religion is far more useful. The road to Hell is paved with religious beliefs and observances.

The common core of the false gospels of this age is a focus on self, not Christ. Long before psychology became fashionable in the churches, they taught self-absorption. Anthropology replaced theology more than a century ago. Instead of proclaiming the Gospel – the good news of what Christ did for his people 2,000 years ago – they proclaimed the false gospel of what God can do for you now. Rome, of course, has taught this false gospel for centuries, saying that what makes a man acceptable to God is God's grace in his heart. That grace is received through the sacraments of the Church, especially baptism and mass, and there is no salvation outside the Roman Church.

But grace is not something infused – like pie filling – into human hearts. It is an attribute of God, not of man – God's unmerited favor toward his people. What makes a man acceptable to God is not God's grace in his heart, but the perfect life and obedient and substitutionary death of Jesus Christ, who fulfilled the law of God perfectly on behalf of his people. This false gospel – that we are saved by something in us, something of allegedly divine origin – replaced the true Gospel – that we are saved only by the perfect life and death of Christ – centuries ago in the Roman Church, and it is now widely accepted in most other churches. Sometimes the false gospel takes the form of the gospel of the new birth – as though being born again makes one acceptable to God – or the baptism of the Spirit, or our own good works, which give evidence of the grace of God in our hearts. Sometimes the false gospel takes the form of preaching that says that belief of the Gospel is not enough, that we must "surrender," that we must "trust," that we must "make Jesus Lord of our life," that we must "put Jesus on the throne of our life."

But the Gospel declares that we are not justified by any psychological exercises, by any infused goodness, by any feelings, intentions, or works, but simply by believing the account of Christ's life and death in the Bible. We are saved by assenting to the truth of the everlasting righteousness of Christ and our own hopeless sinfulness.

Before Martin Luther recovered the Gospel of justification by faith alone, he was the most religious of monks. He performed all that was required of him – prayers, fastings, masses, flagellations and more, for he was seeking evidence of the grace of God in his heart; he was surrendering totally to God. Yet Luther despaired because he saw that all his righteousnesses were as filthy rags before God. Then the light of the Gospel dawned on him, and he realized that he could not be saved by his own good feelings and good intentions, even if those good feelings and good intentions came from God, but only by an alien righteousness – the righteousness of God himself. False gospels cause men to look inside themselves, if not at their own strengths, then for evidence of what God is doing in their lives. The true Gospel is about what Jesus Christ did 2,000 years ago. It focuses our minds on him and his righteousness, not on ourselves.

Because false gospels cause men to look inward rather than outward to Christ, they have taken many different forms: the false gospel of the new birth, the false gospel of the changed life, the false gospel of self-esteem, the false gospel of full surrender, the false gospel of Spirit baptism, the false gospel of grace in the heart, the false gospel of an integrated personality, the false gospel of good works, the false gospel

The Gospel declares that we are not justified by any psychological exercises, by any infused goodness, by any feelings, intentions, or works, but simply by believing the account of Christ's life and death in the Bible.

of good intentions, the false gospel of positive thinking, the false gospel of speaking in tongues, the false gospel of letting Jesus into your heart, the false gospel of a personal relationship (or encounter or experience) with Jesus, the false gospel of following Jesus as a moral example, the false gospel of prosperity and fulfillment, the false gospel of covenantal faithfulness. The variety of subjective gospels is endless, but there is only one true Gospel, the everlasting righteousness of Christ.

John W. Robbins
September 2005

The variety of subjective gospels is endless, but there is only one true Gospel, the everlasting righteousness of Christ.

Preface

THE awakened conscience of the sixteenth century fled to "the righteousness of God."

There it found refuge, at once from condemnation and from impurity.

Only by "righteousness" could it be pacified, and nothing less than that which is divine could meet the case.

At the cross this "righteousness" was found, human, yet divine, provided for man and presented to him by God for relief of conscience and justification of life. On the one word τετέλεσται, "It is finished," as on a heavenly resting place, weary souls sat down and were refreshed. The voice from the tree did not summon them to *do*, but to be satisfied with what was *done*. Millions of bruised consciences there found healing and peace.

Belief in that finished work brought the sinner into favor with God, and it did not leave him in uncertainty as to this. The justifying work of Calvary was God's way, not only of bringing pardon, but of securing certainty. It was the only perfect thing which had ever been presented to God in man's behalf; and so extraordinary was this perfection that it might be used by man in his transactions with God as if it were his own.

The knowledge of this sure justification was life from the dead to multitudes. All over Europe, from the Apennines to the Grampians, from the Pyrenees to the Carpathians, went the glad tidings that man is justified freely, and that God wishes him to know that he is justified. It was not merely

The justifying work of Calvary was God's way, not only of bringing pardon, but of securing certainty.

13

a new thought for man's intellect, but a new discovery for his soul (1) as to the true source of spiritual health, namely, the setting of a man's *conscience* right with God; and (2) as to the continuation of that health, namely, the keeping of the *conscience* right.

The fruit of this was not merely a healthy personal religion, but a renovated intellect and a noble literature, and, above all, a pure worship. It was an era of resurrection. The graves were opened, and the congregation of the dead became the church of the living. Christendom awoke and arose. The resurrection dew fell far and wide, and it has not yet ceased to fall.

For ages, Christianity had grovelled in the dust, smothered with semi-pagan rites, ready to die – if not already dead – bound hand and foot by a semi-idolatrous priesthood; unable to do aught for a world which it had been sent to regenerate. Now, "it was lifted up from the earth, and made to stand upon its feet as a man, and a man's heart was given to it."

The doctrine of another's righteousness reckoned to us for justification before God is one of the links that knit together the first and the sixteenth centuries, the Apostles and the Reformers.

A new *conscience* was born, and with a new conscience came new life and power. Nothing had been seen like this since the age of the Apostles.

The doctrine of another's righteousness reckoned to us for justification before God is one of the links that knit together the first and the sixteenth centuries, the Apostles and the Reformers. The creeds of the Reformation overleap fifteen centuries and land us at once in the *Epistle to the Romans*. Judicial and moral cleansing was what man needed. In that epistle we have both the imputed and imparted righteousness – not the one without the other; both together, and inseparable, but each in its own order, the former the root or foundation of the latter.

It was not Martin Luther merely who took up the old watchword, "The just shall live by faith," and thus found the answer of a good conscience toward God. To thousands of hearts it came like a voice from Heaven, they knew not how. Sunshine from above had fallen upon one grand text, the text which the age needed. Men recognized the truth thus supernaturally lighted up. "The nations came to its light, and kings to the brightness of its rising." The inquiring men of that age, though not borrowing from each other, fled to this truth and text. From every kingdom of Europe came the same voice, and every Protestant Confession bore witness to the unanimity of awakened Christendom. The long-needed, long-missing truth had been found; and ευρηκα [Eureka!] was the cry of gladness announcing the discovery.

Our fathers saw that this truth was the basis of all real spiritual life. That which was superficial, and morbid, and puny, and second-rate, might do with some less deep, less broad foundation; but all that is healthy and noble and daring and happy and successful in religion must rest here: "The just shall live by faith."

Religion is fashionable in our age. But is it that which sprang up, after centuries of darkness, among our fathers in Europe? Is it that of the apostles and prophets? Is it the calm yet thorough religion which did such great deeds in other days? Has it gone deep into the conscience? Has it filled the heart? Has it pervaded the man? Or has it left the conscience unpacified, the heart unfilled, the man unchanged, save with some external appliances of religiousness which leave him *hollow* as before? There is at this moment many an aching spirit, bitterly conscious of this hollowness. Merely understanding the doctrine, the profession, the good report of others, the bustle of work will not fill the soul. God himself must be there with his covering righteousness, his cleansing blood, his quickening Spirit. Without this, religion is but a shell; holy services are dull and irksome. Joy in God, which is the soul and essence of worship, is unknown. Sacraments, prayer meetings, religious services, labors of charity and will not make up for the living God.

How much of *unreality* there may be in the religious life of our age, it is for each individual to determine for himself that he may not be deceived nor lose his reward. All unreality is weakness as well as irksomeness; the sooner that we are stripped of unreality the better, both for peace and for usefulness.

Men with their feet firmly set on Luther's rock, "the

From every kingdom of Europe came the same voice, and every Protestant Confession bore witness to the unanimity of awakened Christendom.

righteousness of God," filled with the Spirit, and pervaded with the peace of God do the great things in the church; others do the little.

The men of robust spiritual health are they who, like Luther, have made sure of their filial relationship to God. They shrink from no battle nor succumb to any toil. The men who go to work with an unascertained relationship give way in the warfare and faint under the labor: Their life is not perhaps a failure or defeat, but it is not a victory; it is not a triumph.

"We do not war after the flesh" (2 *Corinthians* 10:3), and "our weapons are not carnal" (2 *Corinthians* 10:4). Our battle is not fought in the way that the old man would have us to fight it. It is "the fight of *faith*" (1 *Timothy* 6:12). It is not by doubting but by believing that we are saved; it is not by doubting but by believing that we overcome. Faith leads us first of all to Abel's "more excellent sacrifice" (*Hebrews* 11:4). By faith we quit Ur and Egypt and Babylon, setting our face to the eternal city (*Hebrews* 11:16). By faith we offer up our Isaacs, and worship "leaning on the top of our staff," and "give commandment concerning our bones." By faith we choose affliction with the people of God and despise Egypt's treasures. By faith we keep our Passover, pass through the Red Sea, overthrow Jerichos, subdue kingdoms, work righteousness, stop the mouths of lions, quench the violence of fire, turn to flight the armies of the aliens, and refuse deliverance in the day of trial, that we may obtain a better resurrection (*Hebrews* 11:35).

It is "believing" from first to last. We begin, we go on, we end in faith. The faith that justifies is the faith that overcomes (1*John* 5:4). By faith we obtain the "good report" both with God and man. By faith we receive forgiveness; by faith we live; by faith we work, and endure, and suffer; by faith we win the crown – a crown of righteousness which shall be ours in the day of the appearing of him who is *our righteousness*.

The Grange, Edinburgh
November 1872

Men with their feet firmly set on Luther's rock, "the righteousness of God," filled with the Spirit, and pervaded with the peace of God do the great things in the church.

It is "believing" from first to last. We begin, we go on, we end in faith. The faith that justifies is the faith that overcomes (1 John 5:4).

How Shall Man Be Just with God?

1

God's Answer to Man's Question

How may I, a sinner, draw near to him in whom there is no sin, and look upon his face in peace?

This is the great question which, at some time or other, every one of us has asked. This is one of the awful problems that man in all ages has been attempting to solve. There is no evading it; he must face it.

That man's answers to this question should have been altogether wide of the mark is only what might have been expected. He does not really understand the import of the question that he, with much earnestness perhaps, is putting, nor discern the malignant character of that evil that he yet feels to be a barrier between him and God.

That man's many elaborate solutions to the problem that has perplexed the race since evil entered should have been unsatisfactory is not surprising, seeing his ideas of human guilt are so superficial, his thoughts of himself so high, his views of God so low.

But that, when God has interposed as an interpreter to answer the question and to solve the problem, man should be so slow to accept the divine solution as given in the Word of God, betrays an amount of unteachableness and self-will that is difficult to comprehend. The preference which man has always shown for his own theories upon this point is unaccountable, save upon the supposition that he has but a poor discernment of the evil forces with which he professes

How may I, a sinner, draw near to him in whom there is no sin, and look upon his face in peace?

to battle; a faint knowledge of the spiritual havoc which has been wrought in himself; a very vague perception of what law and righteousness are; a sorrowful ignorance of that Divine Being with whom, as lawgiver and judge, he knows that he has to do; and a low appreciation of eternal holiness and truth.

Man has always treated sin as a misfortune, not a crime; as disease, not as guilt; as a case for the physician, not for the judge. Herein lies the essential faultiness of all mere human religions or theologies. They fail to acknowledge the judicial aspect of the question as that on which the answer must hinge and to recognize the guilt or criminality of the evil-doer as that which must first be dealt with before any other answer, or approximation to an answer, can be given.

God is a Father, but he is no less a Judge. Shall the Judge give way to the Father, or the Father give way to the Judge?

God loves the sinner, but he hates the sin. Shall he sink his love to the sinner in his hatred of the sin, or his hatred of the sin in his love to the sinner?

God has sworn that he has no pleasure in the death of the sinner (*Ezekiel* 18:23-32); yet, he has also sworn that the soul that sins, it shall die (*Ezekiel* 18:4). Which of the two oaths shall be kept? Shall the one give way to the other? Can both be kept inviolate? Can a contradiction, apparently so directly be reconciled? Which is the more unchangeable and irreversible, the vow of pity or the oath of justice?

Law and love must be *reconciled*, else the great question as to a sinner's relationship to the Holy One must remain unanswered. The one cannot give way to the other. Both must stand, else the pillars of the universe will be shaken.

The reconciliation man has often tried, for he has always had a glimpse of the difficulty. But he has failed, for his endeavors have always been in the direction of making law succumb to love.

The reconciliation God has accomplished, and, in the accomplishment, both law and love have triumphed. The one has not given way to the other. Each has kept its ground. Each has come from the conflict honored and glorified. Never has

Man has always treated sin as a misfortune, not a crime; as disease, not as guilt; as a case for the physician, not for the judge. Herein lies the essential faultiness of all mere human religions or theologies. They fail to acknowledge the judicial aspect of the question as that on which the answer must hinge.

there been love like this love of God – so large, so lofty, so intense, so self-sacrificing. Never has law been seen so pure, so broad, so glorious, so inexorable.

There has been no compromise. Law and love have both had their full scope. Not one jot or tittle has been surrendered by either. They have both been satisfied to the full – the one in all its severity, the other in all its tenderness. Love has never been more truly love, and law has never been more truly law, than in this conjunction of the two. It has been reconciliation without compromise. God's honor has been maintained, yet man's interests have not been sacrificed.

God has done it all, and he has done it effectually and irreversibly.

Man could not have done it, even though he might have devised it. But truly he could do neither. God only could have devised and done it.

He has done it by moving the whole case into his own courts of law that it might be settled there on a righteous basis. Man could not have gone into court with the case save in the certainty that he would lose it. God comes into court, bringing man and man's whole case along with him, that upon righteous principles and in a legal way the case may be settled, at once in favor of man and in favor of God. It is this *judicial* settlement of the case that is God's one and final answer to man's long unanswered question, "How shall man be just with God?" "Wherewith shall I come before the Lord, and bow myself before the high God?" (*Micah* 6:6).

God provides the basis of the reconciliation – a basis which demonstrates that there is no compromise between law and love, but the full expression of both; a basis which establishes both the authority and the paternity of Jehovah, as Lawgiver and Father; a basis which reveals in infinite awfulness the exceeding sinfulness of sin, the spotless purity of the statute, and the unbending character of God's governmental ordinances; a basis which yet secures, in and by law, the righteous overflow of his boundless love to the lost sons of Adam.

This basis of reconciliation between law and love God has himself not only provided, but brought into his own

It is this judicial settlement of the case that is God's one and final answer to man's long unanswered question, "How shall man be just with God?"

courts of law, proposing to the sinner that all the questions between himself and the sinner should be settled on this basis – so equitable, so friendly, so secure; and settled in judicial form, by a legal process, in which verdict is given in favor of the accused and he is clean absolved – "justified from all things."

The consent of parties to the acceptance of this basis is required in court. The law consents; the Lawgiver consents; Father, Son, and Spirit consent; and man, the chief party interested, is asked for his consent. If he consents, the whole matter is settled. The verdict is issued in his favor, and henceforth he can triumph and say, "It is God that justifies; who is he that condemns?"

Sin is too great an evil for man to meddle with. Man's attempts to remove it do but increase it, and his endeavors to approach God in spite of it aggravate his guilt.

Sin is too great an evil for man to meddle with. His attempts to remove it do but increase it, and his endeavors to approach God in spite of it aggravate his guilt. Only God can deal with sin, either as a disease or as a crime; as a dishonor to himself, or as a hinderer of man's approach to himself. He deals with it not in some arbitrary or summary way, by a mere exercise of will or power, but by bringing it for adjudication into his own courts of law. As judge, seated in his tribunal, he settles the case, and settles it in favor of the sinner – of any sinner on Earth who will consent to the basis which he proposes. Into this court each one may freely come, on the footing of a sinner needing the settlement of the great question between him and God. That settlement is no matter of uncertainty or difficulty; it will at once be granted to each applicant. The guilty man with his case, however bad, thus legally settled, retires from court with his burden removed and his fears dispelled. He is assured that he can never again be summoned to answer for his guilt. It is righteousness that has reconciled God to him, and him to God.

As sin is too great an evil for any but God to deal with, so is righteousness too high for man to reach, too high for any but God to bring down and place at our disposal. God has brought down, and brought nigh, the righteousness. Thus the guilt which we have contracted is met by the righteousness which God has provided. The exclusion from the divine fellowship, which the guilt produced, is more than reversed by the new introduction which the righteousness places at our disposal.

May I then draw near to God and not die? May I draw near and live? May I come to him who hates sin, and yet find that the sin which he hates is no barrier to my coming, no reason for my being shut out from his presence as an unclean thing? May I renew my lost fellowship with him who made me, and made me for himself. May I worship in his holy place with safety to myself and without dishonor to him?

These are the questions with which God has dealt – and dealt with so as to ensure a blessed answer to them all – an answer which will satisfy our own troubled consciences as well as the holy law of God. His answer is final, and it is effectual. He will give no other, nor will he deal with these questions in any other way than he has done. He has introduced them into his courts of law that there they may be finally settled, and out of these courts into which God has taken them, who can withdraw them? Or what end would be served by such a withdrawal on our part? Would it make the settlement more easy, more pleasant, more sure? It would not. It would augment the uncertainty and make the perplexity absolutely hopeless.

Yet the tendency of modern thought and modern theology is to refuse the *judicial* settlement of these questions and to withdraw them from the courts into which God has introduced them. An extra-judicial adjustment is attempted, man declining to admit such a guilt as would bring him within the grasp of law and refusing to acknowledge sin to be of such a nature as to require a criminal process in solemn court, yet admitting the necessity or desirableness of the removal of the sore evil under which humanity is felt to be laboring and under which, if unremoved, it must ere long dissolve.

The history of six thousand years of evil has been lost on man. He refuses to read its awful lesson regarding sin and God's displeasure against the sinner, which that history records. The flood of evil that has issued forth from one single sin he has forgotten. The death, the darkness, the sorrow, the sickness, the tears, the weariness, the madness, the confusion,

The history of six thousand years of evil has been lost on man. He refuses to read its awful lesson regarding sin and God's displeasure against the sinner, which that history records.

the bloodshed, the furious hatred between man and man, making Earth a suburb of Hell – all this is overlooked or misread. Man repels the thought that sin is crime which God hates with an infinite hate and which he, in his righteousness, must condemn and avenge.

If sin is such a surface thing, such a trifle as men deem it, what is the significance of this long sad story? Do Earth's ten thousand graveyards, where human love lies buried, tell no darker tale? Do the millions upon millions of broken hearts and heavy eyes say that sin is but a trifle? Do the moaning of the hospital or the carnage of the battlefield, the blood-stained sword, and the death-dealing artillery proclaim that sin is a mere casualty and the human heart the seat of goodness after all? Do the earthquake, the volcano, the hurricane, the tempest speak nothing of sin's desperate evil? Do not man's aching head, and empty heart, and burdened spirit, and shaded brow, and weary brain, and tottering limbs utter in a voice articulate beyond mistake – that sin is *guilt*? And do they not utter that guilt must be punished – punished by the Judge of all – not as a mere "violation of natural laws," but as a breach of the eternal law, which admits of no reversal: "The soul that sins, it shall die?" For without law, sin is nothing. "The strength of sin is the law" (*1 Corinthians* 15:56), and he who makes light of sin must defend moral confusion and injustice. He who refuses to recognize sin as *guilt* must dissolve the law of the universe or ascribe imbecility and injustice to the Judge of all.

The world has grown old in sin. It has now more than ever begun to trifle with it, either as a necessity which cannot be cured, or a partial aberration from good order which will rectify itself ere long. It is this tampering with evil, this refusal to see sin as God sees it, as the law declares it, and as the story of our race has revealed it, that has in all ages been the root of error and of wide departure from the faith once delivered to the saints. Admit the evil of sin with all its eternal consequences, and you are shut up to a divine way of dealing with it. Deny the evil of sin and the future results of that evil, and you may deny the whole revelation of God, set aside the cross, and abrogate the law.

Do the moaning of the hospital or the carnage of the battlefield, the blood-stained sword, and the death-dealing artillery proclaim that sin is a mere casualty and the human heart the seat of goodness after all?

"By the law is the knowledge of sin." Therefore the connection between sin and law must be maintained both in condemnation and in pardon. God's interposition in behalf of man must be a confirmation (not a relaxation) of law: For law cannot change, even as God cannot change nor deny himself.

Favor to the sinner must be also favor to the law. Favor to the sinner that would simply establish law or leave its sanctities untouched would be much. But favor to him that would deepen its foundations and render it more venerable, more awful than before, is unspeakably higher and surer. Even so has it been. Law has not suffered at the hands of love, nor love been cramped and frozen by law. Both have had full scope, fuller scope than if man had never fallen.

I know that love is not law, and that law is not love. In law, properly, no love inheres. It is like the balance which knows not whether it be gold or iron that is laid upon it. Yet in that combination of the judicial and the paternal, which God's way of salvation exhibits, law has become the source and vehicle of love, and love law's upholder and honorer, so that even in this sense and aspect, "love is the fulfilling of the law."[1]

The law that was against the sinner has come to be upon the sinner's side. It is now ready to take his part in the great controversy between him and God, provided he will conduct his case on the new principles which God has introduced for the settlement of all variances between himself and the sinner; or rather, provided he will put that case into the hands of the Divine Advocate, who alone knows how to conduct it aright and to bring it to a successful issue – who is both "propitiation" and "Advocate" – "the propitiation for our sins" (1 John 2:2), "the Advocate with the Father, Jesus Christ the righteous" (1 John 2:1).

In that combination of the judicial and the paternal, which God's way of salvation exhibits, law has become the source and vehicle of love, and love law's upholder and honorer, so that even in this sense and aspect, "love is the fulfilling of the law."

1. "Of law there can be no less acknowledged than that her seat is the bosom of God, her voice the harmony of the world; all things in Heaven do her homage, the very least as feeling her care, and the greatest as not exempted from her power; both angels and men, and creatures of what condition soever, though each in different sort and manner, yet all, with uniform consent, admiring her as the mother of their peace and joy." — Richard Hooker, *The Laws of Ecclesiastical Polity*, Book I, section 16.

2

God's Recognition of Substitution

The mere bringing the question into the courts of law would have availed nothing had there not been provision made for so ordering their processes and judgments that the sinner might be righteously acquitted.

THE mere bringing the question into the courts of law would have availed nothing had there not been provision made for so ordering their processes and judgments that the sinner might be righteously acquitted; that God might be "just and the justifier" (*Romans* 3:26), "a just God and a Savior" (*Isaiah* 45:21); that law might be brought to bear upon the sinner's side: his absolver and not his condemner.

This provision has been made by means of *substitution*, transference of the penalty from him who had incurred it to one who had not.

In human courts no such provision can be allowed, save in regard to the payment of debt. In that case, there is no difficulty as to the exchange of person and of property. If the creditor receives his money from a third party, he is satisfied, and the law is satisfied, though the debtor himself has not paid one farthing. To a certain extent, this is substitution. The idea of such a thing, therefore, is not unknown in common life and the principle of it not unacknowledged by human law.

But beyond this the law of man does not go. Substitution in any wider aspect is something about which man has never attempted to legislate. Stripe for stripe is *human* law; "by *his* stripes *we* are healed" is *superhuman*, the result of a legislation as gracious as it is divine.

Substitution is not for man to deal with: Its principle he but imperfectly understands; its details he cannot reach. They are far too intricate, too far-reaching, and too mysterious for him to grasp, or, having grasped, to found any system of legislation upon them. In this, even though willing, he must ever be helpless.

But God has affirmed *substitution* as the principle on which he means to deal with fallen man. The arrangements of his holy tribunal, his righteous governmental processes, are such as to bring this effectually and continually into play. It is through substitution that his righteous government displays its perfection in all its transactions with the sinner.

God has introduced the principle of substitution into his courts. There he sits as judge, "just and justifying," acting on the principle of transference or representation; maintaining law, and yet manifesting grace; declaring that "all have sinned and come short of the glory of God" (*Romans* 3:23); that "by the deeds of the law shall no flesh be justified in his sight, for by the law is the knowledge of sin" (*Romans* 3:20); yet presenting a divine Surety, "as a propitiation through faith in his blood, to declare his righteousness for the remission of sins that are past" (*Romans* 3:25).

Salvation by substitution was embodied in the first promise regarding the woman's seed and his bruised heel. Victory over our great enemy, by his subjecting himself to the bruising of that enemy, is then and there proclaimed. The clothing of our first parents with that which had passed through death, in preference to the fig-leaves which had not so done, showed the element of substitution as that on which God had begun to act in his treatment of fallen man. Abel's sacrifice revealed the same truth, especially as contrasted with Cain's. For that which made Abel's acceptable, and himself accepted, was the death of the victim as substituted for his own; that which rendered Cain's hateful, and himself rejected, was the absence of that death and blood. The slain firstling was accepted by God as, symbolically, Abel's substitute, laid on the altar till he should come; the "woman's seed," "made of a woman, made under the law, to redeem them that were under the law, that we might receive the adoption of sons" (*Galatians* 4:4-5).

From the beginning, God recognized this principle in

Salvation by substitution was embodied in the first promise regarding the woman's seed and his bruised heel.

his dealings with man: the just dying for the unjust and the blessed one becoming a curse that the cursed might be blessed. In all subsequent sacrifices it was the same. Noah's burnt offering was like Abel's, and Abraham's resembled Noah's. Transference of guilt from one who could not bear the penalty without being eternally lost, to one who could bear it and yet come forth from under it free and glorious – this was the deep truth into which God educated the patriarchs as that which lay at the foundation of his procedure with the sinner. The consumption of Abraham's sacrifice by the divine fire told him that the divine displeasure which should have rested on him forever had fallen upon a substitute and been exhausted so that there remained no more wrath, no darkness, "no condemnation" for him; nothing but deliverance and favor and everlasting blessedness.

But it was the arrangements of the tabernacle that brought out most fully this great principle of God's actings to the children of Adam.

In the Passover blood, the idea was chiefly that of *protection from peril.* The lamb stood sentinel at the door of each family; the blood was their "shield and buckler." There might be trembling hearts within, wondering perhaps how a little blood could be so efficacious and make their dwelling so impregnable; disquieted, too, because they could not see the blood, but were obliged to be content with knowing that God saw it (*Exodus* 12:13). Yet no amount of fearfulness could alter the potency of that sprinkled blood, and no weakness of faith could make that God-given shield less efficacious against "the enemy and the avenger." The blood – the symbol of substitution – was on the lintel, and that was enough. They did not see it nor feel it, but *they knew that it was there*; and that sufficed. God saw it, and that was better than their seeing it. They were safe, and they knew that they were so. They could feast upon the lamb in peace, and eat their bitter herbs with thankful joy. They could sing by anticipation the church's song, "If God be for us, who can be against us?"

But still it was not in Egypt, but in the wilderness; not in their paschal chamber, but in the sanctuary of their God

The blood – the symbol of substitution – was on the lintel, and that was enough. They did not see it nor feel it, but they knew that it was there; and that sufficed. God saw it, and that was better than their seeing it.

that they were to learn the full and varied truth of pardon, cleansing, acceptance, and blessing through a substitute.

The old burnt offering of the patriarchs, on the footing of which these fathers had in ages past drawn near to God, was split into many parts. In the details of these we see the fulness and variety of the substitution.

The various sacrifices are all connected with the altar. Even that which was "burnt without the camp" was connected with the altar. It was no doubt carried forth without the camp and burnt with fire (*Leviticus* 6:30, 16:27); but "the blood was brought into the tabernacle of the congregation, to reconcile withal in the holy place." "The blood of the bullock was brought in, to make atonement in the holy place." Their connection with the altar is sufficient of itself to show the truth of substitution contained in them, for the altar was the place of transference. But in each of them we find something which expresses this more directly and fully.

In the *burnt offering* we see the perfection of the substitute presented in the place of our imperfection, in not loving God with all our heart.

In the *meat offering* we have the perfection of the substitute, as that on which, when laid upon the altar, God feeds, and on which he invites us to feed.

In the *peace offering* we find the perfection of the substitute laid on the same altar as an atonement, reconciling us to God; removing the distance and the enmity, and providing food for us out of that which had passed through death; for "he is our peace."

In the *sin offering* we see the perfection of the substitute whose blood is sprinkled on the altar and whose body is burnt without, as securing pardon for unconscious sins – sins of ignorance.

In the *trespass offering* there is the same perfection of the substitute in his atoning character procuring forgiveness for conscious and wilful sin.

In the *drink offering* we have the perfection of the substitute poured out on the altar as that by which God is refreshed and by which we are also refreshed. "His blood is drink indeed."

In the peace offering we find the perfection of the substitute laid on the same altar as an atonement, reconciling us to God; removing the distance and the enmity.

In the *incense* we have the "sweet savor" of the substitute going up to God in our behalf; the cloud of fragrance from his life and death with which God is well pleased, enveloping us and making us fragrant with a fragrance not our own; absorbing all in us that is displeasing or hateful and replacing it with a sweetness altogether perfect and divine.

In the *fire* we see the holy wrath of the Judge consuming the victim slain in the place of the sinner. In the *ashes* we have the proof that the wrath had spent itself, that the penalty was paid, that the work was done. "It is finished," was the voice of the ashes on the altar.

In all this we see such things as the following: (1) God's displeasure against sin; (2) that displeasure exhausted in a righteous way; (3) the substitute presented and accepted; (4) the substitute slain and consumed; (5) the transference of the wrath from the sinner to his representative; (6) God resting in his love over the sinner and viewing him in the perfection of his substitute; (7) the sinner reconciled, accepted, complete, enjoying God's favor, and feeding at his table on that on which God had fed; on that which had come from the altar and had passed through the fire.

Thus God's acceptance of this principle, in his preparation of acceptable worshipers for his sanctuary, shows the fitness and value of it as well as the divine intention that it should be available for the sinner in his drawing near to God. In this way God makes the sinner "perfect as pertaining to the conscience" (*Hebrews* 9:9), gives him "no more consciousness of sins" (*Hebrews* 10:2), and "purges his conscience from dead works to serve the living God" (*Hebrews* 9:14). For that which satisfies the holiness of God cannot but satisfy the consciousness of the sinner. God, pointing to the altar, says, "That is enough for me"; the sinner responds and says, "It is enough for me."

As in the *Epistle to the Hebrews* we have this principle of substitution applied to the sanctuary, so in that to the *Romans* we find it applied to the courts of law. In the former we see God making the sinner *perfect* as a worshiper; in the latter, *righteous* as a servant and a son. In the one it is priestly completeness; in

> *In this way God makes the sinner "perfect as pertaining to the conscience" (Hebrews 9:9), gives him "no more consciousness of sins" (Hebrews 10:2), and "purges his conscience from dead works to serve the living God" (Hebrews 9:14).*

the latter it is judicial righteousness. But in both, the principle on which God acts is the same. And as he acts on it in receiving us, so does he invite us to act in coming to him.

It is this truth that the Gospel embodies, and it is this that we preach when, as ambassadors for Christ, we pray men in Christ's stead to be reconciled to God. God's free love to the sinner is the first part of our message; God's righteous way of making that free love available for the sinner is the second. What God is and what Christ has done make up one Gospel. The belief of that Gospel is eternal life. "All that believe are justified from all things" (*Acts* 13:39).

With a weak faith and a fearful heart many a sinner stands before the altar. It is not the strength of his faith but the perfection of the sacrifice that saves; and no feebleness of faith, no dimness of eye, no trembling of hand, can change the efficacy of our burnt offering. The vigor of our faith can add nothing to it, nor can the poverty of it take anything from it. Faith, in all its degrees, still reads the inscription, "The blood of Jesus Christ his Son cleanses us from all sin." If at times the eye is so dim that it cannot read these words, through blinding tears or bewildering mist, faith rests itself on the certain knowledge of the fact that the inscription is still there, or at least that the blood itself (of which these words remind us) remains in all its power and suitableness upon the altar, unchanged and uneffaced. God says that the believing man is justified: Who are we, then, that we should say, "We believe, but we do not know whether we are justified?" What *God* has joined together, let not *man* put asunder.

The question as to the right way of believing puzzles many and engrosses all their anxiety to the exclusion of the far greater questions as to the person and work of him who is the object of their believing. Thus their thoughts run in a self-righteous direction and are occupied, not with what *Christ has done*, but with what *they* have yet *to do* to get themselves connected with his work.

What should we have said to the Israelite, who, on bringing his lamb to the tabernacle, should puzzle himself with questions as to the right mode of laying his hands on the

The question as to the right way of believing puzzles many and engrosses all their anxiety to the exclusion of the far greater questions as to the person and work of him who is the object of their believing. Thus their thoughts run in a self-righteous direction and are occupied, not with what Christ has done, but with what they have yet to do to get themselves connected with his work.

head of the victim and who should refuse to take any comfort from the sacrifice because he was not sure whether he had laid them aright – on the proper place, in the right direction, with adequate pressure, or in the best attitude? Should we not have told him that his own actings concerning the lamb were not the lamb, yet he was speaking as if they were? Should we not have told him that the lamb was everything and his touch nothing as to virtue or merit or recommendation? Should we not have told him to be of good cheer, not because he had laid his hands on the victim in the most approved fashion, but because they had touched that victim – however lightly and imperfectly – and thereby said, Let this lamb stand for me, answer for me, die for me? The touching had no virtue in itself. Therefore the excellency of the act was no question to come up at all: It simply intimated the man's desire that this sacrifice should be taken instead of himself as God's appointed way of pardon. It was simply the indication of his consent to God's way of saving him by the substitution of another. The point for him to settle was not, Was my touch right or wrong, light or heavy? but, Was it the touch of the right lamb – the lamb appointed by God for the taking away of sin?

The quality or quantity of faith is not the main question for the sinner. That which he needs to know is that Jesus died and was buried and rose again, according to the Scriptures. This knowledge is life everlasting.

> *The quality or quantity of faith is not the main question for the sinner. That which he needs to know is that Jesus died and was buried and rose again, according to the Scriptures. This knowledge is life everlasting.*

3
The Completeness of the Substitution

IN PERSON and in work, in life and in death, Christ is the sinner's substitute. His vicariousness is co-extensive with the sins and defects of those whom he represents. It covers all the different periods as well as the varied circumstances of their lives.

He entered our world as the substitute. "There was no room for him in the inn" (*Luke* 2:7) – the inn of Bethlehem, the city of David, his own city. "Though rich, for our sakes he had become poor" (*2 Corinthians* 8:9). In poverty and banishment his life began. He was not to be allowed either to be born or to die, save as an outcast man. "Without the gate" (*Hebrews* 13:12) was his position as he entered and as he left our Earth. Man would not give even a roof to shelter or a cradle to receive the helpless babe. It was as the substitute that he was the outcast from the first moment of his birth. His vicarious life began in the manger. For what can this poverty mean, this rejection by man, this outcast condition, but that his sin-bearing had begun?[1]

The name, too, that met him as he came into our world

In person and in work, in life and in death, Christ is the sinner's substitute. His vicariousness is co-extensive with the sins and defects of those whom he represents.

---

1. The *Heidelberg Catechism* (used in the Scotch Church, along with Calvin's, till superseded by the *Westminster*) asks, "What profit take you by Christ's holy conception and nativity?" and answers, "That he is our mediator, and covers my sins with his innocency and perfect holiness, in which I was conceived, that they may not come into the sight of God."

intimated the same truth: "You shall call his name *Jesus*, for he shall save his people from their sins" (*Matthew* 1:21). His name proclaimed his mission and his work to be salvation; "Jehovah the Savior" (Jesus) is that by which the infant is called. As the Savior, he comes forth from the womb; as the Savior, he lies in the manger; and if he is the Savior, he is the substitute. The name *Jesus* was not given to him merely in reference to the cross, but to his whole life below. Therefore did Mary say, "My soul magnifies the Lord, and my spirit rejoices in God my Savior" (*Luke* 1:46, 47). Therefore also did the angel say to the shepherds, "Unto you is born this day, in the city of David, a Savior, which is Christ the Lord" (*Luke* 2:11).

Why was Jesus circumcised if not as the substitute? That rite proclaimed his vicarious birth as truly as did the cross his vicarious death.

Scarcely is he born when his blood is shed. Circumcision deals with him as one guilty and needing the sign of cleansing.[2] He knew no sin, yet he is circumcised. He was not born in sin nor shapen in iniquity, but was "the holy thing" (*Luke* 1:35); yet he is circumcised as other children of Abraham, for "he took upon him the seed of Abraham" (*Hebrews* 2:16). Why was he circumcised if not as the substitute? That rite proclaimed his vicarious birth as truly as did the cross his vicarious death. "He who knew no sin was made sin for us, that we might be made the righteousness of God in him" (*2 Corinthians* 5:21). This was the beginning of that obedience in virtue of which righteousness comes to us; as it is written, "As by one man's disobedience many were made sinners, so by the obedience of one shall many be made righteous" (*Romans* 5:19). For he himself testified concerning his baptism, "Thus it becomes us

---

2. "These ceremonial observances were so many confessions of sin. Christ, then, who was made sin for us, conformed to these" (Ames, *Medulla Theologica*, Book 1, ch. 21). "Hereby [by circumcision] he was represented to the world not only as a subject, but also as a sinner. For though he was pure and holy, yet this ordinance passing upon him seemed to imply as if corruption had indeed been in him, which must be cut off by mortification.... Thus was he represented as a sinner to the world, though most holy and pure in himself" (John Flavel, *Fountain of Life*, Sermon 19). "He was circumcised, and kept the law to deliver us from the condemnation of it.... Therefore we must seek our righteousness, not in the law, but in Christ, who hath fulfilled the same, and given us there his fulfilling" (Hugh Latimer on *Matthew* 2:1, 2).

to fulfil all righteousness" (*Matthew* 3:15), and what was true of his baptism was no less so of his circumcision. The pain and the blood and the bruising of his tender body connected with that symbol of shame are inexplicable save on the supposition that even in infancy he was the vicarious one, not indeed bearing sin in the full sense and manner in which he bore it on the cross (for without death, sin-bearing could not have been consummated), but still bearing it in measure according to the condition of his years. Even then he was "the Lamb of God."

His banishment into Egypt is referred to once and again by the old divines as part of that life of humiliation by which he was bearing our sins. As the banished one, he bore our banishment that we might return to God. He passed through Earth as an outcast, because he was standing in the outcast's place – "hurried up and down," says an old writer, "and driven out of his own land as a vagabond" (John Flavel). In each part of his sin-bearing life there is something to meet our case. By the first Adam we were made exiles from God and paradise; by the last Adam we are brought back from our wanderings, restored to the divine favor, and replaced in the paradise of God.

His baptism is the same in import with his circumcision. He needed not the symbol of death and cleansing, for he was wholly pure, and not liable to death on his own account. Why, then, should this sign of washing the unclean be applied to him if he was not then standing in the place of the unclean? What had water to do with the spotless one? What had "the figure of the putting away of the filth of the flesh, and of the answer of a good conscience toward God" (1 *Peter* 3:21), to do with him who had no filth of the flesh to put away and on whose conscience not even the very shadow of dispeace had ever rested? But he was the substitute; into all the parts and circumstances of our life he enters, fulfilling all righteousness in the name of those whom he had come to save. The water was poured upon him as standing in our place and fulfilling our obligations.[3]

Jesus was the substitute; into all the parts and circumstances of our life he enters, fulfilling all righteousness in the name of those whom he had come to save.

---

3. The old hymns have not lost sight of those truths. As specimens, I give the following:

In the *Psalms* we find him giving utterance to his feelings while bearing sins that were not his own, but which were felt by him as if they were his own. Again and again he confesses sin. But what had the Holy One to do with confession or with strong crying and tears? What connection had he with the horrible pit and the miry clay, with the overwhelming floods and waves, with the deep waters, and the dust and the darkness, and the lowest pit? Why shrank he from the assembly of the wicked that enclosed him, from the "bulls that compassed him, the strong bulls of Bashan that beset him round," from the power of the dogs, from the sword, from the lion's mouth, from the horns of the unicorns? Why, during the days of his flesh, was he subjected to all this? And why were the powers of Earth and Hell let loose against him? Because he was the substitute who had taken our place, assumed our responsibilities, and undertaken to do battle with our enemies. In these *Psalms* we find the seed of the woman at war with the seed of the serpent and undergoing the varied anguish of the bruised heel.

> *Why, during the days of his flesh, was Jesus subjected to all this? And why were the powers of Earth and Hell let loose against him? Because he was the substitute who had taken our place, assumed our responsibilities, and undertaken to do battle with our enemies.*

Stillat excisos pueri per artus	Efficacious blood drops from
Efficax noxas abolere sanguis;	The pierced limbs of the boy
Obligat morti pretiosa totum	To abolish punishments;
Stilla cruorem.	A precious drop requires the
	whole bloodshed to death.

Again:

Vix natus, ecce lacteum	Behold the infant, scarcely born,
Profundit Infans sanguinem,	Sheds the milk blood,
Libamen est hoc funeris	A sample of death,
Amoris hoc præludium.	A prelude of love

And again:

Dixit; et Patris veneratus iram	He spoke; and having respected
Sustinet vulnus silicis cruentae;	The wrath of the Father endures
	The wound of the bloody rock;
Et jugum legis subit ipse, servis	And he himself submits to the
	Yoke of the law
Ut juga demat.	In order to take away the yokes
	For his servants.

– *Editor*.

Little as these hymns contain of the finished work of the substitute, occasionally the great truth breaks out in connection with different events in the Lord's history.

He speaks not merely of the anguish of the cross when the full flood of wrath descended on him, but of his lifetime's daily griefs: "I am afflicted and ready to die *from my youth up*: I suffer your terrors, I am distracted" (*Psalm* 88:15). "My soul is full of troubles, my life draws nigh the grave," he said in the *Psalms*; just as afterward he cried out, "My soul is exceeding sorrowful, even unto death." "My eye mourns by reason of affliction…. Your fierce wrath goes over me, your terrors have cut me off…. Lover and friend you have put far from me, and my acquaintance into darkness." Thus was he "despised and rejected of men" (that is, *the* despised and rejected one of men), "a man of sorrows and acquainted with grief" (*Isaiah* 53:3). And of the meaning of all this we can have no doubt when we remember that he was always the sinless one bearing our sins, carrying them up to the cross as well as bearing them upon the cross (1 *Peter* 2:24, ανήεγκε); also that it is written of him, "Surely he has borne our griefs and carried our sorrows" (*Isaiah* 53:4); and yet again, that it is written expressly with reference to his daily life, "He healed all that were sick, that it might be fulfilled which was spoken by Esaias the prophet, saying, *he himself took our infirmities and bore our sicknesses*" (*Matthew* 8:17).[4] Vicariousness, or substitution, attached itself to each part of his life as truly as to his death.[5] Our burden he assumed when he entered the manger, and he laid it aside only at the cross. The utterance, "It is finished," pointed back to a whole life's sin-bearing work.

The confessions of our sins which we find in the *Psalms* (where, as "in a bottle," God has deposited the tears of the Son of Man, *Psalm* 56:8) are the distinctest proofs of his work as the substitute. Let one example suffice: "O Lord, rebuke me

Vicariousness, or substitution, attached itself to each part of Christ's life as truly as to his death. Our burden he assumed when he entered the manger, and he laid it aside only at the cross.

---

4. The Evangelist here translates directly from the Hebrew and differs from the *Septuagint*.

5. The *Heidelberg Catechism* asks, "What do you believe when you say, *He suffered*?" and the answer is, "That he, all the time of his life which he led on Earth, but especially at the end thereof, sustained the wrath of God, both in body and soul, against the sin of mankind, that he might by his passion, as the only propitiatory sacrifice, deliver our body and soul from everlasting damnation, and purchase unto us the favor of God, righteousness, and everlasting life."

not in your wrath, neither chasten me in your displeasure; for your arrows stick fast in me, and your hand presses me sore. There is no soundness in my flesh because of your anger; neither is there any rest in my bones because of my sin. For my iniquities are gone over my head; as an heavy burden, they are too heavy for me" (*Psalm* 38:1-4).

These confessions must be either those of the sinner or the sin bearer. They suit the former, and they show what views of sin we should entertain, and what our confessions should be. But they suit the latter no less. As they occur in those *Psalms* which are quoted in the New Testament as specially referring to Christ, we must take them as the confessions of the sin bearer, meant to tell us what he thought of sin when it was laid upon him simply as a substitute for others. The view thus given us of the completeness of the substitution is as striking as it is satisfying. We see here our Noah building his wondrous ark for the salvation of his household. We see its beginning, middle, and end. We see its different parts, external and internal; each plank as it is laid; each nail as it is driven in. Its form is perfect; its structure in all details is complete; its strength and stability are altogether divine. Yet with what labor and amid what mockings is this ark constructed! Amid what strong crying and tears, what blood and agony, is it completed! Thus, however, we are assured of its perfection and security. Through the deep waters of this evil world it floats in peace. No storm can overset it, no billow break it nor so much as loosen one of its planks. They who have fled to it as a hiding place from the wind and a covert from the tempest are everlastingly safe.

When the Lord said, "Now is my soul troubled" (*John* 12:27); and when again he said, "My soul is exceeding sorrowful, even unto death" (*Matthew* 26:38), he spoke as the sin bearer. For what construction can we possibly put upon that trouble and sorrow but that they were for us?[6] Men, false to the great truth of a sin-bearing Christ, may say

> *We see here our Noah building his wondrous ark for the salvation of his household.*

6. The old catechetical exposition of the *Heidelberg Catechism* brings this out fully: "The Godhead has so strengthened the human nature, and upheld it, that it could bear the weight of the wrath of God against sin.

that in the utterance of this anguish he was merely giving us an example of patient endurance and self-sacrifice. But they who own the doctrine of Christ "suffering for sin, the just for the unjust," will listen to these bitter cries as to the very voice of the substitute and learn from the accomplishment of which he took our flesh, and lived our life, and died our death upon the tree.

But the completeness of the substitution comes out more fully at the cross. There the whole burden pressed upon him, and the wrath of God took hold of him, and the sword of Jehovah smote him; he poured out his soul unto death, and he was cut off out of the land of the living.

Then the work was done. "It is finished." The blood of the burnt offering was shed. The propitiation of God's wrath was made, the transgression finished, and the everlasting righteousness brought in.

All that follows is the fruit or result of the work finished on the cross. The grave is the awful pledge or testimony to his death as a true and real death, but it forms no part of the substitution or expiation.[7] Before our substitute reached the tomb, atonement had been completed. The resurrection is the blessed announcement of the Father that the work had been accepted and the substitute set free, but it was no part either of the atonement or the righteousness. The ascension

The grave is the awful pledge or testimony to Jesus' death as a true and real death, but it forms no part of the substitution or expiation. The resurrection of Christ is the blessed announcement of the Father that the work had been accepted and the substitute set free, but it was no part either of the atonement or the righteousness.

It has also given such dignity to the short sufferings of the human nature that it has satisfied for the eternal punishment which we had deserved.... What suffered he in his soul? Very heavy and terrible torments, anxieties, pains, sorrows, distresses, arising from the sense of God's wrath.... When and how long has Christ suffered? The whole time of his life which he led on Earth, but especially at the end thereof. The evangelical histories testify of banishments, Satan's temptations, poverty, disgrace, infirmities, hunger, thirst, fear, perils of life; especially in the garden of Gethsemane, in the judgment hall, on Golgotha.... He not only suffered for sin, but he felt God against him in that suffering as an angry judge.... Has he also purchased righteousness for us? Yes, so that the Father freely gives and bestows the same on us, and reckons it unto us; so that the satisfaction and righteousness of Christ being imputed to us, we may stand in God's judgment."

7. "To what end was he buried? That thereby he might make manifest that he was dead indeed" (*Heidelberg Catechism*).

and the appearing in the presence of God for us with his own blood are the carrying out of the atonement made upon Calvary, but they are no part of the expiation by means of which sin is forgiven and we are justified. All was finished, once and forever, when the substitute said, "Father, into your hands I commend my spirit."

There are some who would separate propitiation from the cross, who maintain that the three days' entombment was part of the sin bearing. But the cry from the cross, "It is finished," silences all such theories. The altar is the only place of expiation, and it is death that is the wages of sin. Burial was but the visible proof of the reality of the death. The substitute's death once given instead of ours, the work is done. The fire has consumed the sacrifice. The ashes which remain are not the prolongation of that sacrifice, but the palpable proof that the fire has exhausted itself, that wrath is spent, and that nothing can now be added to or taken from the perfection of that sacrifice through which pardon and righteousness are henceforth to flow to the condemned and the ungodly.

"Justified by his blood" is the apostolic declaration; and, as the result of this, "saved from wrath through him" (*Romans* 5:9). Here we rest, sitting down beneath the shadow of the cross to receive the benefit of that justifying, saving, protecting sacrifice.

It is at and by the *cross* that God justifies the ungodly. "By his stripes we are healed" (*Isaiah* 53:5), and the symbol of the brazen serpent visibly declares this truth. It was the serpent when uplifted that healed the deadly bite, not the serpent after it was taken down and deposited in the tabernacle. As from that serpent – the figure of him who was "made a curse for us" – so from the cross health and life flow in. It is not resurrection but crucifixion that is the finishing of transgression and the making an end of sin.

"Reconciled to God by the death of his Son" (*Romans* 5:10) is another of the many testimonies to the value and efficacy of the cross. Reconciliation is not connected with resurrection. The "peace was made by the blood of his

There are some who would separate propitiation from the cross, who maintain that the three days' entombment was part of the sin bearing. But Christ's cry from the cross, "It is finished," silences all such theories. The altar is the only place of expiation, and it is death that is the wages of sin.

cross" (*Colossians* 1:20). The fruits and results of the peace offering may be many and various, but they are not the basis of reconciliation. That basis is the sacrificial blood-shedding. What can be more explicit than these three passages which announce justification by the blood, reconciliation by the death, and peace by "the blood of the cross"?

In the cross we see the priest and priesthood; in the resurrection, the king and royal power. To the priest belong the absolution and the cleansing and the justifying; to the king, the impartation of blessing to the absolved and the cleansed and the justified.

To the cross, therefore, do we look and cleave; knowing that out of its death life comes to us, and out of its condemnation, pardon and righteousness. With Christ were we crucified, and in this crucifixion we have "redemption through his blood, the forgiveness of sins, according to the riches of his grace."

Three times over in one chapter (*Leviticus* 1:9, 13, 17) we read these words, "It is a burnt sacrifice, an offering made by fire of a sweet savor unto the Lord." The apostle, referring to these words, says, "Christ has loved us, and has given himself for us, an offering and a sacrifice to God for a sweet-smelling savor" (*Ephesians* 5:2). This sweet savor came from the brazen altar, or altar of burnt-offering. It was the sweet odor of that sacrifice that ascended to God and that encompassed the worshiper so that he was covered all over with this sacrificial fragrance, presenting him perfect before God and making his own conscience feel that he was accepted as such and treated as such. Thus, by that burnt offering there is proclaimed to us justification in a crucified Christ.

The manifold blessings flowing from resurrection and ascension are not to be overlooked, but nowhere does Scripture teach justification by these. The one passage sometimes quoted to prove this declares the opposite (*Romans* 4:25), for the words truly translated run thus: "He was delivered *because* we had sinned, and raised again *because* of our justification." It was because the justifying work was *finished* that resurrection was possible. Had it not been so, he must have remained under the power of the grave. But the cross had completed

The manifold blessings flowing from Christ's resurrection and ascension are not to be overlooked, but nowhere does Scripture teach justification by these. It was because the justifying work was finished that Christ's resurrection was possible.

the justification of his church. He was raised from the dead. Death could no longer have dominion over him. The work was finished, the debt paid, and the surety went forth free. He rose not in order to justify us, but because we were justified. In raising him from the dead, God the Father cleared him from the imputed guilt which had nailed him to the cross and borne him down to the tomb. "He was justified in the Spirit" (*1 Timothy* 3:16). His resurrection was not his justification, but the declaration that he was "justified." That resurrection in which we are one with him does not justify us, but proclaims that we were justified – justified by his blood and death.[8]

Christ rose not in order to justify us, but because we were justified. That resurrection in which we are one with him does not justify us, but proclaims that we were justified – justified by his blood and death.

Insofar, then, as substitution is concerned, we have to do with the cross alone. It was, indeed, the place of *death*, but on that very account it was also to us the place of life and the pledge of resurrection.

The words of the apostle (*Romans* 6:6) are very explicit on this point: "Knowing this, that our old man has been crucified with him, that the body of sin might be destroyed, that henceforth we should not serve sin." Here we have three things connected directly with the *cross*: (1) The death of the old man; (2) the destruction of the body of sin; (3) deliverance from the life-bondage of sin. Then he adds, "For he who dies is freed from sin" (verse 7) . The word "freed" is literally "justified,"[9] teaching us that *death* is the exhaustion of the penalty and the justification of the sinner. Justification in a crucified Christ is the teaching of the Spirit here.

The words of another apostle are no less clear (*1 Peter* 4:1): "Christ suffered for us in the flesh; …he that has suffered in the flesh has ceased from sin." Here Christ on the cross is

---

8. "What other benefits do we receive by the sacrifice and death of Christ? That by virtue of his death our old man is crucified, slain, and buried together with him, that henceforth evil lusts and desires may not reign in us, but we may offer ourselves unto him a sacrifice of thanksgiving.... How does the resurrection of Christ profit us? First, by his resurrection he vanquished death, that he might make us partakers of that righteousness which he had purchased for us; secondly, we are stirred up by his power to a new life" (*Heidelberg Catechism*).

9. δεδιχαίωτιλι has been judicially released, legally set free, having paid the full penalty.

set before us, suffering, the just for the unjust. Having thus suffered, he has exhausted the penalty which he was bearing; and having exhausted it, his connection with sin has ceased: He is now in the state described elsewhere, "without sin" (*Hebrews* 9:28). The word "ceased" means more properly "has rest."[10] The life of our surety was one of sorrow and unrest, for our penalty lay upon him; but when this penalty was paid by his death, he "rested." The labor and the burden were gone; and as one who knew what entering into rest was (*Hebrews* 4:10), he could say to us, "I will give you rest." He carried his life-long burden to the cross and there laid it down, "resting from his labors." Or rather, it was there that the law severed the connection between him and the burden, loosing it from his shoulders that it might be buried in his grave. From that same cross springs the sinner's rest, the sinner's disburdening, the sinner's absolution and justification.

Not for a moment are we to lose sight of the blessings flowing from resurrection or to overlook and undervalue the new position into which we are brought by it. The "power of his resurrection" (*Philippians* 3:10) must be fully recognized and acted on for its own results. We are crucified with Christ. With him we died, were buried, and rose again. "Raised with him through faith in the operation of God, who has raised him from the dead" (*Colossians* 2:12). "He has quickened us together with Christ, and has raised us up together, and made us sit together in heavenly places in Christ Jesus" (*Ephesians* 2:5-6). Such are the terms in which the apostle describes the benefits of Christ's resurrection and in which he reveals to us our oneness with him who died and rose. But nowhere does he separate our justification from the cross; nowhere does he speak of Christ meeting our legal responsibilities by his resurrection; nowhere does he ascribe to his resurrection that preciousness in whose excellency we stand complete. Acceptance and completeness in our standing before God are attributed to the cross and blood and death of the Divine Substitute.

10. See Kypke's *Observations in the New Testament*, who quotes some striking passages in classical Greek to illustrate this. See also Bengel and Winer.

Not for a moment are we to lose sight of the blessings flowing from resurrection or to overlook and undervalue the new position into which we are brought by it. But nowhere does Paul separate our justification from the cross; nowhere does he speak of Christ meeting our legal responsibilities by his resurrection.

Poor as my faith in this Substitute may be, it places me at once in the position of one to whom "God imputes righteousness without works." God is willing to receive me on the footing of his perfection; if I am willing to be thus received, in the perfection of another with whom God is well pleased, the whole transaction is completed. *I am justified by his blood.* "As he is, so am I (even) in *this* world" – even *now*, with all my imperfections and evils.

To be entitled to use another's name when my own name is worthless, to be allowed to wear another's raiment because my own is torn and filthy, to appear before God in another's person – the person of the Beloved Son – this is the summit of all blessing. The sin bearer and I have exchanged names, robes, and persons! I am now represented by him, my own personality having disappeared. He now appears in the presence of God for me (*Hebrews* 9:24). All that makes him precious and dear to the Father has been transferred to me. His excellency and glory are seen as if they were mine. I receive the love and the fellowship and the glory as if I had earned them all. So entirely one am I with the sin bearer that God treats me not merely as if I had not done the evil that I have done, but as if I had done all the good which I have not done, but which my substitute has done. In one sense I am still the poor sinner, once under wrath; in another I am altogether righteous and shall be so forever because of the perfect one in whose perfection I appear before God. Nor is this a false pretence or a hollow fiction which carries no results or blessings with it. It is an exchange which has been provided by the Judge and sanctioned by law; an exchange of which any sinner upon Earth may avail himself and be blest.

God treats me not merely as if I had not done the evil that I have done, but as if I had done all the good which I have not done, but which my substitute has done.

4
The Declaration of the Completeness

THE fifty-third chapter of *Isaiah* is a prophetic vision of the cross.

The book of *Leviticus* had given Israel in detail the standing symbols which were all to be transformed into spiritual substances or verities in Christ crucified. And this chapter of the prophet gives a summary of these truths in Levitical language, connecting them all with the seed of the woman and his bruising upon the tree.

The fifty-third chapter of Isaiah is a prophetic vision of the cross.

For more than three thousand years the "bruised heel" had been held up before the eye of the world, and specially of Israel (in their sacrifices), as their deliverance and hope. But now the interpretation is given in more explicit language. Its meaning – as expressing (in the varied details of this chapter) the transference of the sinner's guilt to the substitute; as setting forth also the mysterious person of the man of sorrows, and, under all this, revealing the deep free love of God to man – is here proclaimed with a clearness and fulness such as had not hitherto been revealed either to the patriarchs or to Israel. Nowhere is the work of Messiah the sin bearer more explicitly revealed. The just one suffering for the unjust is the theme of this prophetic burden.

Abruptly the prophet breaks forth in his description of Messiah, seed of the woman, son of Adam, son of Abraham, son of David: "He shall grow up before him as a tender plant, and as a root out of a dry ground." The soil and the air of

Earth are alike uncongenial to this shoot from the stem of Jesse. Its affinities are all with a purer climate than ours.

He rises up in the midst of us, but not to be appreciated and honored, not to be admired or loved. "He has no form nor comeliness; and when we shall see him, there is no beauty that we should desire him." The light shines in the darkness, and the darkness comprehends it not. "He is [the] despised and rejected [one] of men," that is, of all men, the most despised and rejected; for he came to his own, and his own received him not.

Here is the beginning of his vicarious life – a life of reproach among the sons of men, "a man of sorrows, and acquainted with grief."

Whence all this life-long sadness? When angels visit Earth, are they thus sorrowful? Does the air of Earth infect them with its troubles? Do they weep and groan and bleed? Are they assailed with the blasphemies of Earth? If not, why is it thus? Why is the holy Son of God from his childhood subjected to this contempt and bowed down beneath this burden? Why is the cup of gall and wormwood set beside his cradle? And why, day by day, in youth and manhood, has he to drink the bitter draught? Angels see the sights and hear the sounds of Earth as they attend us in their ministries or execute the errands of their King. Yet they are not saddened, nor when they return to their dwellings of light do they require the tears to be wiped from their eyes or the sweat from their brows. How can we account for the difference between Messiah and the angels, save by the fact that his sin-bearing character made him accessible to and penetrable by grief in a way such as no angel could be?

The difficulty of such a case was obvious, and accordingly the prophet meets it in the next verse. It was *our* griefs that he was bearing; it was *our* sorrows that he was carrying. These were the things that made him the man of sorrows. They that saw him could not understand the mystery. They said, God has smitten him for his sins and afflicted him for some hidden transgression that we know not. But no: "He was wounded for *our* transgressions, he was bruised for *our* iniquities; the chastisement of *our* peace was upon him, and with his stripes

"He was wounded for our transgressions, he was bruised for our iniquities; the chastisement of our peace was upon him, and with his stripes we are healed."
– Isaiah 53

we are healed." The wounding, the bruising, the chastening, and the scourging had their beginnings before he reached the cross; but it was there that they were all completed by "the obedience unto death."

"The Lord [Jehovah] has laid on him the iniquity of us all," or, has made to rush or strike upon him the punishment of us all.

> It was exacted, and he became answerable,
> And [therefore] he opened not his mouth.
> As a lamb to the slaughter he is led;
> And as a sheep before her shearers is dumb,
> So he opened not his mouth.
> From prison and from judgment he is taken,
> And his generation [manner of life] who declares?

These are scenes before the cross, while he was on his way to it. He was silent before his judges because he had made himself legally responsible for our debt or guilt. Nor was there anyone to come forward and declare his innocence. He was carrying, too, our sins to the cross. After this we have the cross itself:

> He was cut off out of the land of the living;
> For the transgression of my people was he stricken.

The sin bearing of the cross is fully brought out here. There he hung as the substitute, "the just for the unjust, that he might bring us to God."

> And there was appointed him a grave with the wicked,
> But with the rich man was he in death.

There was assigned to him a place with the wicked not only on the cross, but in his burial; he was condemned not only to die an ignominious death, but to have a like sepulchre. From this latter, however, he was delivered by the rich man of Arimathea who unexpectedly came forward and begged the body, which would otherwise have been consigned to a malefactor's grave. He was "with the rich in his death"; that is, when he died, or after his death, when he was taken down from the cross.

> Yet it pleased Jehovah to bruise him,

He was silent before his judges because he had made himself legally responsible for our debt or guilt.

He has put him to grief.

Jehovah was well pleased with his bruising – nay, took pleasure in bruising him. Never was Messiah more the "beloved Son" than when suffering on the cross; yet Jehovah was "well pleased" to put him to grief. Though the consciousness of communion was interrupted for a time when he cried, "Why have you forsaken me?" yet there was no breaking of the bond. There was wrath coming down on him as the Substitute, but love resting on him as the Son. Both were together. He knew the love, even while he felt the wrath. It was the knowledge of the love that made him cry out in amazement and anguish, "My God, my God, why have you forsaken me?"

It was the knowledge of the love that made him cry out in amazement and anguish, "My God, my God, why have you forsaken me?"

You shall make his soul an offering for sin;

or more exactly, "a trespass offering"; a sacrifice for wilful, conscious sin. Of this trespass offering it is written, "The priest shall make an atonement for him before the Lord, and he shall be forgiven for anything that he has done in trespassing therein" (*Leviticus* 6:7). The various offerings of the tabernacle and the altar all center in and cluster round the cross. It is *the soul* that is here said to be the trespass offering, implying that when the soul was parted from the body – when Christ commended his spirit to his Father – then the trespass offering was completed. Atonement was made once for all. Before the body of the Surety had reached the tomb, the great work was done. The lying in the grave was the visible and palpable sign or pledge of the work having been already finished; resurrection was the Father's seal from above set to the excellency of that completed sacrifice and to the perfection of him by whom it had been accomplished on the cross.

Upon the labor of his soul he shall look,
He shall be satisfied.

Christ, in the days of his flesh, often used language like this regarding his soul: "My soul is exceedingly sorrowful, even unto death" (*Matthew* 26:38); "Now is my soul troubled" (*John*

46

12:27); "The Son of man came…to give his soul a ransom for many" (*Matthew* 20:28); "The good Shepherd gives his soul for the sheep" (*John* 10:11); "I lay down my soul for the sheep" (*John* 10:15). Thus the life, the soul, the blood, are connected together; and with that which was accomplished by them in life and in death he is satisfied. Whether it is *himself* that is satisfied, or the Father, matters not. The truth taught is the same.

> By his knowledge shall my righteous Servant justify many;
> For he shall bear their iniquities.

It is the Father that here speaks. He calls Messiah, "My righteous servant," and proclaims that by giving the knowledge of himself he shall justify many. The knowledge of Christ is that which secures our justification; the knowledge of Christ as the sin bearer. For it is added, as the justifying thing in this knowledge, "he shall bear their iniquities"; thus again linking justification with the cross, and the finished work there.

The last verse is very remarkable as bringing out fully the Father's reasons for glorifying his Son, reasons connected entirely with the cross and the sin bearing there:

> Therefore will I divide him a portion with the great,
> And he shall divide the spoil with the strong,
> Because he has poured out his soul unto death.
> And he was numbered with the transgressors;
> And he bore the sin of many,
> And made intercession for the transgressors.

So that the resurrection, with all the subsequent glory and honor conferred on him, is the recompense and result of his justifying work upon the cross. On that tree of death and shame the work was *finished*. There he poured out his soul; there he was numbered with the transgressors; there he bore the sin of many; there he made intercession for the transgressors when he cried out, "Father, forgive them, for they know not what they do."[1]

The knowledge of Christ is that which secures our justification; the knowledge of Christ as the sin bearer. For it is added, as the justifying thing in this knowledge, "he shall bear their iniquities"; thus again linking justification with the cross, and the finished work there.

---

1. In these words, "they know not what they do," he is speaking as the sin offering, which was specially for sins of ignorance.

"It is finished," were his words as he died. The justifying work is done! If anything else besides this finished work is to justify, then Christ has died in vain.

"It is finished," he said, and gave up the ghost. "Father, into your hands I commend my spirit," and to the Father that spirit went. The Father received it, and, in receiving it, bore testimony to the completeness of the work. The Roman soldiers, "perceiving that he was dead already," may be said to have testified to the completion of the work of pouring out his soul unto death. The taking down from the cross was another testimony. Joseph and Nicodemus were like the Levites carrying away the ashes from the altar.

The burial was another testimony. The resurrection began the divine and visible testimony to this same thing. The ascension and "sitting at the Father's right hand were the attestations from above – the heavenly responses to the voice from the cross, "It is finished." All after this was the *result* of that finished work. The presentation of his blood was not to complete the sacrifice, but to carry out what was already done. The sprinkling of the blood (at whatever time that may have been done) was the application of the sacrifice, not the sacrifice itself.

"It is finished!" He who makes this announcement on the cross is the Son of God; it is he who but the day before had said in the prospect of this consummation, "I have glorified you on the Earth: I have finished the work which you gave me to do." He knows what he says when he utters it, and he is "the faithful and true witness." His words are true, and they are full of meaning.

He makes this announcement before the Father as if calling on him to confirm it. He makes it before Heaven and Earth, before men and angels, before Jew and Gentile. He makes it to us. Listen, O sons of men! The work that saves is perfected. The work that justifies is done.

The completeness thus announced is a great and momentous one. It is one in which all the ends of the Earth have an interest. Had aught been left unfinished, then what hope for man or for man's Earth? But it is begun, carried on,

The completeness thus announced is a great and momentous one. It is one in which all the ends of the Earth have an interest. Had aught been left unfinished, then what hope for man or for man's Earth?

consummated. No flaw is found in it; no part is left out; not a jot or tittle has failed. It is absolutely perfect.

This perfection or consummation of the Father's purpose is the completion of atonement, the completion of the justifying work, the completeness of the sin bearing and law fulfilling, the completeness of the righteousness, the completeness of the covenant and the covenant seal. All is done, and done by him who is Son of Man and Son of God. It is perfectly and forever done; nothing is to be added to it or taken from it by man, by Satan, or by God. The burial of the substitute does not add to its completeness; resurrection forms no part of that justifying work. It was all concluded on the cross.

It is so finished that a sinner may at once use it for pardon, for rest, for acceptance, for justification. Standing beside this altar where the great burnt offering was laid and consumed to ashes, the sinner feels that he is put in possession of all blessing. That which the altar has secured passes over to him simply in virtue of his taking his place at the altar and thus identifying himself with the victim. There the divine displeasure against sin has spent itself; there righteousness has been obtained for the unrighteous; there the sweet savor of rest is continually ascending before God; there the full flood of divine love is ever flowing out; there God meets the sinner in his fullest grace without hindrance or restraint; there the peace which has been made through blood-shedding is found by the sinner; there reconciliation is proclaimed, and the voice that proclaims it from that altar reaches to the ends of the Earth; there the ambassadors of peace take their stand to discharge their embassy, pleading with the sons of men far off and near, saying, "Now then we are ambassadors for Christ, as though God did beseech you by us; we pray you in Christ's stead, be reconciled to God."

The resurrection was the great visible seal set to this completeness. It was the Father's response to the cry from the cross, "It is finished." As at baptism he spoke from the excellent glory and said, "This is my beloved Son, in whom I am well pleased," so did he speak (though not with audible voice) at

All is done, and done by him who is Son of Man and Son of God. It is perfectly and forever done; nothing is to be added to it or taken from it by man, by Satan, or by God. The burial of the substitute does not add to its completeness; resurrection forms no part of that justifying work. It was all concluded on the cross.

the resurrection, bearing testimony thereby not only to the excellency of the person, but to the completeness of the work of his only begotten Son. The resurrection added nothing to the propitiation of the cross; it proclaimed it already perfect, incapable of addition or greater completeness.

The ascension added to this testimony, especially the sitting at God's right hand. "This man, after he had offered one sacrifice for sins forever, sat down at the right hand of God" (*Hebrews* 10:12). "When he had by himself purged our sins, sat down on the right hand of the Majesty on high" (*Hebrews* 1:3). The standing posture of the ancient priests showed that their work was an unfinished one. The sitting down of our high priest intimated to all Heaven that the work was done and the "eternal redemption obtained." And what was thus intimated in Heaven has been proclaimed on Earth by those whom God sent forth in the power of the Holy Ghost to tell to men the things which eye had not seen nor ear heard. That "sitting down" contained in itself the Gospel. The first note of that Gospel was sounded at Bethlehem from the manger where the young child lay: The last note came from the throne above when the Son of God returned in triumph from his mission of grace to Earth and took his seat upon the right hand of the Majesty in the heavens.

The standing posture of the ancient priests showed that their work was an unfinished one. The sitting down of our high priest intimated to all Heaven that the work was done and the "eternal redemption obtained."

Between these two extremities – the manger and the throne – how much is contained for us! All the love of God is there. The exceeding riches of divine grace are there. The fulness of that power and wisdom and righteousness which have come forth, not to destroy but to save, is there. These are the two boundary walls of that wondrous storehouse out of which we are to be filled throughout the eternal ages.

Of what is contained in this treasure house we know something here in some small measure, but the vast contents are beyond all measurement and all imagination. The eternal unfolding of these to us will be perpetual gladness. Apart from the excellency of the inheritance and the beauty of the city – and the glory of the kingdom – which will make us say, "Truly the lines have fallen unto us in pleasant places," – there will be, in our ever-widening knowledge of "the unsearchable riches of Christ," light and replenishment and satisfaction which, even were all external brightnesses swept away, would be enough for the soul throughout all the ages to come.

The present glory of Christ is the reward of his humiliation here. Because he humbled himself and became obedient unto death, even the death of the cross, God has highly exalted him and given him the name that is above every name. He wears the crown of glory because he wore the crown of thorns. He drank of the brook by the way; therefore, he has lifted up the head (*Psalm* 110:7).

But this is not all. That glory to which he is now exalted is the standing testimony before all Heaven that his work was finished on the cross. "I have finished the work which you gave me to do," he said. Then he added, "Now, O Father, glorify me with your own self, with the glory which I had with you before the world was" (*John* 17:4, 5).

The proofs of the completeness of the sacrificial work upon the cross are very full and satisfying. They assure us that the work was really finished and, as such, available for the most sinful of men. We shall find it good to dwell upon the thought of this completeness for the pacifying of the conscience, for the satisfying of the soul, for the removal of all doubt and unbelief, and for the production and increase of faith and confidence.

There are degrees of rest for the soul, and it is in proportion as we comprehend the perfection of the work on Calvary that our rest will increase. There are depths of peace which we have not yet sounded, for it is "peace which passes all understanding." Into these depths the Holy Spirit leads us, not in some miraculous way or by some mere exertion of power, but by revealing to us more and more of that work in the first knowledge of which our peace began.

We are never done with the cross nor ever shall be. Its wonders will be always new and always fraught with joy. "The Lamb as it had been slain" will be the theme of our praise above. Why should such a name be given to him in such a book as the *Revelation*, which in one sense carried us far past the cross, were it not that we shall always realize our

We are never done with the cross nor ever shall be. Its wonders will be always new and always fraught with joy. "The Lamb as it had been slain" will be the theme of our praise above.

connection with its one salvation; we shall always be looking to it even in the midst of the glory; and we shall always be learning from it some new lesson regarding the work of him "in whom we have redemption through his blood, even the forgiveness of sins, according to the riches of his grace"? What will they who here speak of themselves as being so advanced as to be done with the cross say to being brought face to face with the slain Lamb, in the age of absolute perfection, the age of the heavenly glory?

You fool! Do you not know that the cross of the Lord Jesus Christ endures forever and that you shall eternally glory in it, if you are saved by it at all?

You fool! Will you not join in the song below, "To him who loved us, and washed us from our sins in his own blood"? Will you not join in the song above, "You were slain, and here redeemed us to God by your blood"? And do you not remember that it is from "the Lamb as it had been slain" that "the seven spirits of God are sent forth into all the Earth"? (*Revelation* 5:6).[2]

It is *the Lamb* who stands in the midst of the elders (*Revelation* 5:6) and before whom they fall down. "Worthy is *the Lamb*" is the theme of celestial song. It is *the Lamb* that opens the seals (6:1). It is before *the Lamb* that the great multitude stand clothed in white (7:9). It is the blood of *the Lamb* that washes the raiment white (7:14). It is by the blood of *the Lamb* that the victory is won (12:11). The book of life belongs to *the Lamb slain* (13:8). It was *the Lamb* that stood on the glorious Mount Zion (14:1). It is *the Lamb* that the redeemed multitude are seen following (14:4), and that multitude is the first fruits unto God and unto *the Lamb* (14:4). It is the song of *the Lamb* that is sung in Heaven (15:3). It is *the Lamb* that wars and overcomes (17:14). It is the marriage of *the Lamb* that is celebrated, and it is to the marriage supper of *the Lamb* that we are called (19:7, 9). The church is *the Lamb's* wife (21:9). On the foundations of

> *It is the Lamb who stands in the midst of the elders and before whom they fall down. "Worthy is the Lamb" is the theme of celestial song. It is the Lamb that opens the seals.*

2. Thirty times does the word *Lamb*, as Christ's heavenly name, occur in the *Apocalypse*; bringing perpetually before the redeemed in glory the cross and the blood as if to prevent the possibility of our losing sight of Christ crucified.

the heavenly city are written the names of the twelve apostles of *the Lamb* (21:14). Of this city the Lord God Almighty and *the Lamb* are the temple (21:22). Of that city *the Lamb* is the light (21:23). The book of life of *the Lamb* and the throne of *the Lamb* (21:27, 22: 1, 3) sum up this wondrous list of honors and dignities belonging to the Lord Jesus as the *crucified* Son of God.

Thus the glory of Heaven revolves around the cross, and every object on which the eye lights in the celestial city will remind us of the cross and carry us back to Golgotha. Never shall we get beyond it, or turn our backs on it, or cease to draw from it the divine virtue which it contains.

The tree – be it palm, cedar, or olive – can never be independent of its roots, however stately its growth and however plentiful its fruit. The building – be it palace or temple – can never be separated from its foundation, however spacious or ornate its structure may be. So, never shall the redeemed be independent of the cross or cease to draw from its fulness.

In what ways our looking to the cross hereafter will benefit us; what the shadow of that tree will do for us in the eternal kingdom, I know not, nor do I venture to say. But it would seem as if the cross and the glory were so inseparably bound together that there cannot be the enjoyment of the one without the remembrance of the other. The completeness of the sacrificial work on Calvary will be matter for eternal contemplation and rejoicing long after every sin has been, by its cleansing efficacy, washed out of our being forever.

Shall we ever exhaust the fulness of the cross? Is it a mere stepping-stone to something beyond itself? Shall we ever cease to glory in it (as the apostle gloried), not only because of past, but because of present and eternal blessing? The forgiveness of sin is one thing, but is that all? The crucifixion of the world is another, but is that all? Is the cross to be a relic, useless though venerable, like the serpent of brass laid up in the tabernacle to be destroyed perhaps at some future time and called Nehushtan? (*2 Kings* 18:4). Or is it not rather like the tree of life which bears twelve manner of fruits and

The glory of Heaven revolves around the cross, and every object on which the eye lights in the celestial city will remind us of the cross and carry us back to Golgotha. Never shall we get beyond it, or turn our backs on it, or cease to draw from it the divine virtue which it contains.

yields its fruit every month by the banks of the celestial river? Its influence here on Earth is transforming. But even after the transformation has been completed and the whole church perfected, shall there not be a rising higher and higher, a taking on of greater and yet greater comeliness, a passing from glory to glory – all in connection with the cross and through the never-ending vision of its wonders?

Of the new Jerusalem it is said, *"The Lamb* is the light [or lamp] thereof "* (Revelation* 21:23). *The Lamb* is only another name for *Christ crucified.* Thus it is the cross that is the lamp of the holy city; and with its light the gates of pearl, the jasper wall, the golden streets, the brilliant foundations, and the crystal river are all lighted up. The glow of the cross is everywhere, penetrating every part, reflected from every gem; and by its peculiar radiance transporting the dwellers of the city back to Golgotha as the fountainhead of all this splendor.

The Lamb is only another name for Christ crucified. Thus it is the cross that is the lamp of the holy city.

It is light from Calvary that fills the Heaven of heavens. Yet it is no dim religious light, for the glory of God is to lighten it (*Revelation* 21:23). Its light is "like unto a stone most precious, even like a jasper stone, clear as crystal…. and there is no night there, and they need no candle, neither light of the Sun, for the Lord God gives them light" (*Revelation* 21:11; 22:5). Yes, we shall never be done with the cross and the blood; though, where all are clean and perfect in every sense, these will not be used for purging the conscience or justifying the ungodly.

It is the symbol both of a dying and of a risen Christ that we find in the *Revelation.* The "Lamb as it had been slain" indicates both. But the prominence is given to the former. It is the slain Lamb that has the power and authority to open the seals; implying that it was in his sin bearing or sacrificial character that he exercised his right, and that it was his finished work on which this right rested and by which it was acquired. It is as the Lamb that he is possessed with all wisdom and strength – "the seven horns and the seven eyes, which are the seven Spirits of God" (*Revelation* 5:6); the Holy Spirit, or the Spirit of omniscience and omnipotence.

The Lamb is one of his special and eternal titles; the name by which he is best known in Heaven. As such, we obey and honor and worship him; never being allowed to lose sight of the cross amid all the glories of the kingdom. As such we follow him, and shall follow him eternally. As it is written, "There are they that follow *the Lamb* wherever he goes" (*Revelation* 14:4).

"There are they that follow the Lamb wherever he goes" (Revelation 14:4).

5

Righteousness for the Unrighteous

He who goes to God for forgiveness can use as his plea the righteousness of the righteous Judge, no less than the grace of the loving and merciful Lord God.

IT IS *in* righteousness and *by* righteousness that God saves the sinner.

He justifies the ungodly (*Romans* 4:5), but he does it *in* and *by righteousness*. For "the righteous Lord loves righteousness" (*Psalm* 11:7). He "justifies *freely* by his *grace*" (*Romans* 3:24), but still it is "in and by righteousness." His grace is *righteous* grace; it is grace which condemns the sin while acquitting the sinner; nay, which condemns the sin by means of that very thing which brings about the acquittal of the sinner. His pardon is *righteous* pardon and therefore irreversible. His salvation is *righteous* salvation and therefore everlasting.

It is as the righteous *Judge* that God justifies. He is "faithful and just" in forgiving sin (*1 John* 1:9). By his pardons he magnifies his righteousness, so that he who goes to God for forgiveness can use as his plea the righteousness of the righteous Judge, no less than the grace of the loving and merciful Lord God.

God loves to pardon because he is love; and he loves to pardon because he is righteous, and true, and holy. No sin can be too great for pardon, and no sinner can be too deep or old in sin to be saved and blest because the righteousness out of which the salvation comes is infinite.[1]

1. "How are you righteous before God? Only by a true faith in Jesus Christ: insomuch that if my conscience accuse me that I have grievously transgressed against all the commandments of God, nor have kept any

The sacrifices on which the sinner is called to rest are "the sacrifices of *righteousness*" (*Deuteronomy* 33:19; *Psalm* 4:5). It is from "the God of our salvation" that this righteousness comes (*Psalm* 24:5). It is with the "sacrifices of righteousness" that God is "pleased" (*Psalm* 51:19). It is with righteousness that his priests are clothed (*Psalm* 132:9). It is righteousness that looks down from Heaven to bless us (*Psalm* 85:11), and it is righteousness and peace that kiss each other in bringing deliverance to our world. It is the work of righteousness that is peace, and "the effect of righteousness, quietness, and assurance forever" (*Isaiah* 32:17).

It is with the "robe of righteousness" that Messiah is clothed, over and above the garments of salvation (*Isaiah* 61:10), when he comes to deliver Earth. When he proclaims himself "mighty to save," it is when "speaking in righteousness" (*Isaiah* 63:1). When he came to "finish the transgression, and to make an end of sin, and to make reconciliation for iniquity," he came also to bring in "everlasting righteousness" (*Daniel* 9:24).

"This is the name whereby he shall be called, *The Lord our righteousness*" (*Jeremiah* 23:6); and as if to mark the way in which he blesses and justifies, it is added in another place, "This is the name wherewith *she* shall be called, *The Lord our righteousness*" (*Jeremiah* 33:16) – his name passing over to the sinner, with the sinner's name lost and forgotten in that of his substitute. Oneness in name, in nature, in privilege, in position, in righ-

> It is from "the God of our salvation" that this righteousness comes.

---

one of them, and, moreover, am still prone to evil; yet, notwithstanding, *the full and perfect satisfaction, righteousness, and holiness of Christ is imputed and given to me*, without any merit of mine, of the mere mercy of God, even as if I had never committed any sin, or as if no spot at all did cleave to me, yea, as if I myself had perfectly performed that obedience which Christ performed for me…. Why is Christ's sacrifice and obedience called the material cause of our justification? For that it is the same for which we are made righteous (*Romans* 5:19). – Is Christ's death and last passion only imputed to us, or also the obedience of His life? Both. His satisfaction by punishment merits for us the remission of sin. This is his *passive* obedience. Then there is the obedience called *active* obedience…. We owed to God not only punishment for the transgression, but also a perfect obedience. All this Christ has satisfied for us. But our justification is most ascribed to Christ's suffering, blood-shedding, and death" (*Heidelberg Catechism*).

teousness, and in glory with Messiah his divine sin bearer is the sinner's portion. "Their righteousness is of me, says the Lord" (*Isaiah* 54:17); for "he, of God, is made unto us righteousness" (*1 Corinthians* 1:30). The transference is complete and eternal. From the moment that we receive the divine testimony to the righteousness of the Son of God, all the guilt that was on us passes over to him, and all his righteousness passes over to us. God looks on us as possessed of that righteousness and treats us according to its value in his sight. Men may call this a mere "name" or "legal fiction," but it is such a "name" as secures for us the full favor of the righteous God who can only show favor to us in a righteous way. It is such a "fiction" as law recognizes and God acts upon in dealing with the unrighteous as if they were righteous – supremely and divinely righteous in virtue of their connection with him who, "though he knew no sin, was made sin for us, that we might be made the righteousness of God in him" (*2 Corinthians* 5:21).

This is "the righteousness of God which is revealed from faith to faith" (*Romans* 1:17).[2] This is "the righteousness of God without the law which is manifested and was witnessed by the law and the prophets," (*Romans* 3:21); "the righteousness of God which is by faith of Jesus Christ unto all and upon all them that believe" (*Romans* 3:22).[3] Thus, "in believing" (not in doing) this "righteousness of God" becomes ours; for the promise of it is "to him that works not, but believes on him that justifies the ungodly" (*Romans* 4:5).

On our part there is the "believing"; on God's part, the "imputing" or reckoning. We believe; he imputes; and the whole transaction is done. The blood (as "atoning" or "covering") washes off our guilt. The righteousness presents us before God as legally entitled to that position of righteousness which

> *"In believing" (not in doing) this "righteousness of God" becomes ours; for the promise of it is "to him that works not, but believes on him that justifies the ungodly" (Romans 4:5).*

2. That is, "Therein is the righteousness of God, which is by faith, revealed to be believed."

3. That is, the righteousness which God has provided for us – the righteousness of him who is God and which comes to us by believing in Christ – is presented to all without distinction and is put upon all who believe for a robe or covering. As it is written, "Put on the Lord Jesus Christ" (*Romans* 13:14), and again, "As many of you as have been baptized into Christ have put on Christ" (*Galatians* 3:27).

our Surety holds; as being himself not merely the righteous one, but "Jehovah our righteousness." We get the benefit of his perfection in all its completeness, not as infused into us, but as covering us: "Your beauty was perfect through my comeliness which I had put upon you" (*Ezekiel* 16:14). Applying here the words of the prophet concerning Jerusalem, we may illustrate and extend the figure used by the Holy Spirit as to the "perfection" of him whom this righteousness covers. Spread out, it is as follows:

1. "I said to you, 'Live'" (*Ezekiel* 16:6).
2. "I spread my skirt over you" (16:8).
3. "I entered into a covenant with you, and you became mine" (16:8).
4. "I washed you" (16:9).
5. "I anointed you" (16:9).
6. "I clothed you" (16:10).
7. "I shod you" (16:10).
8. "I girded you" (16:10).
9. "I covered you with silk" (16:10).
10. "I decked you with ornaments, bracelets, chains, jewels, a beautiful crown" (16:11-12).
11. "You were exceedingly beautiful" (16:13).
12. "Your renown went forth for your beauty" (16:14).

Such, in the symbols of Scripture, is a picture of the perfection (not our own) with which we are clothed so soon as we believe in him who is "Jehovah our righteousness." "You are all fair, my love; there is no spot in you" (*Song of Solomon* 4:7).

"He that believes is not condemned" (*John* 3:18). This is the negative side; even were there no more for us, this would be blessedness, seeing our portion was by nature that of "children of wrath." But there is more, for it is written, "All that believe are justified from all things" (*Acts* 13:39); and "Christ is the end [or fulfilling] of the law for righteousness to every one that believes" (*Romans* 10:4). "As by the offence of one, judgment came upon all men to condemnation; even so by the righteousness of one, the free gift came upon all men into justification of life" (*Romans* 5:18).

"All that believe are justified from all things" (Acts 13:39); and "Christ is the end [or fulfilling] of the law for righteousness to every one that believes" (Romans 10:4).

The strength or kind of faith required is nowhere stated. The Holy Spirit has said nothing as to quantity or quality on which so many dwell and over which they stumble, remaining all their days in darkness and uncertainty. It is simply in *believing* – feeble as our faith may be – that we are invested with this righteousness. For faith is not work, nor merit, nor effort, but the cessation from all these and the acceptance in place of them of what another has done – done completely and forever. The simplest, feeblest faith suffices: It is not the excellence of our act of faith that does anything for us, but the excellence of him who suffered for sin – the just for the unjust – that he might bring us to God. His perfection suffices to cover not only that which is imperfect in our characters and lives, but also that which is imperfect in our faith when we believe on his name.

> *The simplest, feeblest faith suffices: It is not the excellence of our act of faith that does anything for us, but the excellence of him who suffered for sin – the just for the unjust – that he might bring us to God.*

Many a feeble hand – perhaps many a palsied one – was laid on the head of the burnt offering (*Leviticus* 1:4), but the feebleness of that palsied touch did not alter the character of the sacrifice or make it less available in all its fulness for him who brought it. The priest would not turn him away from the door of the tabernacle because his hand trembled, nor would the bullock fail to be "accepted for him, to make atonement for him" (*Leviticus* 1:4) because his fingers might barely touch its head by reason of his feebleness. The burnt offering was still the burnt offering. The weakest touch sufficed to establish the connection between it and him. Even that feeble touch was the expression of his consciousness that he was unfit to be dealt with on the footing of what he was himself and of his desire to be dealt with by God on the footing of another, infinitely worthier and more perfect than himself.

On our part there is unrighteousness, condemning us: On God's part there is righteousness, forgiving and blessing us. Thus unrighteousness meets righteousness, not to war with each other, but to be at peace. They come together in love, not in enmity. The hand of righteousness is stretched out not to destroy, but to save.

It is as the *unrighteous* that we come to God; not with goodness in our hands as a recommendation, but with the utter want of goodness; not with amendment or promises of amendment, but with *only evil*, both in the present and the past; not presenting the claim of contrition or repentance or broken hearts to induce God to receive us as something less than unrighteous, but going to him simply as *unrighteous*; and unable to remove that unrighteousness or offer anything either to palliate or propitiate.[4]

It is the conscious absence of all good things that leads us to the fountain of all goodness. That fountain is open to all who thus come; it is closed against all who come on any other footing. It is the want of light and life that draws us

It is the conscious absence of all good things that leads us to the fountain of all goodness. That fountain is open to all who thus come; it is closed against all who come on any other footing.

---

4. "I may boldly glory of all the victory which he obtains over the law, sin, death, the devil; and may challenge to myself all his works, even as if they were my very own, and I myself had done them…. Wherefore, when the law shall come and accuse you that you do not observe it, send it to Christ, and say, 'There is that man who has fulfilled the law; to him I cleave; he has fulfilled it for me, and has given his fulfilling unto me.' When it hears these things, it will be quiet. If sin come, and would have you by the throat, send it to Christ, and say 'As much as you may do against him, so much right shall you have against me; for I am in him, and he is in me.' If death creep upon you and attempt to devour you, say unto it, 'Good mistress Death, do you know this man? Come, bite out his tooth: Have you forgotten how little your biting prevailed with him once? Go to! If it be a pleasure unto you, encounter him again. You have persuaded yourself that you should have prevailed somewhat against him when he did hang between two thieves, and died an ignominious death; but what did you gain thereby? You did bite, indeed, but it turned worst to yourself. I pertain to this man; I am his and he is mine, and where he abides I will abide. You could not hurt him; therefore let me alone….'

"Hereof we may easily understand what kind of works those be which make us entire and righteous before God. Surely they are the works of another…. Salvation has come unto all by Jesus Christ, as by the works of another. Wherefore this is diligently to be noted: Our felicity does not consist in our own works, but in the works of another, namely, of Christ Jesus our Savior, which we obtain through faith only in him…. 'Before God your righteousness is of no estimation. You must set in place thereof another, namely mine. This God my Father allows. I have appeased the wrath of God, and of an angry Judge have made him a gentle, merciful, and gracious Father. Believe this, and it goes well with you; you are then safe, entire, and righteous. Beware that you presume not to deal before God with your own works. But if you will do anything with him, creep into me, put on me, and you shall obtain of my Father whatever you desire.'"
— Martin Luther, *Sermon on John 20:24-29.*

to the one source of both, and both of these are the free gifts of God.

He who comes as partly righteous is sent empty away. He who comes acknowledging unrighteousness but at the same time trying to neutralize it or to expiate it by feelings, prayers, and tears, is equally rejected. But he who comes as an unrighteous man to a righteous yet gracious God, finds not only ready access, but plenteous blessing. The righteous God receives unrighteous man if man presents himself in his own true character as a sinner and does not mock God by pretending to be something less or better than this.

For then the divinely provided righteousness comes in to cover the unrighteous and to enable God to receive him in love and justify him before Earth and Heaven.

In all this we find such things as the following – each of them bringing out a separate aspect of the answer to the great question, "How can man be just with God?"

1. The Justifier – "it is God that justifies." The sentence of acquittal must come from *his* lips and be registered in his books.

2. The justified – man, the sinner, under wrath, the ungodly, the condemned.

3. The justifying fact – the death of him whose name is Jehovah our righteousness.

4. The justifying instrument – faith. Not strong faith, or great faith, or perfect faith, but simply faith, or believing. "We are justified by faith."

5. The justifying medium – the righteousness of God. This is the "best robe" which is prepared for the prodigal. By it he is clothed, beautified, made fit to enter his Father's house, and sit down at his Father's table. Christ is himself our justification. In him we "stand." In him we are "found." Him we "put on"; with him we are clothed; by him we are protected as by a shield; in him we take refuge as in a strong tower.

"Found in Him." What then? Our own "self" has disappeared; instead there is Christ, the beloved Son in whom God is well pleased. Found in ourselves, there was nothing but wrath; found in him, there is nothing but favor. We are

He who comes as partly righteous is sent empty away. He who comes acknowledging unrighteousness but at the same time trying to neutralize it or to expiate it by feelings, prayers, and tears, is equally rejected.

hidden in Christ. God seeks for us; when at last he discovers us in our hiding-place, it is not we that he finds, but Christ, so complete is the exchange of persons, so perfect and so glorious the disguise. Yet it is not a disguise which shall ever be taken off, nor of which we shall have cause to be ashamed. It remains ours forever. It is an everlasting righteousness.[5]

Jehovah is satisfied with Christ's obedience. He is well-pleased with his righteousness. And when we, crediting his testimony to that obedience and that righteousness, consent to be treated by him on the footing of its perfection, then is he satisfied and well-pleased with us.

Jehovah is satisfied – more than satisfied – with Christ's fulfilling of the law which man had broken. For never had that law been so fulfilled in all its parts as it was in the life of the God-man. For man to fulfil it would have been much; for an angel to fulfil it would have been more, but for him who was God and man to fulfil it was yet unspeakably more. So satisfied is Jehovah with this divine law-fulfilling, and with him who so gloriously fulfilled it, that he is willing to pass from or cancel all the law's sentences against us; nay, to deal with us as partakers of or identified with this law-fulfilling if we will but agree to give up all personal claims to his favor, and accept the claims of him who has magnified the law and made it honorable.

5. In this there is no confusion of personalities; no transfer of moral character; no exchange of inherent sin on the one hand or inherent righteousness on the other; no literal or physical identity. Rather a judicial verdict or sentence is given in our favor, constituting us partakers in law of all the results or fruits of the work of him whom God, as Judge, appointed our substitute. "As we are made guilty of Adam's sin, which is not inherent in us, but only imputed to us; so we are made righteous by the righteousness of Christ, which is not inherent in us, but only imputed to us" (John Owen).

The legal or judicial gift of benefits is certainly different from the personal meriting of them; but the benefits are not less real, nor their possession less sure. That they should come to us in a righteous way with the consent and sanction of law is the great thing. The reality is to be measured by the actual possession and enjoyment of the benefits and not by the way in which they come. The security for them lies in this, that they reach us in a legal and honorable way.

Jehovah is satisfied with Christ's obedience. He is well-pleased with his righteousness. And when we, crediting his testimony to that obedience and that righteousness, consent to be treated by him on the footing of its perfection, then is he satisfied and well-pleased with us.

6

The Righteousness of God
Reckoned to Us

*It is not that
so much
righteousness is
reckoned to us
in proportion to
the strength of
our faith, or the
warmth of our
love, or the fervor
of our prayers;
but the whole of
it passes over to
us by imputation.*

THIS "everlasting righteousness" comes to us through believing. We are "justified by faith" (*Romans* 5:1), the fruit of which is "peace with God through our Lord Jesus Christ."

It is of this "everlasting righteousness" that the Apostle Peter speaks when he begins his second epistle thus: "Simon Peter, a servant and an apostle of Jesus Christ, to them that have obtained like precious faith with us, through the righteousness of God and our Savior Jesus Christ" (*2 Peter* 1:1).[1]

This righteousness is "reckoned" or "imputed" to all who believe, so that they are treated by God as if it were actually theirs. They are entitled to claim all that which such a righteousness can merit from God as the Judge of righteous claims. It does not become ours gradually, or in fragments or drops; but is transferred to us all at once. It is not that so much of it is reckoned to us (so much to account, as men in

---

1. "To them that have obtained like precious faith with us," that is, with us Jews, who have believed now, and with all our fathers of the past ages, "through [or more properly *in*] the righteousness of him who is our God and Savior." Thus that which is elsewhere called "the righteousness of God" is here called "the righteousness of our God and Savior," that is, of Christ. So that "the righteousness of Christ" is a Scriptural expression.

business say) in proportion to the strength of our faith, or the warmth of our love, or the fervor of our prayers; but the whole of it passes over to us by *imputation*: We are "accepted in the Beloved" (*Ephesians* 1:6); we are "complete in him, who is the head of all principality and power" (*Colossians* 2:10). In its whole quality and quantity it is transferred to us. Its perfection represents us before God; its preciousness, with all that that preciousness can purchase for us, henceforth belongs to us (1 *Peter* 1:7).[2]

The stone, the chief cornerstone, elect and precious – this stone in all its preciousness is ours, not only for resting on, not only for acceptance, but for whatever its divine value can purchase for us. Possessed of this preciousness (imputed, but still ours), we go into the heavenly market and buy what we need without stint or end. We get everything upon the credit of his name, because not only has our unworthiness ceased to be recognized by God in his dealings with us, but our demerit has been supplanted by the merit of one who is absolutely and divinely perfect. In his name we carry on all our transactions with God and obtain all that we need by simply using it as our plea. The things that he did not do were laid to his charge, and he was treated as if he had done them all; the things that he did do are put to our account, and we are treated by God as if we had done them all.

This is the Scriptural meaning of *reckoning* or *imputing*, both in the Old Testament and the New. Let us look at a few of these passages:

Genesis 15:6: "It was *imputed* to him for righteousness";

The things that he did not do were laid to his charge, and he was treated as if he had done them all; the things that he did do are put to our account, and we are treated by God as if we had done them all.

2. In the high priest's breastplate were twelve precious stones on which the names of the twelve tribes were written. The names thus graven shone with all the glory of the gems which contained them. Thus are our names written on the breastplate of the greater High Priest, not only for remembrance, but for glory. They are enveloped in his glory and shine as if all that glory were their own. The luster of the sardius, the topaz, and the diamond, chased in gold, took away that which was dark and earthly about the name or the person or the tribe. Similarly, the more resplendent luster of the heavenly gems which glitter in the breastplate of the great Intercessor not only hides all that is unlustrous in us, but gives to us a beauty such as belongs only to him.

that is, it was so reckoned to him, that in virtue of it he was treated as being what he was not.

Genesis 31:15: "Are we not *counted* of him strangers?" Are we not treated by him as if we were strangers, not children?

Leviticus 7:18: "Neither shall it be *imputed* unto him that offers it." The excellence of the peace offering shall not be counted to him.

God imputes righteousness without works.

Numbers 18:27: "Your heave-offering shall be *reckoned unto you* as though it were the corn of the threshing-floor." It shall be accepted by God as if it were the whole harvest, and you shall be treated by him accordingly.

2 Samuel 19:19: "Let not my lord *impute* iniquity unto me, neither remember that which your servant did perversely." Do not deal with me according to my iniquity.

Psalm 32:2: "Blessed is the man unto whom the Lord *imputes* not iniquity"; to whom God does not *reckon* his iniquities, but treats him as if they were not (see also *Psalm* 106:31).

Romans 4:3: "It was *counted* to him for righteousness."

Romans 4:5: "His faith is *counted* for righteousness"; that is, not as the righteousness, or as the substitute for it, but as bringing him into righteousness (εἰς δικαιοσύνην).

Romans 4:6: "Unto whom God *imputes* righteousness without works."

Romans 4:8: "Blessed is the man to whom the Lord will *not impute* sin."

Romans 4:11: "That righteousness might be *imputed* to them also."

Romans 4:24: "To whom it shall be *imputed*, if we believe on him who raised up Jesus our Lord from the dead."

2 Corinthians 5:19: "Not *imputing* their trespasses unto them."

Galatians 3:6: "It was *accounted* to him for righteousness."

Thus the idea of reckoning to one what does not belong to him and treating him as if he really possessed all that is reckoned to him comes out very clearly.[3] This is God's way of

3. See the Greek of *Isaiah* 53:3, 4. "He was despised, and we *esteemed* him not"; that is, refused to *reckon* him to be what he was. "We did *esteem* him stricken, smitten of God"; we *reckoned* him to be under the curse

lifting man out of the horrible pit and the miry clay, of giving him a standing and a privilege and a hope far beyond that which mere pardon gives and no less far above that which the first Adam lost. To be righteous according to the righteousness of the first Adam would have been much; but to be righteous according to the righteousness of the last Adam, the Lord from Heaven, is unspeakably and inconceivably more.

"It is God that justifies," and he does so by imputing to us a righteousness which warrants him as the Judge to justify the unrighteous freely.

It is not simply *because* of this righteousness that Jehovah justifies; but he *legally transfers* it to us so that we can use it, plead it, and appear before God in it, just as if it were wholly our own. Romanists and Socinians have set themselves strongly against the doctrine of "imputed righteousness." But there it stands, written clearly and legibly in the divine Word. There it stands, an essential part of the great Bible truth concerning sacrifice and substitution and suretyship. It is as deeply written in the book of *Leviticus* as in the *Epistle to the Romans*. It spreads itself over all Scripture and rises gloriously into view in the cross of our Lord Jesus Christ where the "obedience unto death" which makes up this righteousness was completed.[4] There he, who as our substitute took flesh and was born at Bethlehem, who as our substitute passed through Earth as a man of sorrows and acquainted with grief, consummated his

> "Justifying righteousness is the doing and suffering of Christ when he was in the world. This is clear, because we are said to be justified by his obedience – his obedience to the law."
>
> – John Bunyan

---

of God. The word in these two sentences is the same as is elsewhere rendered "imputed."

4. "Justifying righteousness is the doing and suffering of Christ when he was in the world. This is clear, because we are said to be justified by his obedience – his obedience to the law (*Romans* 5:19, 10:4). This righteousness resides in and with the person of Christ; it is of a justifying virtue only by imputation, that is, by God's reckoning it to us, even as our sins made the Lord Jesus a sinner, nay sin, that is, by God's reckoning it to him. The righteousness of God, that is, a righteousness of God's completing, a righteousness of God's bestowing, a righteousness that God gives unto and puts upon all them that believe – a righteousness that stands in the works of Christ, and that is imputed both by the grace and justice of God. The righteousness by which we stand just before God, from the curse, was performed long ago by the person of Christ."

— John Bunyan, *Sermon on Justification by Imputed Righteousness.*

substitution and brought in the "everlasting righteousness." This is the righteousness of which the apostle spoke when he reasoned that, "as by the disobedience of one many were made sinners, so by the obedience of one shall many be made righteous" (*Romans* 5:19); when he proclaimed his abnegation of all other righteousnesses: "and be found in him, not having my own righteousness, which is of the law, but that which is by the faith of Christ, even the righteousness which is of God by faith" (*Philippians* 3:9). This is "the gift of righteousness" regarding which he says: "If by one man's offence death reigned by one; much more they which receive abundance of grace, and of the gift of righteousness, shall reign in life by one, Jesus Christ" (*Romans* 5:17). The one man's offence rests upon all men "to condemnation" (*Romans* 5:18); so the one Man's righteousness, as the counteraction or removal of this condemnation, is available and efficacious "unto justification of life." The imputation of the first Adam's sin to us, and of the last Adam's righteousness, are thus placed side by side. The transference of our guilt to the Divine Substitute, and the transference of that Substitute's righteousness or perfection to us, must stand or fall together.

This righteousness of God was no common righteousness. It was the righteousness of him who was both God and man; therefore it was not only the righteousness of God, but in addition to this, it was the righteousness of man. It embodied and exhibited all uncreated and all created perfection. Never had the like been seen or heard of in Heaven or on Earth before. It was the two-fold perfection of Creaturehood and Creatorship in one resplendent center, one glorious person. The dignity of that person gave a perfection, a vastness, a length and breadth, a height and depth, to that righteousness which never had been equalled and which never shall be equalled forever. It is the perfection of perfection, the excellency of excellency, the holiness of holiness. It is that in which God pre-eminently delights. Never had his law been so kept and honored before. Son of God and Son of Man in one person, he in this twofold character keeps the Father's law and in keeping it provides a righteousness so large and full that

This righteousness of God was no common righteousness. It was the righteousness of him who was both God and man; therefore it was not only the righteousness of God, but in addition to this, it was the righteousness of man. It embodied and exhibited all uncreated and all created perfection.

it can be shared with others, transferred to others, imputed to others; and God be glorified (as well as the sinner saved) by the transference and imputation. Never had God been so loved as now, with all divine love and with all human love. Never had God been so served and obeyed, as now he has been by him who is "God manifest in flesh." Never had God found one before who for love to the holy law was willing to become its victim that it might be honored; who for love to God was willing not only to be made under the law, but by thus coming under it, to subject himself to death, even the death of the cross; who for love to the fallen creature was willing to take the sinner's place, bear the sinner's burden, undergo the sinner's penalty, to assume the sinner's curse, die the sinner's death of shame and anguish, and go down in darkness to the sinner's grave.

The objections against *imputation* all resolve themselves into objections against *substitution* in any form. Vicarious suffering is even more unreasonable to some than vicarious obedience, and the arguments used in assailing the former apply with greater force against the latter. Yet human law recognizes both; the "laws of nature" show the existence of both; and the divine law, as interpreted by the great Lawgiver himself, acknowledges both. Man is willing to act on the principle of substitution or representation by another in earthly transactions – such as the payment of debt or the performance of duty or the descent of property; but he is not so willing to admit it, or proceed upon it, in the great transaction between him and God as to condemnation and righteousness. That to which he objects not in temporal things – giving one man the benefit of another's doings or another's sufferings; treating the man who has not paid the debt as if he had done so because another has paid it for him; or recognizing the legal right of a man to large wealth or a vast estate, no part of which he had earned or deserved, but which had come to him as the gift and fruit of another's lifetime's toil – he repudiates in spiritual things as unjust and unreasonable.

Men do not object to receive any kind or amount of this world's goods from another, though they have done nothing

Men do not object to receive any kind or amount of this world's goods from another, though they have done nothing to deserve them and everything to make them unworthy of them; but they refuse to accept the favor of God.

to deserve them and everything to make them unworthy of them; but they refuse to accept the favor of God, and a standing in righteousness before him on the ground of what a substitute has done and suffered. In earthly things they are willing to be represented by another, but not in heavenly things. The former is all fair, and just, and legal; the latter is absurd, an insult to their understanding, and a depreciation of their worth! Yet if they prized the heavenly as much as they do the earthly blessing, they would not entertain such scruples nor raise such objections as to receiving it from another as the result of his work. If God is willing that Christ should represent us, who are we that we should refuse to be represented by him? If God is willing to deal with us on the footing of Christ's obedience and to reckon that obedience to us as if it had been our own, who are we that we should reject such a method of blessing and call it unjust and impossible? This principle or theory of representation, of one man being treated far beyond his deserts in virtue of his being legally entitled to use the name or claims of another, runs through all earthly transactions. Why should it not in like manner pervade the heavenly?

Rejection of "imputed righteousness" because the words do not actually occur in Scripture is foolish and weak. Such terms as *Christianity*, the *Trinity*, the *Eucharist*, and *Plenary Inspiration* are not to be found in the Bible; yet, inasmuch as the thing, or object, or truth which these words truly and accurately cover is there, the term is received as substantially accurate and made use of without scruple. Such an objection savors more of little-minded cavilling than of the truth-seeking simplicity of faith. [5]

> *In earthly things unbelievers are willing to be represented by another, but not in heavenly things. The former is all fair, and just, and legal; the latter is absurd, an insult to their understanding, and a depreciation of their worth!*

5. Thus old Anthony Burgess, in 1655, wrote regarding imputation: "The righteousness the believer hath is imputed. It is an *accounted* or *reckoned* righteousness to him; it is not that which he hath inherently in himself, but God through Christ doth esteem of him as if he had it, and so deals with him as wholly righteous. This is a passive, not an active righteousness – a righteousness we *receive*, not that we *do*. This doctrine of imputed righteousness is by all erroneous persons judged to be like the abomination of desolation. Howsoever heretical persons contradict one another in other things, yet against this they are unanimously conspiring.

Refusal to accept the divine "theory" or doctrine of representation in and by another indicates in many cases mere indifference to the blessing to be received; in others, resentment of the way in which that doctrine utterly sets aside all excellency or merit on our part. Men will win the kingdom for themselves; they will deserve eternal life; they will not take forgiveness or righteousness freely from another's hands or be indebted to a substitute for what they are persuaded they can earn by their personal doings. Because the plan of representation or substitution is distasteful and humbling, they call it absurd and unjust. They refuse a heavenly inheritance on such terms, while perhaps at the very moment they are accepting an earthly estate on terms as totally irrespective of their own labor or goodness.

The Judge must either be the justifier or the condemner. That Judge is Jehovah. It is his office to condemn; it is his office also to justify. He does not condemn by infusing sin into the person who appears before him; so he does not justify by infusing righteousness into the sinner whom he acquits. It is as *Judge* that he acquits. But he does not merely acquit or absolve. He goes beyond this. The marvelous way in which he has met the claims of justice so as to enable him to pronounce a righteous acquittal enables him to replace, either on his own former place of innocence or on a higher, the sinner whom he absolves so freely and so completely. It was by representation

Because the plan of representation or substitution is distasteful and humbling, sinners call it absurd and unjust.

It is well enough known what reproaches and mocks are put upon it by the Popish party, calling it the putative and chimerical righteousness. The Socinians abominate it. The Castellians flout at it, saying they have an imputed learning and imputed modesty that hold imputed righteousness. The Arminians, though they grant faith to be accounted for righteousness, yet think it an idol of the Protestants' brain to say that Christ's righteousness is imputed to us, and say that it is nowhere expressed in Scripture…. Let this satisfy us, that the Scripture doth often mention an imputed righteousness, and therefore that it should not be matter of reproach, but worthy of all acceptation; and certainly, seeing none of us has such an inherent righteousness within ourselves as is able to endure before so perfect and holy a God, we ought greatly to rejoice in the goodness and mercy of God, who had provided such glorious robes for us, that when we were wholly naked and undone, hath procured a righteousness for us that neither men nor angels could bring about."

or substitution of the just for the unjust that he was enabled to acquit, and it is by the same representation or substitution that he lifts into a more glorious position the acquitted man.

The representative or substitute being the Son of God and therefore of infinite dignity in his person, the excellency of that which he is and does, when conveyed or reckoned to another, gives that other a claim to be treated far higher than he could otherwise in any circumstances have possessed. Some may have expressed his transference in terms too strong and absolute, as if we actually became as righteous as he is, as near to God as he is, as infinitely the objects of the Father's love as he is. But though there may have been unwise utterances on this point, which have needlessly afforded cause of offence and objection, it remains true that the man who believes in Jesus Christ – from the moment that he so believes – not only receives divine absolution from all guilt, but is so made legally possessor of his infinite righteousness that all to which that righteousness entitles becomes his, and he is henceforth treated by God according to the perfection of the perfect one, as if that perfection had been his own. "As he is, so are we [even] in *this world*" (*1 John* 4:17), that is, even *now*, in our state of imperfection, though men of unclean lips, and though dwelling among a people of unclean lips. As it is elsewhere written, "There is therefore *now* no condemnation to them that are in Christ Jesus" (*Romans* 8:1). Not only are we "delivered from the wrath to come" (*1 Thessalonians* 1:10), not only shall we "not come into condemnation" (*John* 5:24), not only are we "justified from all things" (*Acts* 13:39), but we are "made[6] *the righteousness of God* in him" (*2 Corinthians* 5:21).

The transaction is not one of *borrowing*. The perfection made over to us is *given*, not *lent*, by God. It becomes ours *in law*, ours for all legal ends, ours as efficaciously as if it had been from first to last our own in very deed.

The transaction is a real one between the sinner and God and carries with it all legal consequences, just as if the sinner

> *The transaction is not one of borrowing. The perfection made over to us is given, not lent, by God. It becomes ours in law, ours for all legal ends, ours as efficaciously as if it had been from first to last our own in very deed.*

6. Literally, we "become" – γινωμεθα.

had personally discharged his own debts and obtained a judicial *absolvitor* from all further claims whatever, a receipt in full from him to whom the great debt was due.

The transaction is one to which all the parties concerned have consented as being fully satisfied that injury has been done to none; nay, that all have been greatly more benefited by this mode of settlement than by the more direct one of the parties punishable undergoing the punishment in their own persons. When thus not merely no injustice is done to anyone, but when more than justice is done to all; when no one is defrauded, but when each gets far more than his due; how foolish, how preposterous, to speak of imputation as a violation of law and a subversion of the principles of righteous government!

The transaction is not one of indifference to sin or obliterative of the distinction between righteousness and unrighteousness. It is one which, of all that can be imagined, is most fitted to show the evil of evil, the malignity of sin, the divine hatred of all departure from perfection, the regard which God has to his law, his awful appreciation of justice, and his determination to secure at any cost – even the death of his Son – the righteous foundations of the universe and the sanctities of his eternal throne.

If the Christ of God, in his sorrowful life below, be but a specimen of suffering humanity or a model of patient calmness under wrong, not one of these things is manifested or secured. He is but one fragment more of a confused and disordered world where everything has broken loose from its anchorage, and each is dashing against the other in unmanageable chaos without any prospect of a holy or tranquil issue. He is an example of the complete triumph of evil over goodness, of wrong over right, of Satan over God – one from whose history we can draw only this terrible conclusion: God has lost the control of his own world; sin has become too great a power for God either to regulate or extirpate; the utmost that God can do is to produce a rare example of suffering holiness which he allows the world to tread upon without being able effectually to interfere; righteousness, after ages of buffeting

If the Christ of God, in his sorrowful life below, be but a specimen of suffering humanity or a model of patient calmness under wrong, not one of these things is manifested or secured. He is but one fragment more of a confused and disordered world where everything has broken loose from its anchorage, and each is dashing against the other in unmanageable chaos.

and scorn, must retire from the field in utter helplessness and permit the unchecked reign of evil.

If the cross be the mere exhibition of self-sacrifice and patient meekness, then the hope of the world is gone. We had always thought that there was a potent purpose of God at work in connection with the sin-bearing work of the holy sufferer which, allowing sin for a season to develop itself, was preparing and evolving a power which would utterly overthrow it – and sweep Earth clean of evil – moral and physical. But if the crucified Christ be the mere self-denying man, we have nothing more at work for the overthrow of evil than has again and again been witnessed when some hero or some martyr rose above the level of his age to protest against evils which he could not eradicate and to bear witness in life and death for truth and righteousness – in vain.

The transaction is, in all its aspects and in its bearings on all parties and interests, strictly and nobly righteous. It provides a righteous channel through which God's free love may flow down to man. It lays a righteous foundation for the pardon of sin. It secures a righteous welcome for the returning sinner. It makes the justification of the justified even more righteous than his condemnation would have been; while it makes the condemnation of the condemned not only doubly righteous, but at once a vindication and an exhibition of infinite and immutable justice.

There can be no justification without some kind of righteousness, and according to the nature or value of that righteousness will the justification be. That justification will necessarily partake of the value of the righteousness which justifies. If the righteousness be poor and finite, our standing as justified men will be the same. If it be glorious and divine, even such will our standing be. God the justifier, acting according to the excellency of that righteousness and recognizing its claims in behalf of all who consent to be treated according to its value, deals with each believing man – weak as his faith may be – in conformity with the demands of that righteousness. All that it can claim for us we may ask and expect; all that it can claim for us God will assuredly bestow. He

If the crucified Christ be the mere self-denying man, we have nothing more at work for the overthrow of evil than has again and again been witnessed when some hero or some martyr rose above the level of his age to protest against evils which he could not eradicate and to bear witness in life and death for truth and righteousness – in vain.

by whom, in believing, we consent to be represented puts in the claim for us in his name; and the demands of that name are as just as they are irresistible.

Our legal responsibilities as transgressors of the law are transferred to him; and his legal claims, as the fulfiller of the law, pass over to us. It is not a transference of characters nor an exchange of persons that we mean by this; but a transference of liabilities, an exchange of judicial demands. Very strikingly is the case between the sinner and God put in our Lord's parable of the two debtors, of which these words are the sum: "When they had nothing to pay, he frankly forgave them both" (*Luke* 7:42). Here is our thorough bankruptcy and God's full discharge. What can law say to us after this? "It is God that justifies." We are bankrupts; our assets are nothing; God looks at the case, pities us, and clears everything.

The epithet "fictitious" which some have applied to this representation need not trouble or alarm us. The question with us is not, Can we clear up fully the abstract principles which the transaction embodies? but, Does it carry with it legal consequences by which we are set in a new standing before God and entitled to plead, in all our dealings with God, the meritoriousness of an infinitely perfect life the payment effected in behalf of those who had nothing to pay, by an infinitely perfect death?

Thus "grace reigns through righteousness unto eternal life through Jesus Christ our Lord" (*Romans* 5:21).[7] God's free love has found for itself a righteous channel along which it flows in all its fulness to the ungodly. For while all that the believing man receives, he receives from grace; yet it is no less true that all that he receives, he receives from righteousness, from the hand of a righteous God acting according to the claims of a righteousness which is absolutely and divinely perfect.

He who refuses to be represented by another before God must represent himself and draw near to God on the strength

> *He who refuses to be represented by another before God must represent himself and draw near to God on the strength of what he is in himself or what he has done.*

---

7. "Through (διa) righteousness," and also "through (διa) Jesus Christ our Lord"; the one the active instrument, the other the efficient cause: (1) God the justifier; (2) Christ the cause; (3) righteousness the instrument.

of what he is in himself or what he has done. How he is likely to fare in such an approach, let his own conscience tell him if he will not believe the explicit declaration of the Holy Spirit that "through him [Christ] we have access by one Spirit to the Father" (*Ephesians* 2:18); or Christ's own affirmation concerning this: "I am the way," and "I am the door" (*John* 14:6; 10:9).

As for him who, conscious of unfitness to draw near to God by reason of personal imperfection, is willing to be represented by the Son of God and to substitute a divine claim and merit for a human; let him know that God is willing to receive him with all his imperfection because of the perfection of another, legally transferred to him by the just God and Judge; that God is presenting to him a righteousness not only sufficient to clear him from all guilt and to pay his penalty to the full, but to exalt him to a new rank and dignity such as he could not possibly acquire by the labors or prayers or goodnesses of ten thousand such lives as his own.

"Christ is all and in all" (*Colossians* 3:11). He who knows this, knows what fully satisfies and cheers. He who knows this best has the deepest and truest peace: He has learned the secret of being always a sinner, yet always righteous; always incomplete, yet always complete; always empty, yet always full; always poor, yet always rich. We would not say of that fulness, Drink deep or taste not; for even to taste is to be blest. But yet we say, Drink deep; for he who drinks deepest is the happiest as well as the holiest man.[8]

> "*Think not that to live always on Christ for justification is a low and beggarly thing – a staying at the foundation. For, let me tell you, depart from a sense of the meritorious means of your justification before God, and you will quickly grow light, and frothy, and vain; you will be subject to errors and delusions.*"
> – *John Bunyan*

---

8. "Think not that to live always on Christ for justification is a low and beggarly thing – a staying at the foundation. For, let me tell you, depart from a sense of the meritorious means of your justification before God, and you will quickly grow light, and frothy, and vain; you will be subject to errors and delusions, for this is not to 'hold the head,' from which nourishment is administered. Why not live upon Christ alway and especially as he standeth the Mediator between God and the soul, defending thee with the merit of his blood, and covering thee with His infinite righteousness from the wrath of God and the curse of the law? Can there be any greater comfort ministered to thee, than to know that thy person stands just before God; just, and justified from all things that would otherwise swallow thee up? Is peace with God and assurance

Recognition of the perfection of the Lord Jesus Christ, as to personal excellency, official suitableness, and vicarious value, is that only which satisfies the heart and conscience of the sinner. It satisfies the former by presenting it with the most lovable of all lovable objects on which a heart can rest, and the latter by furnishing it with that which can alone remove from the trembling conscience every possible ground for claim. True knowledge of the person of him who is "the Christ of God," appreciation of his completed sacrifice and living attachment to himself, can alone meet the evil condition into which man has sunk; not only lifting him out of the horrible pit and out of the miry clay; not only setting his feet upon the eternal rock; but raising him up into a region of peace and holiness such as no less costly means could have accomplished for the fallen son of Adam.

The assumption of all our legal responsibilities by a divine substitute is that which brings us deliverance.

"He who knew no sin was made sin for us." On this basis we build for eternity. The assumption of all our legal responsibilities by a divine substitute is that which brings us deliverance. These responsibilities were great, and no effort of ours to rid ourselves of them could possibly succeed. They must all be fully met. Such judicial claims as are brought against the sinner cannot be waived. They are righteous claims and must be settled righteously. God offers to settle them for us by transferring them to one who can be answerable for them. The basis of this eternal settlement was laid at the cross, and on that basis God is willing to deal with any sinner for the complete canceling of all his liabilities.

The second Man came, as the Righteous One, to undo by his righteousness all that the first Man, as the unrighteous one, had done by his unrighteousness. Yet such is the power of sin that it took thirty-three years of righteousness to undo what one act of unrighteousness had done. One act of disobedience to one statute had done the evil; a lifetime's obedience to the whole law of God is required for the undoing. Only by

---

of Heaven of so little respect with thee, that thou slightest the very foundation thereof, even faith in the blood and righteousness of Christ?"
– John Bunyan, *Justification by Imputed Righteousness*

this can man be replaced in that condition of righteousness in which God can accept him and the law recognize him as entitled to blessing.

Our *characters* are not transferred to Christ, but our *liabilities* are; and in our acceptance of God's mode of transference, we make the complete exchange by which we are absolved from all guilt and enter into a state of "no condemnation." Sin reckoned to Christ as our substitute, and righteousness reckoned to us as the acceptors of that substitute: This is deliverance, and peace, and life eternal.[9]

"Christ the Son of God was given, not for the righteous and holy, but for the unrighteous and sinners."
– Martin Luther

9. "Labor therefore diligently, that not only out of the time of temptation, but also in the danger and conflict of death, when your conscience is thoroughly afraid with the remembrance of your sins past, and the devil assaults you with great violence, going about to overwhelm you with heaps, floods, and whole seas of sins, to terrify you, to draw you from Christ, and to drive you to despair; that then, I say, you may be able to say with sure confidence, Christ the Son of God was given, not for the righteous and holy, but for the unrighteous and sinners. If I were righteous and had no sin, I should have no need of Christ to be my reconciler. Why then, O you peevish "holy" Satan, will you make me to be holy, and to seek righteousness in myself, when in very deed I have nothing in me but sins, and most grievous sins? Not feigned or trifling sins, but such as are against the first table; to wit, great infidelity, doubting, despair, contempt of God, hatred, ignorance, and blaspheming of God, unthankfulness, abusing of God's name, neglecting, loathing, and despising the Word of God, and such like."
— Martin Luther

7

Not Faith, But Christ

O<small>UR</small> justification is the direct result of our believing the Gospel; our knowledge of our own justification comes from our believing God's promise of justification to everyone who believes these glad tidings. For there is not only the divine testimony, but there is the promise annexed to it, assuring eternal life to every one who receives that testimony. There is first, then, a believed *Gospel*, and then there is a believed *promise*. The latter is the "appropriation," as it is called; which, after all, is nothing but the acceptance of the *promise* which is everywhere coupled with the Gospel message. The believed Gospel *saves*, but it is the believed promise that *assures* us of this salvation.

Yet, after all, faith is not our righteousness. It is accounted to us *in order to* (εἰς) righteousness (*Romans* 4:5), but not as righteousness; for in that case it would be a *work* like any other doing of man. As such, it would be incompatible with the righteousness of the Son of God; the "righteousness which is by faith." Faith connects us with the righteousness and is therefore totally distinct from it. To confound the one with the other is to subvert the whole Gospel of the grace of God. Our act of faith must ever be a separate thing from that which we believe.

God reckons the believing man as having done all righteousness, though he has not done any and though

Faith connects us with the righteousness and is therefore totally distinct from it. To confound the one with the other is to subvert the whole Gospel of the grace of God. Our act of faith must ever be a separate thing from that which we believe.

79

his faith is not righteousness. In this sense it is that faith is counted to us for, or in order to, righteousness; and that we are "justified by faith." Faith does not justify as a work, or as a moral act, or a piece of goodness, or as a gift of the Spirit; but simply because it is the bond between us and the substitute – a very slender bond in one sense, but strong as iron in another. The work of Christ *for us* is the object of faith; the Spirit's work *in us* is that which produces this faith: It is out of the former, not out of the latter, that our peace and justification come. Without the touch of the rod the water would not have gushed forth; yet it was the rock, and not the rod, that contained the water.

The bringer of the sacrifice into the tabernacle was to lay his hand upon the head of the sheep or the bullock. Otherwise the offering would not have been accepted for him. But the laying on of his hand was not the same as the victim on which it was laid. The serpent-bitten Israelite was to look at the uplifted serpent of brass in order to be healed. But his looking was not the brazen serpent. We may say it was his looking that healed him, just as the Lord said, "Your faith has saved you"; but this is figurative language. It was not his act of looking that healed him, but the object to which he looked. So faith is not our righteousness. It merely knits us to the Righteous One and makes us partakers of his righteousness. By a natural figure of speech, faith is often magnified into something great; whereas it is really nothing but our consenting to be saved by another. Its supposed magnitude is derived from the greatness of the object which it grasps, the excellence of the righteousness which it accepts. Its preciousness is not its own, but the preciousness of him to whom it links us.

Faith is not our physician; it only brings us to the Physician. It is not even our medicine; it only administers the medicine, divinely prepared by him who "heals all our diseases." In all our believing, let us remember God's words to Israel: "I am Jehovah, who heals you" (*Exodus* 15:26). Our faith is but our touching Jesus; and what is even this, in reality, but his touching us?

> *The work of Christ for us is the object of faith; the Spirit's work in us is that which produces this faith: It is out of the former, not out of the latter, that our peace and justification come. Without the touch of the rod the water would not have gushed forth; yet it was the rock, and not the rod, that contained the water.*

Faith is not our savior. It was not faith that was born at Bethlehem and died on Golgotha for us. It was not faith that loved us and gave itself for us, that bore our sins in its own body on the tree, that died and rose again for our sins. Faith is one thing, and the Savior is another. Faith is one thing, and the cross is another. Let us not confound them nor ascribe to a poor, imperfect act of man that which belongs exclusively to the Son of the living God.

Faith is not perfection. Yet only by perfection – either our own or another's – can we be saved. That which is imperfect cannot justify, and an imperfect faith could not in any sense be a righteousness. If it is to justify, it must be perfect. It must be like "the Lamb, without blemish and without spot." An imperfect faith may connect us with the perfection of another; but it cannot of itself do anything for us, either in protecting us from wrath or securing the divine acquittal. All faith here is imperfect. Our security is this: It matters not how poor or weak our faith may be; if it touches the perfect one, all is well. The touch draws out the virtue that is in him, and we are saved. The slightest imperfection in our faith, if faith were our righteousness, would be fatal to every hope. But the imperfection of our faith, however great, if faith be but the approximation or contact between us and the fulness of the substitute, is no hindrance to our participation in his righteousness. God has asked and provided a perfect righteousness; he nowhere asks nor expects a perfect faith. An earthenware pitcher can convey water to the traveler's thirsty lips as well as one of gold; nay, a broken vessel even, if there be but "a shard to take water from the pit" (*Isaiah* 30:14) will suffice. So a feeble, very feeble faith will connect us with the righteousness of the Son of God – the faith, perhaps, that can only cry, "Lord, I believe; help my unbelief."

Faith is not *satisfaction to God*. In no sense and in no aspect can faith be said to satisfy God or to satisfy the law. Yet if it is to be our righteousness, it must satisfy. Being imperfect, it cannot satisfy; being merely human, it cannot satisfy even though it were perfect. That which satisfies must be capable of bearing our guilt; and that which bears our guilt must be

It matters not how poor or weak our faith may be; if it touches the perfect one, all is well. The touch draws out the virtue that is in him, and we are saved.

not only perfect, but divine. It is a sin bearer that we need, and our faith cannot be a sin bearer. Faith can expiate no guilt, can accomplish no propitiation, can pay no penalty, can wash away no stain, can provide no righteousness. It brings us to the cross, where there is expiation and propitiation, and payment, and cleansing, and righteousness; but in itself it has no merit and no virtue.

Faith is not Christ, nor the cross of Christ. Faith is not the blood, nor the sacrifice. It is not the altar, nor the laver, nor the mercy-seat, nor the incense. It does not work, but accepts a work done ages ago; it does not wash, but leads us to the fountain opened for sin and for uncleanness. It does not create; it merely links us to that new thing which was created when the "everlasting righteousness" was brought in (*Daniel* 9:24).

And as faith goes on, so it continues; always the beggar's outstretched hand, never the rich man's gold; always the cable, never the anchor; the knocker, not the door, or the palace, or the table; the handmaid, not the mistress; the lattice which lets in the light, not the Sun.

Without worthiness in itself, faith knits us to the infinite worthiness of him in whom the Father delights; and so knitting us, it presents us perfect in the perfection of another.

Without worthiness in itself, it knits us to the infinite worthiness of him in whom the Father delights; and so knitting us, it presents us perfect in the perfection of another. Though it is not the foundation laid in Zion, it brings us to that foundation and keeps us there, "grounded and settled" (*Colossians* 1:23), that we may not be moved away from the hope of the Gospel. Though it is not "the Gospel," the "glad tidings," it receives the good news as God's eternal verities and bids the soul rejoice in them; though it is not the burnt offering, it stands still and gazes on the ascending flame which assures us that the wrath which should have consumed the sinner has fallen upon the substitute.

Though faith is not "the righteousness," it is the tie between it and us. It realizes our present standing before God in the excellency of his own Son, and it tells us that our eternal standing in the ages to come is in the same excellency and depends on the perpetuity of that righteousness which can never change. For never shall we put off that Christ whom we put on when we believed (*Romans* 13:14; *Galatians* 3:27).

This divine raiment is "to everlasting." It grows not old, it cannot be torn, and its beauty fades not away.

Nor does faith lead us away from that cross to which at first it led us. Some in our day speak as if we soon get beyond the cross and might leave it behind; that the cross having done all it could do for us when first we came under its shadow, we may quit it and go forward; that to remain always at the cross is to be babes, not men.

But what is the cross? It is not the mere wooden pole, or some imitation of it, such as Romanists use. These we may safely leave behind us. We need not pitch our tent upon the literal Golgotha or in Joseph's garden. But the great truth which the cross represents we can no more part with than we can part with life eternal. In this sense, to turn our back upon the cross is to turn our back upon Christ crucified – to give up our connection with the Lamb that was slain. The truth is that all that Christ did and suffered – from the manger to the tomb – forms one glorious whole, no part of which shall ever become needless or obsolete and no part of which we can ever leave without forsaking the whole. I am always at the manger, and yet I know that mere incarnation cannot save; always in Gethsemane, and yet I believe that its agony was not the finished work; always at the cross with my face toward it and my eye on the crucified one, and yet I am persuaded that the sacrifice there was completed once for all; always looking into the grave, though I rejoice that it is empty, and that "he is not here, but is risen"; always resting (with the angel) on the stone that was rolled away, and handling the graveclothes, and realizing a risen Christ, an ascended and interceding Lord: yet on no pretext whatever leaving any part of my Lord's life or death behind me, but unceasingly keeping up my connection with him, as born, living, dying, buried, and rising again, and drawing out from each part some new blessing every day and hour.

Man, in his natural spirit of self-justifying legalism, has tried to get away from the cross of Christ and its perfection, or to erect another cross instead, or to set up a screen of ornaments between himself and it, or to alter its true

Some in our day speak as if we soon get beyond the cross and might leave it behind; that the cross having done all it could do for us when first we came under its shadow, we may quit it and go forward; that to remain always at the cross is to be babes, not men.

meaning into something more congenial to his tastes, or to transfer the virtue of it to some act or performance or feeling of his own. Thus the simplicity of the cross is nullified and its saving power denied.

The cross saves completely, or not at all. Our faith does not divide the work of salvation between itself and the cross. It is the acknowledgment that the cross alone saves, and that it saves alone. Faith adds nothing to the cross or to its healing virtue. It owns the fulness, and sufficiency, and suitableness of the work done there and bids the toiling spirit cease from its labors and enter into rest. Faith does not come to Calvary to *do* anything. It comes to see the glorious spectacle of all things done and to accept this completion without a misgiving as to its efficacy. It listens to the "It is finished!" of the sin bearer and says, "Amen." Where faith begins, there labor ends – labor, I mean, *for* life and pardon. Faith is rest, not toil. It is the giving up of all the former weary efforts to do or feel something good in order to induce God to love and pardon; the calm reception of the truth so long rejected that God is not waiting for any such inducements, but loves and pardons of his own goodwill and is showing that goodwill to any sinner who will come to him on such a footing, casting away his own poor performances or goodnesses and relying implicitly upon the free love of him who so loved the world that he gave his only begotten Son.

Faith is the acknowledgment of the entire absence of all goodness in us and the recognition of the cross as the substitute for all the want on our part. Faith saves because it owns the complete salvation of another, not because it contributes anything to that salvation. There is no dividing or sharing the work between our own belief and him in whom we believe. The whole work is his, not ours, from first to last. Faith does not believe in itself, but in the Son of God. Like the beggar, it receives everything, but gives nothing. It consents to be a debtor forever to the free love of God. Its resting place is the foundation laid in Zion. it rejoices in another, not in itself. Its song is, "Not by works of righteousness which we have done, but by his mercy he saved us."

Faith saves because it owns the complete salvation of another, not because it contributes anything to that salvation. There is no dividing or sharing the work between our own belief and him in whom we believe.

Christ crucified is to be the burden of our preaching, and the substance of our belief, from first to last. At no time in the saint's life does he cease to need the cross, though at times he may feel that his special need (in spiritual perplexity or the exigency of conflict with evil) may be the incarnation, or the agony in the garden, or the resurrection, or the hope of the promised advent, to be glorified in his saints, and admired in all them that believe.

But the question is not, What truths are we to believe? but, What truths are we to believe *for justification*?

That Christ is to come again in glory and in majesty, as Judge and King, is an article of the Christian faith, the disbelief of which would almost lead us to doubt the Christianity of him who disbelieves it. Yet we are not in any sense justified by the second advent of our Lord, but solely by his first. We believe in his ascension, yet our justification is not connected with it. So we believe his resurrection, yet are we not justified by faith in it, but by faith in his death – that death which made him at once our propitiation and our righteousness.

"He was raised again on account of our having been justified" (*Romans* 4:25) is the clear statement of the Word. The resurrection was the visible pledge of a justification already accomplished.

"The power of his resurrection" (*Philippians* 3:10) does not refer to atonement, or pardon, or reconciliation; but to our being renewed in the spirit of our minds, to our being "begotten again unto a living hope, by the resurrection from the dead" (*1 Peter* 1:3). That which is *internal*, such as our quickening, our strengthening, our renewing, may be connected with resurrection and resurrection power; but that which is *external*, such as God's pardoning, and justifying, and accepting, must be connected with the cross alone.

The doctrine of our being justified by an infused resurrection righteousness,[1] or, as it is called, justification in

The doctrine of our being justified by an infused resurrection righteousness, or, as it is called, justification in a risen Christ, is a complete subversion of the Surety's work.

1. Mr. Edward Irving, Dr. John Henry Newman, and the followers of Mr. John Nelson Darby are the modern upholders of this new form of old heresy. Formerly it was simply justification by an infused righteousness;

a risen Christ, is a complete subversion of the Surety's work when "he died for our sins, according to the Scriptures," or when "he washed us from our sins in his own blood," or when he gave us the robes "washed white in the blood of the Lamb."

It is *the* blood that justifies (*Romans* 5:9). It is the blood that pacifies the conscience, purging it from dead works to serve the living God (*Hebrews* 9:14). It is the blood that emboldens us to enter through the veil into the holiest and go up to the sprinkled mercy-seat. It is the blood that we are to drink for the quenching of our thirst (*John* 6:55). It is the blood by which we have peace with God (*Colossians* 1:20). It is the blood through which we have redemption (*Ephesians* 1:7), by which we are brought nigh (*Ephesians* 2:13), by which we are sanctified (*Hebrews* 13:12). It is the blood which is the seal of the everlasting covenant (*Hebrews* 13:20). It is the blood which cleanses (*1 John* 1:7), which gives us victory (*Revelation* 12:11), and with which we have communion in the Supper of the Lord (*1 Corinthians* 10:16). It is the blood which is the purchase money or ransom of the church of God (*Acts* 20:28).

The blood and the resurrection are very different things; for the blood is death, and the resurrection is life.

It is remarkable that in the book of *Leviticus* there is no reference to resurrection in any of the sacrifices. It is death throughout. All that is needed for a sinner's pardon, and justification, and cleansing, and peace, is there fully set forth in symbol – and that symbol is death upon the altar. Justification by any kind of infused or inherent righteousness is wholly inconsistent with the services of the tabernacle – most of all justification by an infused resurrection-righteousness.

The sacrifices are God's symbolical exposition of the way of a sinner's approach and acceptance, and in none of these does resurrection hold any place. If justification be in a *risen* Christ, then assuredly that way was not revealed to Israel; and the manifold offerings, so minutely detailed, did not answer

Justification by any kind of infused or inherent righteousness is wholly inconsistent with the services of the tabernacle – most of all justification by an infused resurrection-righteousness.

---

now it is by an infused righteousness derived from Christ's resurrection. See Dr. Newman's sermon, *Christ's Resurrection the Source of Justification.*

the question, How may man be just with God? nor give to the worshipers of old one hint as to the way by which God was to justify the ungodly.

"Christ in us, the hope of glory" (*Colossians* 1:27) is a well-known and blessed truth; but Christ in us, our justification, is a ruinous error, leading men away from a crucified Christ – a Christ crucified *for us*. Christ *for us* is one truth; Christ *in us* is quite another. The mingling of these two together, or the transposition of them, is the nullifying of the one finished work of the substitute. Let it be granted that Christ *in us* is the source of holiness and fruitfulness (*John* 15:4); but let it never be overlooked that first of all there must be Christ *for us* as our propitiation, our justification, our righteousness. The risen Christ in us, our justification, is a modern theory which subverts the cross. Washing, pardoning, reconciling, justifying, all come from the one work of the cross, not from resurrection. The dying Christ completed the work for us from which all the above benefits flow. The risen Christ but sealed and applied what, three days before, he had done once for all.

It is somewhat remarkable that in the Lord's Supper (as in the Passover) there is no reference to resurrection. The broken body and the shed blood are the Alpha and Omega of that ordinance. In it we have communion (not with Christ as risen and glorified, but) with the body of Christ and the blood of Christ (1 *Corinthians* 10:16), that is, Christ *upon the cross.* "This do in remembrance of me." "As often as you eat this bread, and drink this cup, you show the Lord's death till he come." If, after we have been at the cross, we are to pass on and leave it behind us as no longer needed, seeing we are justified by the risen Christ in us, let those who hold that deadly error say why all reference to resurrection should be excluded from the great feast and why the death of the Lord should be the one object presented to us at the table.

"Life in a risen Christ" is another way of expressing the same error. If by this were meant only that resurrection has been made the channel or instrument through which the life and the justification are secured for us on and by the cross – as when the apostle speaks of our being begotten again unto

The risen Christ in us, our justification, is a modern theory which subverts the cross. Washing, pardoning, reconciling, justifying, all come from the one work of the cross, not from resurrection.

a lively hope by the "resurrection of Christ from the dead," or when we are said to be "risen with Christ" – one would not object to the phraseology. But when we find it used as expressive of dissociation of these benefits from the cross and derivation of them from resurrection solely, then do we condemn it as untrue and anti-scriptural. For concerning this "life" let us hear the words of the Lord: "The bread that I will give is my flesh, which I will give for the life of the world" (*John* 6:51). "Except you eat the flesh of the Son of Man and drink his blood, you have no life in you. Whoever eats my flesh and drinks my blood has eternal life, and I will raise him up at the last day. For my flesh is meat indeed, and my blood is drink indeed. He that eats my flesh, and drinks my blood, dwells in me, and I in him" (*John* 6:53-56).

This assuredly is not the doctrine of "life in a risen Christ," or "a risen Christ in us, our justification and life." I do not enter on the exposition of these verses. I simply cite them. They bear witness to the cross. They point to the broken body and shed blood as our daily and hourly food, our life-long feast from which there comes into us the life which the Son of Man, by his death, has obtained for us. That flesh is life imparting; that blood is life imparting; and this not once, but forevermore. It is not incarnation on the one hand, nor is it resurrection on the other, on which we are thus to feed and out of which this life comes forth; it is that which lies between these two – death – the sacrificial death of the Son of God. It is not the personality nor the life history of the Christ of God which is the special quickener and nourishment of our souls, but the blood shedding. Not that we are to separate the former from the latter, but still it is on the latter that we are specially to feed, and this all the days of our lives.

"Christ, our Passover, has been sacrificed for us." Here we rest, protected by the paschal blood and feeding on the paschal lamb, with its unleavened bread and bitter herbs, from day to day. "Let us keep the feast" (*1 Corinthians* 5:8). Wherever we are, let us keep it. For we carry our Passover with us, always ready, always fresh. With girded loins and staff in hand, as wayfarers, we move along through the rough or the smooth

> *It is not incarnation on the one hand, nor is it resurrection on the other, on which we are thus to feed and out of which this life comes forth; it is that which lies between these two – death – the sacrificial death of the Son of God.*

of the wilderness, our face toward the land of promise.

That paschal lamb is Christ crucified. As such he is our protection, our pardon, our righteousness, our food, our strength, our peace. Fellowship with him upon the cross is the secret of a blessed and holy life.

We feed on that which has passed through the fire, on that which has come from the altar. No other food can quicken or sustain the spiritual life of a believing man. The unbroken body will not suffice, nor will the risen or glorified body avail. The broken body and shed blood of the Son of God are the viands on which we feast; and it is under the shadow of the cross that we sit down to partake of these and find refreshment for our daily journey, strength for our hourly warfare. His flesh is meat indeed; his blood is drink indeed.

The unbroken body will not suffice, nor will the risen or glorified body avail.

8

What the Resurrection of the Substitute Has Done

Oneness is not substitution; and it is not by the former, but by the latter, that we are justified.

DEATH is not resurrection, and the benefits of the Surety's death are not the same as those of his resurrection. Yet let us not overlook the "glorious things" spoken concerning the latter.

Our justified life, or our life as justified men, is certainly in one sense resurrection life, produced and sustained by resurrection power. But not for a moment is that justified life severed from the cross, nor is the justified man to lose sight of his indebtedness to the cross for justification.

That we are risen with Christ is the truth of God. Oneness with him who rose is our privilege and our standing. But oneness is not substitution; and it is not by the former, but by the latter, that we are justified. Resurrection points us back to a finished substitution and seals its blessings to us.

"Justified in the Spirit" is one of the apostle's references to Christ's resurrection. As he was brought again from the dead by the blood of the everlasting covenant (*Hebrews* 13:20), so was he justified in or by the Spirit in raising him from the dead. He died as a criminal and went down to the grave as such; but the Spirit raises him and thereby declares him righteous, free from the imputed guilt under which he went down to the tomb.

But let us look a little more minutely into Christ's

resurrection, lest we should be led to undervalue it. The resurrection must not hide the cross; neither must the cross hide the resurrection.

The words of the angel to the women are meant for us: "He is not here, for he is risen" (*Matthew* 28:6).

Man did all that he could to hinder the resurrection of the Son of God. He had succeeded in slaying the prince of life; and he is resolved that, if he can help it, the dead shall not arise. Samson is in prison, and must be kept there. The great stone, the watch, the Roman seal are all proofs of this determination.

But he knows not his prisoner. He might as well bind the whirlwind with a cord of silk, or shut up the lightning in one of his chambers and say to it, Thou shalt not go forth. Death itself, stronger than man, could not hold its prey. Before the dawn of the third day, the earthquake shook the tomb (the earthquake of *Psalm* 18:6, 7), the angel of the Lord descended, the stone was rolled away, the seal was broken, and the dead came forth.

Even his own believe not that he will rise. They would not try to hinder his resurrection, but, treating it as a thing incredible, they act as those who believe that all is over and that the cross has destroyed their hopes. They would not close the sepulchre, nor seal it; they would roll away the stone and break the seal, but this is only to anoint him for his final burial. It is not the expression of hope, but of despair.

But the tomb of the Son of God is the place of light, not of darkness; of hope, not of despair; of life, not of death. They come to look on the dead; they find the living. The seekers of the crucified Jesus find the risen Son of God. The garments of death are all that the tomb contains; the linen clothes – still stained with blood – and the carefully folded napkin – folded by angels' hands, if not by his own. They had brought their myrrh and aloes and spices to keep corruption from entering; forgetful that it is the Incorruptible whose body they are thus needlessly though lovingly embalming, ignorant of the meaning of the ancient promise, "You will not allow your Holy One to see corruption."

His friends would roll away the stone and break the seal, but this is only to anoint him for his final burial. It is not the expression of hope, but of despair.

The earthquake and the brightness were too terrible for man to bear. "For fear of him, the keepers did shake and became as dead men." Nor does he try to allay their terror. Let them tremble on. But for those who are seeking the crucified one, he has words of love and peace.

But friend and enemy are both at fault. The unbelief of the former and the resistance of the latter are met equally with a strange surprise. For God's thoughts are not our thoughts nor his ways our ways. The angel of the Lord descends; he rolls back the stone; he sits upon it to show himself in his brightness to the watchers; he opens the gate that the Holy One may go forth. Not that he raises or assists in raising the Son of God. That is beyond the mightiest of these mighty ones, those angels that excel in strength. But he is honored to have a share in the scene as porter or doorkeeper of that glorious shrine. With him came the earthquake, the second that had occurred during these three days – the first being when the prince of life entered the chambers of death, and at the open door many of the dead saints of other days came forth; the second being when this same prince of life left these chambers and burst the bands of death, shaking creation with the tread of his feet as he marched forth in triumph.

The earthquake and the brightness were too terrible for man to bear. "For fear of him, the keepers did shake and became as dead men." Nor does he try to allay their terror. Let them tremble on. But for those who are seeking the crucified one, he has words of love and peace. To the keepers he was as the lightning; to the women he was as the dayspring from on high. "Fear not; I know that you seek Jesus, who was crucified."

That which follows is the angel's message to these women – and to us no less in these last days. It is the reason for the cheer, the comfort he had spoken. It is the blessed contents of the cup, the ingredients of the heavenly wine, which he was giving them to drink. And the substance of it is, "Jesus lives." The comfort with which the Lord himself once comforted the sorrowing father of Capernaum was, "The maid is not dead, but sleeps"; so the comfort ministered by the angel is like this, only it goes far beyond it: "He is not dead; he does not even sleep: He has awakened; he has arisen." And as the Lord calmed the fears of his disciples once with, "Be of good cheer; it is I; be not afraid"; so did the angel here. As in Patmos the Lord allayed the alarm of the beloved disciple with "Fear not, I am the First and the Last; I am he that lives, and was dead; and behold, I am alive forevermore"; so does the angel soothe the fear of the trembling women: "Fear not; he is not here; he is risen: Come, see the place where the Lord lay."

Let us mark, then, the glad tidings which the angel brings us regarding him who died and was buried.

He is not here. This is the only place regarding which it could be accounted good news to say, Christ is *not* here. Christ is *here*, was good news at Bethany, at Jericho, at Nain, at Capernaum, or on the Sea of Galilee; but Christ is *not* here is the good news from Joseph's tomb. A *present* Christ would be accounted the joy and security of other places; it is an *absent* Christ that is announced as the blessing, the consolation, here. He is *not* here is one of the gladdest sounds that ever fell on human ears. Were he still here, what and where should we have been?

And who is it that you are seeking here? The mortal or the immortal? And what place is this in which you expect to find the Son of God? In a grave? Is this the place for immortality? Is it likely that there should be life in the dwellings of death? Why seek ye the living among the dead? No; not here – not *here*; not in this place of death can the prince of life be found. He *was* here, indeed; but he *is* not. These rock walls and this rock gate cannot hold him. He *was* in Gethsemane, in Pilate's palace, on the cross; but not now. These he has visited, but in none of them has he remained. He has left them all behind. With him it is all life, and incorruption, and glory now. He is not here!

If not here, where? That we soon discover when we follow him to Emmaus and to Galilee. But even though we knew not, does it matter save for this: that we may learn that his disappearance has not been a forsaking of Earth, nor a turning his back upon the children of men? His disappearance from the tomb is only the carrying out of his love.

He is risen. He was laid down upon that rocky floor, but only to rest there for a day. For that tomb was his first earthly resting place; all before that was weariness. Having rested

"He is not here" is one of the gladdest sounds that ever fell on human ears. Were he still here, what and where should we have been?

there for a short season, he rises; and with renewed strength, into which hereafter no element of weariness can enter, he resumes his work. He has not been carried off, either by friend or enemy. He has been raised by the Father as the righteous one; the fulfiller of his purpose; the finisher of his work; the destroyer of death; the conqueror of him who has the power of death; the Father's beloved Son in whom he is well pleased. This true temple has been destroyed, only to be rebuilt in greater and more undecaying magnificence. This true Siloam has only for three days intermitted the flow of its missioned waters, that it might gush forth in larger fulness. This true Sun has only for three days been darkened, that it might be relighted in its incorruptible glory.

In Christ's resurrection we read the Father's testimony to his Sonship; the Father's seal set to his completed propitiation; the Father's declaration of satisfaction and delight in the work of Calvary.

He is risen! Yes; and now we see more fully the meaning of his own words spoken at a tomb over one whom death had bound: "I am the resurrection and the life" – himself at once the raiser and the raised, the quickener and the quickened, the possessor and the giver of an infinite life – a higher kind of life than that which the first Adam knew – a life which can force its way into the dungeons of death, transforming them by its resistless power into the dwellings, the palaces, the temples of immortality and glory.

He is risen! He has tasted death, but he has not seen corruption; for he is the Holy One of God, and upon holiness corruption cannot fasten. As the beloved of the Father, he rises from the dead; for the Father loves him because he gives his life for the sheep. And in this resurrection we read the Father's testimony to his Sonship; the Father's seal set to his completed propitiation; the Father's declaration of satisfaction and delight in the work of Calvary.

It was henceforth with a risen Master that the disciples had to do. It was a risen Christ who was their companion on the way to Emmaus; it was a risen Christ who entered the upper chamber with "Peace be unto you" on his lips; it was a risen Christ who appeared to five hundred brethren at once; it was a risen Christ who saluted them by the Sea of Galilee and prepared for them their morning meal on the fire of coals; it was a risen Christ with whom they companied during the forty days when he went out and in among them. And it is now with a risen Christ that we have to do in the pathways of our daily pilgrimage. At every turn of the way, resurrection meets us in the person of the Lord Jesus and says to us, "Because I live, you shall live also." For the life that is in him is resurrection life.

It is with this risen life that faith connects us from the moment that we believe in him who died and rose again. Let us note, then, such things as these:

1. *The security of this risen life.* It is not mere life out of nothingness as in the case of the first Adam, but life out of death. And it is this life which Scripture presents to us as higher, fuller, and more secure. The soil out of which the tree of immortality springs is not the common soil of earth; it is the mold of the graveyard, the dust of the tomb. This far securer life, this life that no death can touch, comes to us from the risen life of him who died and rose again. The faith that knits us to him makes us partakers of his resurrection life; nay, does it so fully that his resurrection becomes ours: We are risen with him, and with him have put on a divine immortality.

2. *The power of the risen life.* It was as the risen one that he spoke, "All *power* is given unto me." It was as possessor of this power that he went forth from the sepulchre; a power like that by which he overcame death; "the power of an endless life." This corn of wheat had fallen into the ground and died; though sown in weakness, it was raised in power. It was with this power of the risen life that he ascended on high, leading captivity captive. It is this power of the risen life that he now wields upon the throne. It is in this power of the risen life that he comes again in his glory: Redeemer, King, Judge of all. It is this power of the risen life that he puts forth in his church – that he exercises in the begetting us again to a lively hope, and in sustaining each begotten one in a world of hostility and death, amid fightings without and fears within. It is to the power of this risen life that we flee in the day of weakness and conflict so that, strong in the Lord and in the power of his might, we are made more than conquerors.

3. *The love of the risen life.* Resurrection was a new and

This far securer life, this life that no death can touch, comes to us from the risen life of him who died and rose again.

higher stage of being; and with the perfection of the life, there came the perfection of the love. The instrument was now more perfectly tuned and fitted both for containing and giving forth new measures of love. The love of the risen life is the largest and the highest of all. It is of this love that we are made partakers – a love beyond all that is earthly and human, a love that passes knowledge.

4. *The sympathies of the risen life.* Resurrection does not form a gulf or throw up a wall between us and the risen one. It is not the shepherd withdrawing from his flock to some inaccessible height. It is the filling up of every gulf, the throwing down of every wall; it is the shepherd bringing himself into closer and fuller sympathy with his flock. True, they are evil, and he is good; they are earthly, and he is heavenly. But that which resurrection laid aside was not anything of true humanity. It was but the sinless infirmities which weighed down his true humanity and kept its sympathies from coming out into full development and play. The risen life, then, is the life of truest and largest sympathy. In its perfection there is the perfection of sympathy, the development of the full round of fellow feeling existing in the being of the Word made flesh.

5. *The affinities of the risen life.* The resurrection breaks no bonds save those of mortality. It is the strengthening, not the weakening, of the links that fasten the Son of God to us, and us to the Son of God. Resurrection ties are the strongest of all. The risen life of Christ alters none of the affinities between himself and his saints; it has not lessened the number of the points at which we come in contact with him; it has not made him less human, nor stopped certain channels of communication between us and him. His immortality has not unlinked him from those who are still here in flesh. His risen life has not shaken or loosened the relationship he bears to the unrisen. All that he was before, he is still, with something superadded of new love, new power, new perfection, new glory. The difference between his unrisen and his risen life is only that between the Sun at dayspring and at noon. Let us rejoice at the remembrance of his risen life as the truest, the fittest, the most blessed for us. The more that we realize our

The risen life of Christ alters none of the affinities between himself and his saints; it has not lessened the number of the points at which we come in contact with him; it has not made him less human, nor stopped certain channels of communication between us and him.

own mortality, the more let us feel the preciousness and the suitableness of his immortality as the risen one; and the more let us realize the identity between us and him, in virtue of which not merely we shall rise, but we have risen with him.

6. *The joys of the risen life.* In the tomb, the man of sorrows left all his sorrows as he left all our sins. There they were buried with him. At his resurrection his full joy began, and in the *Psalms* this connection between his resurrection and his joy is more than once proclaimed. In *Psalm* 16 the two things are placed very strikingly together; for after it is said, "You will not allow your Holy One to see corruption," it is added, "You will show me the path of life [resurrection]; in your presence is fulness of joy" (see also *Psalms* 30:3-5; 116:3-7). For him resurrection was joy, not merely because it ended his connection with death, but because it introduced him into the fulness of joy – a joy peculiar to the risen life and of which only a risen man can be capable. Into the joy of his risen life, we in some measure enter here by faith; but the fulness of that risen joy is yet in reserve for us, awaiting the resurrection of the just when the body as well as the head shall have done with tribulation and with death forever.

7. *The hopes of the risen life.* We are "begotten again to a lively [or living and life-giving] hope by the resurrection of Jesus Christ from the dead" (*1 Peter* 1:3). With Christ's resurrection and with his risen life our "hope" is connected – a "hope" which contains and imparts "life" here; a "hope" which, like a flower from the bud, opens out into the fulness of the glorious life hereafter. The hope of which we are partakers through the risen life of the second Adam far transcends any hope which the unrisen life of the first Adam could have given. It is the hope of an inheritance, a kingdom, a city, a glory such as belongs only to the risen offspring of the second Adam and such as can be possessed only by the redeemed and the risen. The resurrection of the Son of God is to us the earnest and the pledge of this blessed hope. Hence our watchword is, "Christ in us, the hope of glory."

For the church of God, the words "he is risen" are full of health and gladness. The more that we dwell upon our

The hope of which we are partakers through the risen life of the second Adam far transcends any hope which the unrisen life of the first Adam could have given.

Surety's resurrection, the more shall we realize the life and immortality which have been brought to light by his Gospel. The oftener that we visit his empty tomb and see for ourselves that he is not here, he is risen, the more shall we be penetrated by that wondrous truth that we are risen with him; and that this fellowship in resurrection is as truly the source of spiritual life, health, and holiness, as it is of joy unspeakable and full of glory.

Christ is the same Savior still as when, by the Sea of Galilee, he said to sinners as far off as you can be, "Come unto me, and I will give you rest."

For each sad sinner, still buried in the grave of sin, the words contain a Gospel – glad tidings of great joy. The empty tomb of Jesus gives forth a voice which reaches to the very ends of the Earth. Everlasting life through him who died and rose again; forgiveness and righteousness and reconciliation through the accepted work of the great substitute, finished on the cross, but sealed and attested by resurrection; peace with God through him who left the tomb and went up to the Father's right hand, as at once the maker and the giver of peace – all this we preach without condition or restriction to a world lying in wickedness that each condemned one may hear and live! Through this man is preached unto you the forgiveness of sins! Take the free pardon now; and in taking it, exchange at once, without one moment's delay or uncertainty, life for death, liberty for bondage, sonship for alienation, joy for sorrow, a hope that does not make ashamed, for heaviness here and eternal despair hereafter. He is risen, sinner, he is risen! Go, deal with this risen Christ; go, transact the great business for eternity with him; go, receive life and blessing at his hands. For truly he is the same Savior still as when, by the Sea of Galilee, he said to sinners as far off as you can be, "Come unto me, and I will give you rest."

9

The Pardon and the Peace Made Sure

CHRIST for us," the obedient in the place of the disobedient, is the *first* part of our message. His assumption of the legal claims, which otherwise would have been made good against us, is the security for our deliverance. That deliverance becomes an actual thing to us immediately upon our consenting to allow him to undertake our case.

"Christ in us" is the *second* part of our message. This second is of mighty moment, yet is not to be confounded with the first. That which is done *for* us is not the same as that which is done *in* us. By the former we are constituted righteous; by the latter we are made holy. The one is properly the Gospel, in the belief of which we are saved; the other, the carrying out of that Gospel in the soul.

Christ "for us" is our justification. "Christ in us, and we in Christ," is our holiness. The former is the external substitution; the latter, the internal energy or operation, taking its rise from the former, yet not to be confounded with it or substituted for it.

Christ the substitute, giving his life for ours upon the cross, is specially the object of faith. The message concerning this sacrificial work is the Gospel, the belief of which brings pardon to the guilty.

God has given us this Gospel not merely for the purpose of securing to us life hereafter, but of making us sure of this life

That which is done for us is not the same as that which is done in us…. The one is properly the Gospel, in the belief of which we are saved; the other, the carrying out of that Gospel in the soul.

even now. It is a true and sure Gospel so that he who believes it is made sure of being saved. If it could not make us sure, it would make us miserable; for to be told of such a salvation and such a glory, yet kept in doubt as to whether they are to be ours or not, must render us truly wretched. What a poor Gospel it must be which leaves the man who believes it still in doubt as to whether he is a child of God, an unpardoned or a pardoned sinner! Till we have found forgiveness, we cannot be happy; we cannot serve God gladly or lovingly; but must be in sore bondage and gloom.

The Bible gives no quarter to unbelief or doubting. It does not call it humility. It does not teach us to think better of ourselves for doubting.

This is the view of the matter which Scripture sets before us; telling us that salvation is a free, a sure, and a present gift. "He that believes is justified" (*Acts* 13:39). "He that believes has everlasting life" (*John* 3:36). The Bible gives no quarter to unbelief or doubting. It does not call it humility. It does not teach us to think better of ourselves for doubting. It does not countenance uncertainty or darkness.

This was the view taken of the subject by our fathers from the Reformation downwards. They held that a man ought to *know* that he is justified; that it was popery to teach uncertainty, or to set aside the full assurance of faith, or to hold that this sureness was not to be had from the beginning of a man's conversion, but only to be gathered up in process of years by summing up his good feelings and good deeds and concluding from his own excellences that he must be one of the elect, a man in favor with God. Our fathers believed that the jailor at Philippi rejoiced as soon as he received the good news which Paul preached to him (*Acts* 16:34). Our fathers believed that, "being justified by faith, we have peace with God" (*Romans* 5:1), and that the life of a believing man is a life of known pardon; a life of peace with God; a life of which the outset was the settlement of the great question between himself and God; a life in which, as being a walk with God, the settlement of that question did not admit of being deferred or kept doubtful. For without felt agreement, without conscious reconciliation, intercourse was impossible.

All the Reformation creeds and confessions take this for granted; assuming that the doctrine of uncertainty was one of the worst lies of popery,[1] the device and stronghold of a money-loving priesthood who wished to keep people in suspense in order to make room for the dealings of priests and payments for pardon. If assurance be the right of every man who believes, then the priest's occupation is at an end; his craft is not only in danger, but gone. It was the want of assurance in his poor victims that enabled him to drive so prosperous a trade and to coin money out of people's doubts. It was by this craft he had his wealth and hence the hatred with which Rome and her priests have always hated the doctrine of assurance. It took the bread out of their mouths. If God pardons so freely, so simply, so surely, so immediately upon believing, alas for the priesthood! Who will pay them for absolution? Who will go to them to make sure that which God has already made sure in a more excellent way than theirs?

Romanists have always maintained that assurance is presumption. It is remarkable that they quote, in defense of their opinion, the same passages which many modern Protestants do, such as, "Work out your salvation with fear and trembling"; the apostle's expression about being "a castaway"; "Let him that thinks he stands"; and the like.

If assurance be the right of every man who believes, then the priest's occupation is at an end; his craft is not only in danger, but gone.

---

1. "What do you think of the doctrine of the papists, whereby they teach the people to doubt and fear? It is a comfortless doctrine, placing a believer at his departure no higher than an unbeliever" (*Heidelberg Catechism*). Elsewhere in the same *Catechism* we have the following quotation: "What comfort have the papists here? Continual doubting, an unquiet mind, and the wreck of conscience. They say:

    Three things there are that trouble my mind
    The first, that I the grave must find;
    The second troubleth me more yet –
    That I know not the time of it;
    The third above all troubleth me –
    That whither I must I cannot see.
What doth a believer set against this?
    Three things there are that cheer my mind:
    First, that in Christ I pardon find;
    The second cheers me much more yet –
    That Christ my Lord for me is fit;
    The third above all cheereth me –
    That I my place in Heaven do see."

One of them, in reasoning with one of the English Reformers, speaks of "the presumptuous opinion of the certainty of grace and salvation, contrary to that which St. Paul counselleth, Phil. ii. 12." The great Romish controversialists give the following reasons against assurance, which we abridge and translate:

(1) No man certainly ought to disbelieve God's mercy and Christ's merits; but on account of his own imperfections, he ought to be fearful about his own grace, so that no one can certainly know that he has found favor with God.

(2) It is not expedient that men should have certainty about their own grace; for certainty produces pride, while ignorance of this secret preserves and increases humility.

(3) Assurance is the privilege of only a few favored ones to whom God has revealed the singular benefit of the pardon of their sins.

(4) The most perfect men, when dying, have been humbled because of this uncertainty; and if some of the honest men have been uncertain, is it credible that all believers ought to have assurance of their justification?

(5) The best men may fall from faith; therefore, there can be no assurance.

(6) The following passages confute the error of assurance: *1 Corinthians* 10:12; *2 Corinthians* 6:1; *Romans* 11:20; *Philippians* 2:12.

Such are the popish arguments against assurance. The conclusion to which the Council of Trent came was: "If any man shall say that justifying faith is confidence in the mercy of God, who remitteth sins for Christ's sake, or that it is by such confidence alone that we are justified, let him be accursed."

Old John Foxe, who three hundred years ago wrote the history of the martyrs, remarks concerning the Pope's Church, that it "left the poor consciences of men in perpetual doubt" (vol. 1, p. 78).

This is a true saying. But it is true of many who earnestly protest against the Church of Rome. They not only teach doctrines which necessarily lead to doubting and out of which no poor sinner could extract anything but uncertainty;

They not only teach doctrines which necessarily lead to doubting and out of which no poor sinner could extract anything but uncertainty; but they inculcate doubting as a humble and excellent thing.

but they inculcate doubting as a humble and excellent thing; a good preparation, even an indispensable qualification, for faith. The duty of doubting is in their theology much more obligatory than that of believing. The propriety and necessity of being uncertain they strongly insist upon; the blessedness of certainty they undervalue; the sin of uncertainty they repudiate; the duty of being sure they deny.

This same John Foxe, after showing that a man is saved not by working but by believing, gives us the following specimen of "the horrible blindness and blasphemy" of the Church of Rome:

> That faith wherewith a man firmly believeth and certainly assureth himself, that for Christ's sake his sins be forgiven him, and that he shall possess eternal life, is not faith, but rashness; not the persuasion of the Holy Ghost, but the presumption of human audacity.

The above extract is from a popish book of the time and is a fair specimen of the Romish hatred of the doctrine of assurance. Its language is almost the same as that employed by many Protestants of our day.

The Romanists held that a man is to believe in the mercy of God and the merits of Christ, but that this belief brought with it no assurance of justification; though possibly – if the man lived a very holy life – God might before he died reveal his grace to him and give him assurance. This is precisely what many Protestants hold.

In opposition to this our forefathers not only maintained that a man is justified by faith, but that he ought to know that he is justified, and that this knowledge of justification is the great root of a holy life. The Romanists did not quarrel with the word assurance; they did not hold it to be impossible: They held that men might get it, even that some very holy men had got it. But they affirmed that the only means of reaching the grace of assurance was by a holy life; that with the slow development of a holy life, assurance might develop itself; and that in the course of years, a man by numbering his good deeds, and ascertaining the amount of his holiness, might

The Romanists held that a man is to believe in the mercy of God and the merits of Christ, but that this belief brought with it no assurance of justification.

perhaps come to the conclusion that he was a child of God; but perhaps not. They were very strenuous in contending for this life of *religious suspense* – sad and dismal as it must be – because *conscious justification*, such as Luther contended for, shut out priesthood and penance; giving a man the joy of true liberty and divine fellowship at once without the intervention of another party or the delay of an hour.

This *conscious* justification started the man upon a happy life because relieved from the burden of doubt and the gloom of uncertainty, it made his religion bright and tranquil; because springing so sweetly from the certainty of his reconciliation to God, it delivered him from the cruel suspense and undefined fears which the want of assurance carries always with it. It rescued him from all temptations to self-righteousness, because, not arising from any good thing in himself, it preserved him from pride and presumption; because it kept him from trying to magnify his own goodness in order to extract assurance out of it, it drew him away from self to Christ – from what *he* was doing to what *Christ* had done; thus making Christ, not self, the basis and the center of his new being. It made him more and more dissatisfied with self, and all that self contained, but more and more satisfied with Jesus and his fulness. It taught him to rest his confidence toward God, not on his satisfaction with self, not on the development of his own holiness, not on the amount of his graces and prayers and doings, but simply on the completed work of him in whom God is well-pleased.

The Romanists acquiesced in the general formula of the Protestants – that salvation was all of Christ, and that we are to believe on him in order to get it. But they resisted the idea that a man, on believing, knows that he is saved.

The Romanists acquiesced in the general formula of the Protestants – that salvation was all of Christ, and that we are to believe on him in order to get it. But they resisted the idea that a man, on believing, knows that he is saved. They might even have admitted the term "justification by faith," provided it was conceded that this justification was to be known only to God, hidden from the sinner who believes. They did not much heed the mere form of words, and some of them went apparently a long way to the Protestant doctrine. But that which was essential to their system was that in whatever way justification took place, it should be kept secret from the sinner himself so that he should remain without assurance for years, perhaps all his life. Unconscious justification by faith suited their system of darkness quite as well as justification by works. For it was not merely the kind of justification that they hated, but the sinner's knowing it and having peace with God simply in believing without waiting for years of doing. No doubt they objected to free justification in the Protestant sense; but the force of their objection lies not so much against its being *free*, as against the sinner being *sure* of it. For they saw well enough that if they could only introduce uncertainty at any part of the process, their end was gained. For to remove such uncertainty the Church must be called in, and this was all they wanted.

The doctrine, then, that makes uncertainty necessary and that affirms that this uncertainty can only be removed by the development of a holy life, is the old popish one, though uttered by Protestants. Luther condemned it; Bellarmine maintained it. And many of the modern objections to assurance, on the part of some Protestants, are a mere reproduction of old Romish arguments, urged again and again, against justification by faith.

There is hardly one objection made to a man's being sure of his justification which would not apply, and which has not been applied, against his being justified by faith at all. If the common arguments against assurance turn out valid, they cannot stop short of establishing justification by works. Salvation by believing, and assurance only by means of working, are not very compatible.

The interval which is thus created between God's act of justifying us and his letting us know that he has justified us is a singular one of which Scripture certainly takes no cognizance. This interval of suspense (be it longer or shorter) which Romanists have created for the purpose of giving full scope to priestly interposition and which some Protestants keep up in order to save us from pride and presumption, is not acknowledged in the Bible any more than purgatory. An intermediate state in the life to come during which the soul is neither pardoned nor unpardoned, neither in Heaven nor

Many of the modern objections to assurance, on the part of some Protestants, are a mere reproduction of old Romish arguments, urged again and again, against justification by faith.

Hell, is thought needful by Romanists for purging out sin and developing holiness; but this interval of gloom is one of man's creation. An intermediate state in this life during which a sinner, though believing in Jesus, is not to know whether he is justified or not, is reckoned equally needful by some Protestants as a necessary means of producing holiness and, through holiness, leading perhaps, ere life close, to assurance; but then of this sorrowful interval, this present purgatory, which would make a Christian's life so dreary and fearful, the Scripture says nothing. It is a human delusion borrowed from popery and based upon the dislike of the human heart to have immediate peace, immediate adoption, and immediate fellowship.

The self-righteous heart of man craves an interval of the above kind as a space for the exercise of his religiousness while free from the responsibility for a holy and unworldly life which *conscious* justification imposes on the conscience.

It will be greatly worth our while to see what Romanists have said upon this subject, for their errors help us much in understanding the truth.

But it will be greatly worth our while to see what Romanists have said upon this subject, for their errors help us much in understanding the truth. It will be seen that it was against present peace with God that Rome contended; and that it was in defense of this present peace, this immediate certainty, that the Reformers did battle so strenuously as a matter of life and death. The great popish assembly, the Council of Trent, in 1547, took up these points concerning faith and grace. Nor was that body content with condemning assurance; they proclaimed it an accursed thing and pronounced an anathema against everyone who affirmed that justifying faith is "confidence in the mercy of God." They denounced the man as a heretic who should hold "the confidence and certainty of the remission of his sins."

Yet they had a theory of a justification by faith. We give it in their own words, as it corresponds strikingly with the process which is prescribed by some Protestants as the means of arriving, after long years, at the knowledge of our justification:

> The beginning of justification proceedeth from preventing [preceding] grace. The manner of the preparation is, first to believe the divine revelations and promises, and knowing

oneself to be a sinner, to turn from the fear of God's justice to his mercy, to hope for pardon from him, and therefore to begin to love him and hate sin, to begin a new life, and keep the commandments of God. Justification follows this preparation.

This theory of a gradual justification, or a gradual approach to justification, is that held by many Protestants and made use of by them for resisting the truth of immediate forgiveness of sin and peace with God.

Then comes another sentence of the Council, which expresses truly the modern theory of non-assurance and the common excuse for doubting when men say, "We are not doubting Christ; we are only doubting ourselves." The Romish divines assert:

> No one ought to doubt the mercy of God, the merits of Christ, and the efficacy of the sacraments; but in regard to his own indisposition he may doubt, because *he cannot know by certainty, of infallible faith*, that he has obtained grace.

Here sinners are taught to believe in God's mercy and in Christ's merits, yet still to go on doubting as to the results of that belief; namely, sure peace with God. Truly self-righteousness, whether resting on works or on feelings, whether in popery or Protestantism, is the same thing, the root of the same errors, and the source of the same determination not to allow immediate certainty to the sinner from the belief of the good news.

This popish Council took special care that the doctrine of assurance should be served with their most pointed curses. All the "errors of Martin" were by them traced back to this two-fold root, that a man is justified. They thus accuse the German Reformer of *inventing* his doctrine of immediate and conscious justification for the purpose of destroying the sinner's works of repentance, which by their necessary imperfection make room for indulgences. They call this free justification, a thing unheard of before – a thing which not only makes good works unnecessary, but sets a man free from any obligation to obey the law of God.

This theory of a gradual justification, or a gradual approach to justification, is that held by many Protestants and made use of by them for resisting the truth of immediate forgiveness of sin and peace with God.

It would appear that the learned doctors of the Council were bewildered with the Lutheran doctrine. The Schoolmen had never discussed it, nor even stated it. It had no place either among the beliefs or misbeliefs of the past. It had not been maintained as a truth, nor impugned as a heresy, so far as they knew. It was an absolute novelty. They did not comprehend it and of course misrepresented it. As to original sin, *that* had been so often discussed by the Schoolmen that all Romish divines and priests were familiar with it in one aspect or another. On it, therefore, the Council were at home and could frame their curses easily and with some point. But the Lutheran doctrine of justification brought them to a stand. Thus the old translator of Paul Sarpi's *History* puts it:

> The opinion of Luther concerning justifying faith, that it is a confidence and certain persuasion of the promise of God, with the consequences that follow, of the distinction between the law and the gospel, etc., had never been thought of by any school writers, and therefore never confuted or discussed, so that the divines had work enough to understand the meaning of the Lutheran propositions.

Luther's doctrine of the will's bondage they were indignant at as making man a stone or a machine. His doctrine of righteousness by faith horrified them as the inlet of all laxity and wickedness.

Luther's doctrine of the will's bondage they were indignant at as making man a stone or a machine. His doctrine of righteousness by faith horrified them as the inlet of all laxity and wickedness. Protestant doctrines were to them absurdities no less than heresies.

Nor was it merely the church, the fathers, and tradition that they stood upon. The Schools and the Schoolmen! This was their watchword; for hitherto these Scholastic doctors had been, at least for centuries, the bodyguard of the Church. Under their learning and subtleties and casuistries, priests and bishops had always taken refuge. Indeed, without them the church was helpless so far as logic was concerned. When she had to argue, she must call in these metaphysical divines; though generally by force and terror she contrived to supersede all necessity for reasoning.

Three men in the Council showed some independence: a Dominican friar, by name Ambrosius Catarinus; a Spanish Franciscan, by name Andreas de Vega; and a Carmelite, by name Antonius Marinarus. The "Heremites" of the order to which Luther originally belonged were especially blind and bitter, their leader Seripandus outdoing all in zeal against Luther and his heresy.

Compelled in the investigation of the subject to pass beyond Luther to Luther's master, they were sorely puzzled. To overlook him was impossible, for the Protestants appealed to him; to condemn him would not have been wise.

They were obliged to admit the bitter truth that Paul had said that a man is justified by faith. They had maintained the strict literality of "This is my body"; must they admit the equal literality of "justified by faith"? Or may this latter expression not be qualified and overlaid by Scholastic ingenuity, or set aside by an authoritative denial in the name of the Church? At the Council of Trent both these methods were tried.

It was not Luther only who laid such stress upon the doctrine of free justification. His adversaries were wise enough to do the same. They saw in it the root or foundation stone of the whole Reformation. If it falls, popery stands erect and may do what she pleases with the consciences of men. If it stands, popery is overthrown; her hold on men's consciences is gone; her priestly power is at an end, and men have directly to do with the Lord Jesus Christ in Heaven and not with any pretended vicar upon Earth, or any of his priests or seven sacraments. "All the errors of Martin are resolved into that point," said the bishops of the Council; and they added, "He that will establish the Catholic doctrine must overthrow the heresy of righteousness by faith only."

But did not Paul say the same things as Luther has said? Did he not say, *"To him that works not, but believes* on him that justifies the ungodly, his faith is counted for righteousness"? (*Romans* 4:5).

Yes, but we may use some liberties with Paul's words which we cannot do with Luther's. It would not do to refute Paul, but it is quite safe to demonstrate that Luther is wrong and is at variance with the Church.

Let us then assail Luther, and leave Paul alone. Now Luther has said such things as the following:

If the doctrine of justification falls, popery stands erect and may do what she pleases with the consciences of men. If it stands, popery is overthrown; her hold on men's consciences is gone; her priestly power is at an end.

1. Faith without works is sufficient for salvation and alone justifies.

2. Justifying faith is a sure trust by which one believes that his sins are remitted for Christ's sake, and they that are justified are to believe certainly that their sins are remitted.

3. By faith only we are able to appear before God, who neither regards nor has need of our works; faith only purifying us.

4. No previous disposition is necessary to justification; neither does faith justify because it disposes us, but because it is a means or instrument by which the promise and grace of God are laid hold on and received.

5. All the works of men, even the most sanctified, are sin.

6. Though the just ought to believe that his works are sins, yet he ought to be assured that they are not imputed.

7. Our righteousness is nothing but the imputation of the righteousness of Christ, and the just have need of a continual justification and imputation of the righteousness of Christ.

8. All the justified are received into equal grace and glory, and all Christians are equally great with the mother of God and as much saints as she.

These were some of Luther's propositions, which required to be confuted. That they looked wonderfully like the doctrines of the Apostle Paul only made the confutation more necessary. That "faith justifies," the bishops said, we must admit because the apostle has said so; but as to what faith is, and how it justifies, is hard to say. *Faith* has many meanings (some said nine, others fifteen; some modern Protestants have said the same); and then, even admitting that faith justifies, it cannot do so without good dispositions, without penance, without religious performances, without sacraments. By introducing all these ingredients into faith, they easily turned it into a work; or by placing them on the same level with faith, they nullified (without positively denying) justification by faith.

Ingenious men! Thus to overthrow the truth, while professing to admit and explain it! In this ingenious perversity they have had many successors, and that in churches which rejected Rome and its Council.

Faith has many meanings (some said nine, others fifteen; some modern Protestants have said the same); and then, even admitting that faith justifies, it cannot do so without good dispositions, without penance, without religious performances, without sacraments.

"Christ crucified" is the burden of the message which God has sent to man. "Christ died for our sins, according to the Scriptures." The reception of this Gospel is eternal life; the non-reception or rejection of it is everlasting death. "This is the record, that God has given to us eternal life, and this life is in His Son." The belief of the Gospel saves; the belief of the promise annexed to that Gospel makes us sure of this salvation personally. It is not the *belief of our belief* that assures us of pardon and gives us a good conscience toward God; *but our belief of what God has promised to everyone who believes his Gospel* – that is eternal life. "Believe in the Lord Jesus Christ, and *you shall be saved."*

What is God to me? That is the first question that rises up to an inquiring soul. And the second is like unto it: What am I to God? On these two questions hangs all religion, as well as all joy and life to the immortal spirit.

If God is for me, and I am for God, all is well. If God is not for me, and if I am not for God, all is ill (*Romans* 8:31). If he takes my side, and if I take his, there is nothing to fear – either in this world or in that which is to come. If he is not on my side, and if I am not on his, then what can I do but fear? Terror in such a case must be as natural and inevitable as in a burning house or a sinking vessel.

Or, if I do not know whether God is for me or not, I can have no rest. In a matter such as this, my soul seeks certainty; not uncertainty. I must know that God is for me, else I must remain in the sadness of unrest and terror. Insofar as my actual safety is concerned, everything depends on God being for me; and insofar as my present peace is concerned, everything depends on my knowing that God is for me. Nothing can calm the tempest of my soul save the knowledge that I am his, and that he is mine.

Our relationship to God is then to us the first question; till this is settled, nothing else can be settled. It is the question of questions to us, in comparison with which all other personal questions are as moonshine. When the health of a beloved child is in danger, I seem for the time to lose sight of everything around me while wholly absorbed in the thought,

It is not the belief of our belief that assures us of pardon and gives us a good conscience toward God; but our belief of what God has promised to everyone who believes his Gospel – that is eternal life.

Will he live, or will he die? I move about the house as one who sees nothing, hears nothing. I go to and I come from the sickroom incessantly; watching every symptom for the better or the worse. I eagerly inquire at the physician, Is there hope, or is there none? I am paralyzed in everything and indifferent to the things which in other circumstances might interest me. What matters it to me whether it rains or shines, whether my garden flowers are fading or flourishing, whether I am losing or making money, so long as I am uncertain whether that beloved child is to live or die?

And if uncertainty as to my child's health be so important to me, and so engrossing as to make me forget everything else; oh, what must be the engrossment attending the unsettled question of the life or death of my own immortal soul! I must know that my child is out of danger before I can rest, and I must know that my soul is out of danger before I can be quieted in spirit. Suspense in such case is terrible; and, were our eyes fully open to the eternal peril, absolutely unendurable. Not to know whether we are out of danger must be as fatal to peace of soul as the certainty of danger itself. Suspense as to temporal calamities has often in a night withered the fresh cheek of youth and turned the golden hair to grey. And shall time's uncertainties work such havoc with their transient terrors, and shall eternal uncertainties pass over us as the idle wind?

In the great things of eternity nothing but certainty will do. Nothing but certainty can soothe our fears or set us free to attend to the various questions of lesser moment which every hour brings up. The man who can continue to go about these lesser things while uncertainty still hangs over his everlasting prospects and the great question between his soul and God is still unsettled must be either sadly hardened or altogether wretched.

He who remains in this uncertainty remains a burdened and weary man. He who is contented with this uncertainty is contented with misery and danger. He who clings to this uncertainty as a right thing can have no pretensions to the name of son, or child, or saint of God. For in that

In the great things of eternity nothing but certainty will do. Nothing but certainty can soothe our fears or set us free to attend to the various questions of lesser moment which every hour brings up.

uncertainty, is there any feature of resemblance to the son or the saint; anything of the spirit of adoption, whereby we cry, Abba, Father; any likeness to the filial spirit of the beloved Son of God?

He who resolves to remain in this uncertainty is a destroyer of his own soul, and he who tries to persuade others to remain in this uncertainty is a murderer of souls. He who does his best to make himself comfortable without the knowledge of his reconciliation and relationship to God is a manifest unbeliever, and he who tries to induce others to be comfortable without this knowledge is something worse – if worse can be. That there are many among professing Christians who have not this knowledge is a painful fact; that there are some who, instead of lamenting this, make their boast of it is a fact more painful still; that there are even some who proclaim their own uncertainty in order to countenance others in it is a fact the most painful of all.

Thus the questions about assurance resolve themselves into that of the knowledge of our relationship to God. To an Arminian, who denies election and the perseverance of the saints, the knowledge of our present reconciliation to God might bring with it no assurance of final salvation. According to him, we may be in reconciliation today and out of it tomorrow. To a Calvinist there can be no such separation. He who is once reconciled is reconciled forever; the knowledge of filial relationship just now is the assurance of eternal salvation. Indeed, apart from God's electing love, there can be no such thing as assurance. It becomes an impossibility.

By nature we have no peace: "There is no peace to the wicked." Man craves peace, longs for it. God has made it for us and presents it to us.

Many are the causes of dispeace; sin is the root of all. Where unpardoned sin is, there cannot be peace. Many are the subordinate causes. An empty soul, disappointment, wounded affection, worldly losses, bereavement, vexations, cares, weariness of spirit, broken hopes, deceitful friendships, our own blunders and failures, the misconduct or unkind-

To an Arminian, who denies election and the perseverance of the saints, the knowledge of our present reconciliation to God might bring with it no assurance of final salvation.

nesses of others. These produce dispeace; these are the winds that ruffle the surface of life's sea.

Many are the efforts and appliances to obtain peace. Man's whole life is filled up with these. His daily cry is, "Give me peace!" He tries to get it in such ways as the following:

1. *By forgetting God.* It is the remembrance of God that troubles a sinner. He could get over many of his disquietudes if he could keep God at a distance. He tries to thrust him out of his thoughts, his heart, his mind, his conscience. Though he could succeed, what would it avail? He would only bring himself more surely into the number of those who shall be "turned into Hell," for they are they who "forget God." What will forgetting God do for a soul? What will it avail to thrust him out of our thoughts?

2. *By following the world.* The heart must be filled by someone or in some way. Man runs to the world as that which is most congenial and most likely to satisfy his cravings. Pleasure, gaiety, business, folly, change, gold, friends – these man tries; but in vain. Peace comes not.

3. *By working hard and denying self.* The dispeace of a troubled conscience comes from the thought of evil deeds done or good deeds left undone. This dispeace he tries to remove by trying to shake off the evil that is in him and to introduce the good that is not in him. But the hard labor is fruitless. It does not pacify the conscience or assure him of pardon, without which there can be no peace.

4. *By being very religious.* He does not know that true religion is the fruit or result of peace found, not the way to it or the price paid for it. He may be on his knees from morn til night, and may make long fastings and vigils, or prosecute his devotional performances till body and soul are worn out; but all will not do. Peace is as far off as ever.

He wants peace; but he takes his own way of getting it, not God's. He thinks there is a resting place; but he overlooks the free love that said, "Come unto me, and I will give you rest."[2]

2. "I believe these words on the divine testimony. My conscience bears witness to their truth. It is a good conscience; it agrees with God; and

The peace of the cross, what is it? What does it do for us?

What is it? It is peace of conscience, peace with God, peace with the law of God, peace with the holiness of God. It is reconciliation, friendship, fellowship; and all this in a way which prevents the dread or possibility of future variance or distance or condemnation. For it is not simply peace, but the peace of the cross; peace extracted from the cross; peace founded on and derived from what the cross reveals and what the cross has done. It is peace whose basis is forgiveness, "no condemnation." It is peace which comes from our knowledge of the peacemaking work of Calvary. It is true peace, sure peace, present peace, righteous peace, divine peace, heavenly peace, the peace of God, the peace of Christ, complete peace, pervading the whole being.

What does it do for us?

1. *It calms our storms.* In us tempests rage perpetually. The storms of the unforgiven spirit are the most fearful of all: whirlwind, earthquake, rushing blast, lightning, raging waves – these are the emblems of a human heart. But peace comes, and all is still. The great Peacemaker comes, and there is a great calm. The holy pardon which he bestows is the messenger of rest.

2. *It removes our burdens.* A sinner's heaviest burdens must ever be dread of God, lack of conscious reconciliation with him, uncertainty as to the eternal future. Peace with God is the end of all these. A sight of the cross relieves us of our burdens, and connection with the sin bearer assures us that these shall never be laid on us again.

3. *It breaks our bonds.* Sharp and heavy are the chains of sin, not merely because sin is a disease preying upon our spiritual

A sinner's heaviest burdens must ever be dread of God, lack of conscious reconciliation with him, uncertainty as to the eternal future.

---

looks upon him as reconciled perfectly. It fears to dishonor him by calling into question the infinite value of Christ's righteousness and atonement, or doubting of their being mine, while they are freely offered to me, while I find my want of them, and have my dependence upon them. Thus the peace of God rules, takes the lead in the conscience, rules always, the offer being always the same, the righteousness and atonement of Jesus always the same, my want of them always the same, and mine interest in them always the same; which I daily learn to maintain by all means, against all corruptions, enemies, and temptations from every quarter."

nature, but because it is guilt which must be answered for before a righteous Judge. Unpardoned guilt is both prison and fetters. Forgiveness brings with it peace, and with peace every chain is broken. Our prison doors are opened; we walk forth into liberty.

4. *It strengthens us for warfare.* Without peace we cannot fight. Our hands hang down, and our weapons fall from them. Our courage is gone. So long as God is our enemy, or so long as we know not whether God is our friend, we are disabled men. We are without heart and without hope. But when reconciliation comes and God becomes our assured friend, then we are strong, well nerved for battle, fearless in the conflict, full of hope and heart. "If God be for us, who can be against us?"

5. *It cheers us in trial.* The peace of God within is our chiefest consolation when sorrows crowd in upon us. Lighted up with this true lamp, we are not greatly moved because of the darkness without. Peace with God is our anchor in the storm, our strong tower in adverse times, the soother of our hearts, and the dryer-up of our tears. We learn to call affliction light, and to find that it works for us an exceeding and eternal weight of glory.

Is my soul at rest? If so, whence has the rest come? If not, why is it not at rest? Is *unrest* a necessity after Christ has said, "I will give you rest"?

Am I satisfied with the Gospel? Is my heart content with Christ himself and my conscience with what he has done? If *not* content, why? What bothers me about him and his work? Would I have something added to that work, or something taken from it? Is it not, at this moment, exactly the thing for me; exactly the thing which contains all the peace and rest I need? And am I not, at this moment, exactly the person whom it suits; to whom, without any change or delay, it offers all its fulness?

The propitiation and the righteousness finished on the cross, and there exhibited as well as presented to me freely, are such as entirely meet my case: offering me all that which is fitted to remove dispeace and unrest from heart and

When reconciliation comes and God becomes our assured friend, then we are strong, well nerved for battle, fearless in the conflict, full of hope and heart. "If God be for us, who can be against us?"

conscience; revealing as they do the free love of God to the sinner and providing for the removal of every hindrance in the way of that love flowing down; proclaiming aloud the rent veil, the open way, the gracious welcome, the plenteous provision, and the everlasting life.

Peace does not save us, yet it is the portion of a saved soul.

Assurance does not save us; they have erred who have spoken of assurance as indispensable to salvation. For we are not saved by believing in our own salvation, nor by believing anything whatsoever about ourselves. We are saved by what we believe about the Son of God and his righteousness. The Gospel believed saves, not the believing in our own faith.

Nevertheless, let us know that assurance was meant to be the portion of every believing sinner. It was intended not merely that he should be saved, but that he should *know* that he is saved, and so delivered from all fear and bondage and heaviness of heart.

Assurance does not save us; they have erred who have spoken of assurance as indispensable to salvation. For we are not saved by believing in our own salvation…. We are saved by what we believe about the Son of God and his righteousness. The Gospel believed saves, not the believing in our own faith.

10

The Holy Life of the Justified

"To him that *works not*, but *believes*," says the apostle speaking of the way in which we are reckoned just before God.

Does he by this speech make light of good works? Does he encourage an unholy walk? Does he use a rash word which had better been left unspoken?

No, truly. He is laying the foundation of good works. He is removing the great obstacle to a holy life, namely, the bondage of an unforgiven state. He is speaking, by the power of the Holy Ghost, the words of truth and soberness. The difference between working and believing is that which God would have us learn, lest we confound these two things and so destroy them both. The order and relation of these two things are here very explicitly laid down so as to anticipate the error of many who mix up working and believing together or who make believing the result of working, instead of working the result of believing.

We carefully distinguish, yet we as carefully connect the two. We do not put asunder what God has joined together; yet we would not reverse the divine order, nor disturb the divine relation, nor place that last which God has set first.

It was not to depreciate or discourage good works that the apostle spoke of "not working, but believing," or of a man being "justified by faith, *without the deeds of the law*"

The difference between working and believing is that which God would have us learn, lest we confound these two things and so destroy them both.

(*Romans* 3:28), or of God "imputing righteousness *without works*" (4:6). It was to distinguish things that differ; it was to show the true use of faith in connecting us for justification with what another has done; it was to prevent us from doing anything in order to be justified. In this view, then, faith is truly a ceasing from work, and not a working; it is not the doing of anything in order to be justified, but the simple reception of the justifying work of him who "finished transgression and made an end of sin." For the one justifying work was completed eighteen hundred years ago, and any attempt on our part to repeat or imitate this is vain. The one cross suffices.

Nor was it to undervalue good works that our Lord gave what many may deem such a singular answer to the question of the Jews, "What shall we do, that we may work the works of God?" "This is the work of God, that you believe on him whom he hath sent" (*John* 6:29). They wanted to work their way into the favor of God. The Lord tells them that they may have that favor without waiting or working by accepting at once his testimony to his only begotten Son. Till then, they were not in a condition for working. They were as trees without a root and as stars whose motions, however regular, would be useless if they themselves were unlighted.

To say to a groping, troubled spirit, You must first believe before you can work, is no more to encourage ungodliness or laxity of walk than to say to an imprisoned soldier, You must first get out of your dungeon before you can fight; or to a swimmer, You must throw off that millstone before you can attempt to swim; or to a racer, You must get quit of these fetters before you can run the race.

Yet these expressions of the apostle have often been shrunk from; dreaded as dangerous; quoted with a guarding clause or cited as seldom as possible under the secret feeling that, unless greatly diluted or properly qualified, they had better not be cited at all. But why are these bold utterances there, if they are perilous, if they are not meant to be as fearlessly proclaimed now as they were fearlessly written eighteen centuries ago? What did the Holy Spirit mean by

Faith is truly a ceasing from work, and not a working; it is not the doing of anything in order to be justified, but the simple reception of the justifying work of Christ.

the promulgation of such "unguarded" statements, as some seem disposed to reckon them? It was not for nothing that they were so boldly spoken. Timid words would not have served the purpose. The glorious Gospel needed statements such as these to disentangle the great question of acceptance and to relieve troubled consciences and purge them from dead works, yet at the same time to give to works their proper place.

Perhaps some of Luther's statements are too unqualified. Yet their very strength shows how much he felt the necessity of so speaking of works as absolutely and peremptorily to exclude them from the office of justifying the sinner. He saw and testified how the papacy, by mixing the two things together, had troubled and terrified men's consciences and had truly become a "slaughterhouse of souls."

Luther saw and testified how the papacy, by mixing the two things [faith and works] together, had troubled and terrified men's consciences and had truly become a "slaughterhouse of souls."

In another's righteousness we stand, and by another's righteousness we are justified. All accusations against us, founded upon our unrighteousness, we answer by pointing to the perfection of the righteousness which covers us from head to foot, in virtue of which we are unassailable by law as well as shielded from wrath.

Protected by this perfection, we have no fear of wrath, either now or hereafter. It is a buckler to us, and we cry, "Behold, O God, our shield; look upon the face of your Anointed"; as if to say, Look not on me, but on my substitute; deal not with me for sin, but with my sin bearer; challenge not me for my guilt, but challenge *him*; *he* will answer for me. Thus we are safe beneath the shield of his righteousness. No arrow, either from the enemy or from conscience, can reach us there.

Covered by this perfection, we are at peace. The enemy cannot invade us; or if he try to do so, we can triumphantly repel him. It is a refuge from the storm, a covert from the tempest, a river of water in a dry place, the shadow of a great rock in a weary land. The work of righteousness is peace, and in the Lord we have righteousness and strength.

Beautified with this perfection, which is the perfection of God, we find favor in his sight. His eye rests on the comeliness which he has put upon us; and as he did at viewing the first creation, so now, in looking at us clothed with this divine excellency, he pronounces it "very good." He sees "no iniquity in Jacob, and no transgression in Israel." "The iniquity of Jacob may be sought for, and there shall be none; and the sins of Judah, and they shall not be found" (*Jeremiah* 50:20). This righteousness suffices to cover, to comfort, and to beautify.[1]

But there is more than this. We are justified *that we may be holy*. The possession of this legal righteousness is the beginning of a holy life. We do not live a holy life in order to be justified, but we are justified that we may live a holy life. That which *man* calls holiness may be found in almost any circumstances – of dread, or darkness, or bondage, or self-righteous toil and suffering; but that which God calls holiness can only be developed under conditions of liberty and light, and pardon and peace with God. Forgiveness is the mainspring of holiness. Love, as a motive, is far stronger than law and far more influential than fear of wrath or peril of Hell. Terror may make a man crouch like a slave and obey a hard master lest a worse thing come upon him, but only a sense of forgiving love can bring either heart or conscience into that state in which obedience is either pleasant to the soul or acceptable to God.

The possession of this legal righteousness is the beginning of a holy life. We do not live a holy life in order to be justified, but we are justified that we may live a holy life.

1. Every time we say "for your name's sake," or "for Christ's sake," we are making use of another's claim, another's merit, and conceding or accepting the whole doctrine of imputed righteousness. Every man is daily getting, in some way or other, what he personally has no title to. When a son gets an inheritance from his father, he gets what does not belong to him and what could easily and legally be diverted from him. When one who is not a son gets an estate by will, he gets what he has no claim to simply by a legal deed. Human jurisprudence recognizes these transferences as competent and proper, not fictitious or absurd. Man daily acts on these principles of getting what he has no right to simply because a fellow man wills it, and law acknowledges that will. Why then should he speak of fictitious transferences in spiritual blessings proceeding on precisely the same principle? Why should he deny the law or process of the divine jurisprudence by which forgiveness of sin is conferred on him according to the will of another and secured to him by the claims of another? If earthly law deals thus with him in earthly things, why should not heavenly law deal thus with him in heavenly things?

Forgiveness relaxes no law, nor interferes with the highest justice. Human pardons may often do so; God's pardons never.

False ideas of holiness are common, not only among those who profess false religions, but among those who profess the true. For holiness is a thing of which man by nature has no more idea than a blind man has of the beauty of a flower or the light of the Sun. All false religions have had their "holy men" whose holiness often consisted merely in the amount of pain they could inflict upon their bodies, or of food which they could abstain from, or of hard labor which they could undergo. But with God, a saint or holy man is a very different being. It is in filial, full-hearted love to God that much of true holiness consists. And this cannot even begin to be until the sinner has found forgiveness and tasted liberty and has confidence toward God. The spirit of holiness is incompatible with the spirit of bondage. There must be the spirit of liberty, the spirit of adoption, whereby we cry, Abba, Father. When the fountain of holiness begins to well up in the human heart and to fill the whole being with its transforming, purifying power, "We have known and believed the love that God has to us" (1 John 4:16) is the first note of the holy song which, commenced on Earth, is to be perpetuated through eternity.

We are bought with a price that we may be new creatures in Jesus Christ. We are forgiven, that we may be like him who forgives us. We are set at liberty and brought out of prison that we may be holy. The free, boundless love of God pouring itself into us, expands and elevates our whole being; and we serve him, not in order to win his favor, but because we have already won it in simply believing his record concerning his Son. If the root is holy, so are the branches. We have become connected with the holy root and by the necessity of this connection are made holy too.

Forgiveness relaxes no law, nor interferes with the highest justice. Human pardons may often do so; God's pardons never.

Forgiveness doubles all our bonds to a holy life; only they are no longer bonds of iron, but of gold. It takes off the heavy yoke in order to give us the light and easy.

Love is stronger than law. Whatever connects our obedience

with love must be far more influential than what connects us with law.

The love of God to us, and our love to God, work together for producing holiness in us. Terror accomplishes no real obedience. Suspense brings forth no fruit unto holiness. Only the certainty of love, forgiving love, can do this. It is this certainty that melts the heart, dissolves our chains, disburdens our shoulders so that we stand erect, and makes us to run in the way of the divine commandments.

Condemnation is that which binds sin and us together. Forgiveness looses this fearful tie and separates us from sin. The power of condemnation which the law possesses is that which makes it so strong and terrible. Cancel this power, and the liberated spirit rises into the region of love. In that region it finds both will and strength for the keeping of the law – a law which is at once old and new, old as to substance ("You shall love the Lord with all your heart") and new as to mode and motive ("The law of the Spirit of life in Christ Jesus has made me free from the law of sin and death," *Romans* 8:2); that is, the law of the life-giving Spirit which we have in Christ Jesus has served the condemning connection of that law which leads only to sin and death. "For what the law could not do, in that it was weak through the flesh [that is, unable to carry out its commandments in our old nature], God sending his own Son in the likeness of sinful flesh, and for sin, condemned sin in the flesh; that the righteousness of the law might be fulfilled in us, who walk not after the flesh, but after the Spirit" (*Romans* 8:3, 4).

The removal of condemnation is the dissolution of legal bondage and of that awful pressure upon the conscience which at once enslaved and irritated; disenabling as well as disinclining us from all obedience; making holiness both distasteful and dreadful, to be submitted to only through fear of future woe.

Sin, when unforgiven, oppresses the conscience and tyrannizes over the sinner. Sin forgiven in an unrighteous way would be but a slight and uncertain as well as imperfect relief. Sin righteously and judicially forgiven loses its dominion. The

Sin, when unforgiven, oppresses the conscience and tyrannizes over the sinner.

conscience rises up from its long oppression and expands into joyous liberty. Our whole being becomes bright and buoyant under the benign influence of this forgiving love of God. "The winter is past, the rain is over and gone, the flowers appear on the earth, the time of the singing of birds is come" (*Song of Solomon* 2:11, 12).

Condemnation is the dark cloud that obscures our heavens. Forgiveness is the sunshine dissolving the cloud and by its brilliance making all good things to grow and ripen in us.

Condemnation makes sin strike its roots deeper and deeper. No amount of terror can extirpate evil. No fear of wrath can make us holy. No gloomy uncertainty as to God's favor can subdue one lust or correct our crookedness of will. But the free pardon of the cross uproots sin and withers all its branches. The "no condemnation to them that are in Christ Jesus" is the only effectual remedy for the deadly disease of an alienated heart and stubborn will.

They who would rely on law to awaken trust know nothing either of law or love, nor do they understand how the suspicions of the human heart are to be removed and its confidence won.

The lack of forgiveness, or uncertainty as to it, are barriers in the way of the removal of the heart's deep enmity to a righteous God. For enmity will only give way to love; and no suspense, however terrible, will overcome the stout-hearted rebelliousness of man. Threats do not conquer hearts, nor does austerity win either confidence or affection. They who would rely on law to awaken trust know nothing either of law or love, nor do they understand how the suspicions of the human heart are to be removed and its confidence won. The knowledge of God simply as Judge or Lawgiver will be of no power to attract, of no avail to remove distrust and dread.

But the message, "God is love," is like the sun bursting through the clouds of a long tempest. The good news, "Through this man is preached unto you the forgiveness of sins," is like the opening of the prisoner's dungeon gate. Bondage departs, and liberty comes. Suspicion is gone, and the heart is won. "Perfect love has cast out fear." We hasten to the embrace of him who loved us; we hate that which has estranged us; we put away all that caused the distance between us and him; we long to be like one so perfect and to partake of his holiness. To be "partakers of the divine nature" (*2 Peter* 1:4), once so distasteful, is henceforth most grateful and pleasant; nothing seems now so desirable as to escape the corruptions that are in the world through lust.

We undergo many false changes which look like holiness, but which are not really so. The poison tree drops its leaves, yet remains the same. The sea of Sodom glistens in the sunshine with surpassing splendor, yet remains salt and bitter as before. Time changes us, yet does not make us holy. The decays of age change us, but do not break the power of evil. One lust expels another; frailty succeeds to frailty; error drives out error. One vanity pales, another comes freshly in its place; one evil habit is exchanged for a second, but our old man remains the same. The cross has not touched us with its regenerating power; the Holy Spirit has not purified the inner sources of our being and life.[2]

We undergo many false changes which look like holiness, but which are not really so.

Fashion changes us; the example of friends changes us; society changes us; excitement changes us; business changes us; affection changes us; sorrow changes us; dread of coming evil changes us; yet the heart is just what it was. Of the numerous changes in our character or deportment, how many are deceitful, how few are real and deep!

Only that which can go down into the very depths of our spiritual being can produce any change that is worthy of the name.

The one spell that can really transform us is the cross. The one potent watchword is, "I, if I be lifted up, will draw all men unto me" (*John* 12:32). The one physician for all our maladies is he who died for us, and the one remedy which he applies is the blood that cleanses from all sin. The one arm of power

2. "All divine life, and all the precious fruits of it, pardon, peace, and holiness, spring from the cross.... Holiness as well as pardon is to be had from the blood of the cross.... All fancied sanctification which does not arise wholly from the blood of the cross is nothing better than Pharisaism.... If we would be holy, we must get to the cross, and dwell there; else, notwithstanding all our labor and diligence, and fasting, and praying, and good works, we shall be yet void of real sanctification, destitute of those humble, gracious tempers which accompany a clear view of the cross."

that can draw us out of the horrible pit and the miry clay is "the Spirit of holiness."

"For their sakes I sanctify myself, that they also might be sanctified through the truth" (*John* 17:19). Christ presents himself to God as the Holy One and the Consecrated One that his people may partake of his sanctification and be like himself. saints, consecrated ones, men set apart for God by the sprinkling of the blood. Through the truth they are sanctified by the power of the Holy Ghost.

"By one offering he has perfected forever them that are sanctified" (*Hebrews* 10:14) so that the perfection of his saints, both as to the conscience and as to personal holiness, is connected with the one offering and springs out of the one work finished upon Calvary. "By the which will we are sanctified, through the offering of the body of Jesus Christ once for all" (*Hebrews* 10:10). Here again the sanctification is connected with the offering of the body of Christ. Whatever place "the power of his resurrection" may hold in our spiritual history, it is the cross that is the source of all that varied fulness by which we are justified and purified. The secret of a believer's holy walk is his continual recurrence to the blood of the Surety and his daily intercourse with a crucified and risen Lord.

Nowhere does Scripture, either in its statements of doctrine or lives of the saints, teach us that here we get beyond our need of the blood or may safely cast off the divine raiment that covers our deformity. Even should we say at any time, "I am free from sin," this would be no proof of our being really holy; for the heart is deceitful above all things, and there may be ten thousand sins lurking in us, seen by God, though unseen by ourselves. "I know nothing of myself," says the apostle; that is, I am not conscious of any failure. "But," he adds, "I am not hereby justified"; that is, my own consciousness is no proof of my sinlessness; for "he that judges me is the Lord," and the Lord may condemn me in many things in which I do not condemn myself.

Let me say to one who thinks he has reached sinlessness, "My friend, are you *sure* that you are perfectly holy? For noth-

It is the cross that is the source of all that varied fulness by which we are justified and purified. The secret of a believer's holy walk is his continual recurrence to the blood of the Surety.

ing but absolute certainty should lead you to make so bold an affirmation regarding your freedom from all sin. Are you sure that you love the Lord your God with all your heart and soul? For unless you are absolutely sure of this, you have no right to say, I am perfectly holy; and it will be a perilous thing for you to affirm, I have no longer any need of the blood, and I refuse to go to the fountain for cleansing, seeing my going thither would be mockery. For the cross and the blood and the fountain are for the imperfect, not for the perfect; for the unrighteous, not for the righteous; and if your self-consciousness is correct, you are no longer among the imperfect or the unrighteous.

My friend, do you never sin in thought, or in word, or in desire, or in deed? Have you never a wandering thought? Is your heart as warm and are your affections as heavenly as you could possibly desire them to be? What! not one stray thought from morn to night, from night to morn? Not one wrong word, nor look, nor tone? What! no coldness, no want of fervor, no flagging of zeal, no momentary indulgence of self and sloth? What! no error (for error is sin), no false judgment, no failure of temper, no improper step, no imperfect plan, nothing to regret, nothing to wish unsaid or undone in the midst of a world like ours with all its provocations, its crosses, its worries, its oppositions, its heated atmosphere of infectious evil?

And are you sure, quite sure, that all this is the case; that your conscience is so perfectly alive, so divinely sensitive, that the faintest expressions of evil in the remotest corner of your heart would be detected? If so, you are an extraordinary man and far above him who was less than the least of all saints. You are far above him who said, "The good that I would, that I do not; and the evil that I would not, that I do." You are one whose history will require to be written by some immortal pen, as that of the man who, after a few years' believing, ceased to require any application to the cross or to be indebted to the blood for cleansing, who could look at altar and laver and mercy seat as one who had no longer any interest in their provisions; as one to whom a crucified Christ

Are you sure that you love the Lord your God with all your heart and soul? For unless you are absolutely sure of this, you have no right to say, I am perfectly holy.

127

was a thing of the past, of whom he had now no need as a sin bearer or high priest or advocate or intercessor, but only as a companion and friend.

God's processes are not always rapid. His greatest works rise slowly. Swiftness of growth has been one of man's tests of greatness; not so is it with God. His trees grow slowly; the stateliest are the slowest. His creatures grow slowly, year by year; man, the noblest, grows the most slowly of all. God can afford to take his time. Man cannot. He is hasty and impatient. He will have everything to be like Jonah's gourd or like one of those fabled oriental palaces which magicians are said to call up by a word or a stamp out of the sand. He forgets how slowly the palm tree and the cedar grow. They neither spring up in a night nor perish in a night. He forgets the history of the temple: "Forty and six years was this temple in building." He insists that, because it is God's purpose that his saints should be holy, therefore they ought to be holy at once.

It is true that our standard is, and must be, perfection, for our model is the Perfect One. But the question is, Has God in Scripture anywhere led us to expect the rapidity of growth, the quick development of perfection in which some glory and because of the confessed lack of which in others they look down on these others as babes or loiterers?

Is there in Scripture any instance of a perfect man, excepting him who was always and absolutely without sin?

If Christians were perfect, where is the warfare, and the adversary, and the sword, and the shield? Are angels exposed to this warfare when they visit Earth? Or is it not our imperfection that in great measure produces this? And are we anywhere in Scripture led to believe that we are delivered from "the body of this death," from the battle of flesh and spirit, from the wrestling with principalities and powers, till death sets us free or our Lord shall come?

Yet we are called with a holy calling (2 Timothy 1:9) and, as so called, are bound to take the highest standard for our model of life. The slowness or swiftness of the progress does not alter the standard, nor affect our aiming at conformity to it.

It is true that our standard is, and must be, perfection, for our model is the Perfect One. But the question is, Has God in Scripture anywhere led us to expect the rapidity of growth, the quick development of perfection in which some glory?

This progress, rapid or gradual, springs from the forgiveness we have received and the new life imparted by the Holy Spirit. Our life is to be fruit bearing; the fruitfulness coming from our ascertained acceptance, our being "rooted and grounded in love." We taste and see that the Lord is good; that in his favor is life; that the joy of the Lord is our strength; and so we move on and up, rising from one level to another. "We know and believe the love that God has to us," and we find in this the source of goodness no less than of gladness and liberty.

The life of the justified should be a peaceful one. Being justified by faith, we have peace with God – the God of peace and the God of all grace. The world's storms have not been stilled, nor our way smoothed, nor our skies brightened, nor our enemies swept away; but the peace of God has come in and taken possession of the soul. We are cheered and comforted. God is for us, and who can be against us? The name of the Lord is our strong tower; we run into it and are safe. No evil can happen to us; no weapon that is formed against us can prosper.

The life of the justified should be a holy one, all the more because of the extent of previous unholiness. "And such were some of you: But you are washed, but you are sanctified, but you are justified in the name of the Lord Jesus, and by the Spirit of our God" (1 *Corinthians* 6:11). All that these marvelous and mysterious words "holy" and "holiness" imply is to be found in the life of one who has been "much forgiven." There is no spring of holiness so powerful as that which our Lord assumes: "Neither do I condemn you: Go, and sin no more" (*John* 8:11). Free and warm reception into the divine favor is the strongest of all motives in leading a man to seek conformity to him who has thus freely forgiven him all trespasses. A cold admission into the paternal house by the father might have repelled the prodigal and sent him back to his lusts; but the fervent kiss, the dear embrace, the best robe, the ring, the shoes, the fatted calf, the festal song – all without one moment's suspense or delay, as well as without one upbraiding word – could not but awaken shame

The fervent kiss, the dear embrace, the best robe, the ring, the shoes, the fatted calf, the festal song – all without one moment's suspense or delay, as well as without one upbraiding word – could not but awaken shame for the past and true-hearted resolution to walk worthy of such a father and of such a generous pardon.

for the past and true-hearted resolution to walk worthy of such a father and of such a generous pardon. "Revellings, banquetings, and abominable idolatries" come to be the abhorrence of him around whom the holy arms of renewed fatherhood have been so lovingly thrown. Sensuality, luxury, and the gaieties of the flesh have lost their relish to one who has tasted the fruit of the tree of life.

The life of the justified should be a loving one. It is love that has made him what he is, and shall he not love in return? Shall he not love him that begat and him also that is begotten of him? The deep true spring of love is thus revealed to us by the Lord himself: "A certain creditor had two debtors; the one owed five hundred pence, the other fifty. And when they had nothing to pay, *he frankly forgave them both*. Tell me, therefore, which of them will *love* him most?" (*Luke* 7:41-42). Thus love produces love. The life of one on whom the fulness of the free love of God is ever shining must be a life of love. Suspense, doubt, terror, darkness must straiten and freeze; but the certainty of free and immediate love dissolves the ice, and kindles the coldest spirit into the warmth of love. "We love him because he first loved us." Love to God, love to the brethren, love to the world, spring up within us as the heavenly love flows in. Malevolence, anger, envy, jealousy, receive their death blow. The nails of the cross have gone through all these, and their deadly wound cannot be healed. They that are Christ's have crucified the flesh with its affections and lusts. Sternness, coldness, distance, depart. They are succeeded by gentleness, mildness, guilelessness, meekness, ardor, long-suffering. The tempers of the old man quit us, we know not how; in their place comes the

> charity which suffers long, and is kind, which envies not, which vaunts not itself, which is not puffed up, which does not behave itself unseemly, which seeks not her own, which is not easily provoked, which thinks no evil, which rejoices not in iniquity, but rejoices in the truth, which bears all things, which believes all things, which never fails [1 Corinthians 13:4-8].

"A certain creditor had two debtors; the one owed five hundred pence, the other fifty. And when they had nothing to pay, he frankly forgave them both. Tell me, therefore, which of them will love him most?" (Luke 7:41-42). Thus love produces love.

Gentle and loving and simple should be the life of the justified; meek and lowly should they be who have been loved with such a love.

The life of the justified should be an earnest one, for everything connected with his acceptance has been earnest on the part of God; and the free forgiveness on which he has entered in believing nerves and cheers and animates. It is a spring of courage and hardihood and perseverance. It makes the coward brave. It says to the weak, Be strong! to the indolent, Arise! making the forgiving man ready to face danger and toil and loss; arming him with a new-found energy and crowning him with sure success. "Ready to spend and to be spent" is his motto now. "I am debtor" is his watchword – debtor first of all to him who forgave me, and after that, to the church of God, redeemed with the same blood, and filled with the same Spirit; and then after that to the world around, still sunk in sin and struggling with a thousand sorrows under which it has no comforter and of whose termination it has no hope. How thoroughly in earnest should be the life of one thus pardoned – pardoned so freely, yet at such a cost to him who "gave his life a ransom for many!"

The life of the justified should be a generous one. All connected with his justification has been boundless generosity on the part of God. He spared not his own Son, and will he not with him also freely give us all things? The love of God has been of the largest, freest kind; shall this not make us generous? The gifts of God have been all of them on the most unlimited scale; shall not this boundless liberality make us liberal in the highest and truest sense? Can a justified man be covetous or slow to part with his gold? God has given his Son; he has given his Spirit; he has given us eternal life; he has given us an everlasting kingdom. And shall these gifts not tell upon us? Shall they not expand and elevate us? Or shall they leave us narrow and shriveled as before? Surely we are called to a noble life; a life far above the common walk of humanity; a life far above that of those who, disbelieving the liberality of God, are trying to merit his favor or to purchase his kingdom by moral goodnesses or ceremonial performances

Surely we are called to a noble life; a life far above the common walk of humanity; a life far above that of those who, disbelieving the liberality of God, are trying to merit his favor or to purchase his kingdom by moral goodnesses or ceremonial performances of their own.

of their own. Not unselfish merely, but self-denying men, we are called to be; not self pleasers, nor man pleasers, nor flesh pleasers, nor world pleasers; but pleasers of God, like Enoch (*Hebrews* 11:5) or like a greater than Enoch – as it is written, "Even Christ pleased not himself" (*Romans* 15:3). "We then that are strong ought to bear the infirmities of the weak, and *not to please ourselves*; let every one of us please his neighbor for his good to edification," that is, to the edification or building up of the body of Christ (*Romans* 15:2).

Large-heartedness and open handedness may surely be looked for from those whom the boundless liberality of God has made partakers of the unsearchable riches of Christ and heirs of the kingdom which cannot be moved.

Selfishness, self-love, self-seeking have been in all ages the scandal of the church of God. "All seek their own, not the things that are Jesus Christ's" (*Philippians* 2:21) was the sad testimony of the apostle to the Philippian church even in early days, so little had God's marvelous love told even upon those who believed it, so obstinate was the contraction of the human heart and so unwilling to yield to the enlarging pressure of an influence which men in common things deem irresistible. To love warmly, to give largely, to sympathize sincerely, to help unselfishly – these are some of the noble fruits to be expected from the belief of a love that passes knowledge. Self-sacrifice ought not to seem much to those for whom Christ has died and whom he now represents upon the throne. Generous deeds and gifts and words ought to be as natural as they are becoming in those who have been so freely loved, so abundantly pardoned, and so eternally blest. Narrow hearts are the fruits of a narrow pardon and of an uncertain favor; poor gifts are the produce of stinted and grudging giving; but large-heartedness and open handedness may surely be looked for from those whom the boundless liberality of God has made partakers of the unsearchable riches of Christ and heirs of the kingdom which cannot be moved.

The life of the justified should be a lofty one. Littleness and meanness and earthliness do not become the pardoned. They must mount up on wings as eagles, setting their affection on things above. Having died with Christ and risen with him, they sit with him in heavenly places (*Ephesians* 2:6). In the world, and yet not of it, they rise above it; possessed of a heavenly citizenship (*Philippians* 3:20) and expecting an unearthly recompense at the return of him who has gone to prepare a place for them. High thoughts, high aims, high longings become them of whom Christ was not merely the substitute upon the cross, but the representative upon the throne – the forerunner who has entered within the veil and ever lives to intercede for us. Shall he who has been freely justified grovel in the dust, or creep along the polluted soil of earth? Shall such a justification as he has received not be the source of superhuman elevation of character, making him unworldly in his hopes, in his tastes, in his works, in the discharge of his daily calling? Shall not such a justification act upon his whole being and pervade his life, making him a thoroughly consistent man in all things; each part of his course becoming his name and prospects; his whole man symmetrical, his whole Christianity harmonious?

Shall not such a justification act upon his whole being and pervade his life, making him a thoroughly consistent man in all things?

The life of the justified is a decided one. It does not oscillate between goodness and evil, between Christ and the world. The justifying cross has come between him and all evil things; and that which released him from the burden of guilt has, in so doing, broken the bondage of sin. Even if at any time he feels as if he could return to that country from which he set out, the cross stands in front and arrests his backward step. Between him and Egypt rolls the Red Sea, flowing in its strength so that he cannot pass. At the door of the theater or the ballroom or the revel hall stands the cross. It forbids his entrance. The world is crucified to him, and he unto the world, by the saving cross. His first look to the cross committed him. He began, and he cannot go back. It would be mean as well as perilous to do so. There is henceforth to be no mistake about him. His heart is no longer divided, and his eye no longer roams. He has taken up his cross, and he is following the Lamb. He has gone in at the strait gate and is walking along the narrow way; at the entrance thereof stands the cross barring his return. Over his entrance there was joy in Heaven; shall he at any time turn that joy into sorrow by even seeming to go back?

The life of the justified is a useful one. He has become a witness for him who has thrown over him the shadow of

He by whom he is justified is himself the Truth, and every man who receives that truth becomes a witness for it. By the truth he is saved; by the truth he is made free; by the truth he is made clean; by the truth he is sanctified. Therefore it is precious to him in every jot and tittle.

his cross. He can tell what the bitterness of sin is and what is the burden of guilt. He can speak of the rolling away of the stone from the sepulchre of his once dead soul and of the angel sitting on that stone clothed in light. He can make known the righteousness which he has found, and in finding which he has been brought into liberty and gladness. Out of the abundance of his heart and in the fulness of his liberated spirit, his mouth speaks. He cannot but speak of the things which he now possesses that he may induce others to come and share the fulness. He is bent on doing good. He has no hours to throw away. He knows that the time is short, and he resolves to redeem it. He will not waste a life that has been redeemed at such a cost. It is not his own, and he must keep in mind the daily responsibilities of a life thus bought for another. As one of the world's lights, in the absence of the true light, he must be always shining to lessen in some degree the darkness of Earth and to kindle heavenly light in souls who are now excluding it. As one of the sowers of the heavenly seed, he must never be idle, but watching opportunities – making opportunities for sowing it as he goes out and in; it may be in weakness; it may be in tears.

The life of the justified is the life of wisdom and truth. He has become "wise in Christ." "Christ has been made unto him wisdom" as well as righteousness. It is thus that he has become "wise unto salvation," and he feels that he must hold fast the truth that saves. To trifle with that truth, to tamper with error, would be to deny the cross. He by whom he is justified is himself *the Truth*, and every man who receives that truth becomes a witness for it. By the truth he is saved; by the truth he is made free; by the truth he is made clean; by the truth he is sanctified. Therefore it is precious to him in every jot and tittle. Each fragment broken off is so much lost to his spiritual well-being, and each new discovery made in the rich field of truth is so much eternal gain. He has bought the Earth, and he will not sell it. It is his life; it is his heritage; it is his kingdom. He counts all truth precious and all error hateful. He dreads the unbelief that is undermining the foundations of truth and turning its spacious palaces into a chaos of human speculations. He calls no truth obsolete or out of date, for he knows that the truths on which he rests for eternity are the oldest of the old and yet the surest of the sure. To introduce doubts as to the one sacrifice on which he builds is to shake the cross of Calvary. To lay another foundation than that already laid is to destroy his one hope. To take the sacrificial element out of the blood is to make peace with God impossible because he is unrighteous. To substitute the church for Christ, or the priest for the herald of pardon, or the rite for the precious blood, or the sacrament for the living Christ upon the throne, or the teachings of the church for the enlightenment of the Holy Ghost – this is to turn light into darkness and then to call that darkness light. Thus taught by that Spirit who has led him to the cross, the justified man knows how to discern truth from error. He has the unction from the Holy One and knows all things (1 John 2:20); he has the anointing which is truth and is no lie (1 John 2:27); and he can try the spirits, whether they are of God (1 John 4:1).

Want of sensitiveness to the difference between truth and error is one of the evil features of modern Protestantism. Sounding words, well-executed pictures, and pretentious logic carry away multitudes. The distinction between Gospel and no Gospel is very decided and very momentous; yet many will come away from a sermon in which the free Gospel has been overlaid and not be sensible of the lack, praising the preacher. The conversions of recent years have not the depth of other days. Consciences are half-awakened and half-pacified; the wound is slightly laid open, and slightly healed – hence the want of spiritual discernment as to truth and error. The conscience is not sensitive, else it would at once refuse and resent any statement, however well argued or painted, which encroached in the slightest degree upon the free Gospel of God's love in Christ; which interposed any obstacle between the sinner and the cross; or which merely declaimed about the cross without telling us especially how it saves and how it purifies. We need *sensitive* but not *morbid* consciences to keep us stedfast in the faith and to preserve our spiritual eyesight unimpaired, remembering the apostle's

To substitute the church for Christ, or the priest for the herald of pardon, or the rite for the precious blood, or the sacrament for the living Christ upon the throne, or the teachings of the church for the enlightenment of the Holy Ghost – this is to turn light into darkness and then to call that darkness light.

words, "He that lacks these things is *blind, and cannot see afar off*, and has forgotten that he was purged from his old sins" (*2 Peter* 1:9). Censoriousness is one thing, and spiritual discernment is quite another. To avoid the first we do not need to give up the second; though the "liberality" of modern times would recommend us to be charitable to error and not very tenacious of any Bible truth, seeing that nothing in an age of culture can be received but that which has been pronounced credible by philosophy or science and which the "verifying faculty" has adjudged to be true!

The life of the justified must be one of praise and prayer. His justification has drawn him near to God. It has opened his lips and enlarged his heart. He cannot but praise; he cannot but pray. He has ten thousand things to ask for; he has ten thousand things for which to give thanks. He knows what it is to speak in psalms and hymns and spiritual songs, singing with grace in his heart to the Lord (*Colossians* 3:16).

The life of the justified is one of watchfulness. Forgiveness has altered all his circumstances and hopes. It has brought him into a new world from which are shut out things he was formerly familiar with and into which are introduced things which he knew not. He sees and hears what he never saw nor heard before, and he ceases to see and hear what but lately he delighted in. He is no longer satisfied with things as they are. He expects changes and wishes that they were come. The present has become less to him, the future more; and in that future the one absorbing object is the reappearing of him, whom not having seen he loves.

That the future should be a mere repetition of the present – with a few scientific and political improvements – is quite enough for the worldly man. But the man who, by his new connection with the cross, has been transported into a new region is not content that it should be so. He wants a better future and a more congenial world; he desires a state of things in which the new object of his love shall be all. And learning from Scripture that such a new condition of things is to be expected, and that of that new state Christ is himself to be the first and last, he looks eagerly out for the fulfilment

The "liberality" of modern times would recommend us to be charitable to error and not very tenacious of any Bible truth, seeing that nothing in an age of culture can be received but that which has been pronounced credible by philosophy or science.

of these hopes. Learning, moreover, that the arrival of this King and his kingdom is to be sudden, he is led to wait and watch – all the more because everything here, in the world's daily history of change and noise and revelry is fitted to throw him off his guard. His justification does not lull him asleep. His faith does not make him heedless of the future. It is the substance of things hoped for, the evidence of things not seen. It says, Let us not sleep, as do others; but let us watch and be sober: Watch, for you know neither the day nor the hour when the Son of Man comes. Many a trial of her watchfulness has the church had, many a disappointment has her faith sustained; but she does not despond nor give way, remembering the promise, "He that shall come will come, and will not tarry." Her faith keeps up her vigilance, and her vigilance invigorates her faith. In the darkest hour faith says, "I am my beloved's, and my beloved is mine"; and hope adds, "Make haste, my beloved, and be thou like to a roe or a young hart upon the mountains of spices."

The church watches because of present evil and coming good, that she may be kept undefiled from the one and may attain unto the other.

The church watches because of present evil and coming good, that she may be kept undefiled from the one and may attain unto the other. Danger from enemies and the prospect of speedy victory over them keep her awake. Fear of losing sight of the cross and so again walking in darkness; suspicion both of the good and the evil things of Earth – its flatteries and its menaces, its toils, its cares, its amusements, its pleasures; anxiety about keeping her garments unspotted and her conscience clean; the sight of the sleeping millions around; and the knowledge that it is upon a sleeping world that the Lord is to come – these things act powerfully as stimulants and bid her be watchful.

To be among the foolish virgins, without oil and with a dying lamp, when the midnight cry goes forth; to be near the door and yet shut out; to hear the announcement, "The marriage of the Lamb is come, and his wife has made herself ready," and yet not be ready; to be summoned to the festival and yet to be without the bridal and the festal dress; to love and then to fall from love; to draw the sword and then in faint heartedness to sheathe it; to run well for a while and then to slacken speed; to war against Satan as the prince of darkness and yield to him as an angel of light; to set out with condemning the world and then to mingle with it; to cleave like Demas to the saints and then to forsake them; to be among the twelve for a season and then to be a traitor at the last; to be lifted up like Capernaum to Heaven and then to be thrust down to Hell; to be among the sons of light and then to fall from Heaven like Lucifer, son of the morning; to sit down in the upper chamber with the Lord and then to betray the Son of Man with a kiss; to put on a goodly garment of fair profession and then to walk naked in shame – these are the solemn thoughts that crowd in upon the justified man and keep him watchful.

They who know not what it is to be "accepted in the Beloved" and to "rejoice in hope of the glory of God" may fall asleep. He dare not; he knows what he is risking and what one hour of slumber may cost him, and he must be wakeful. He does not make election his opiate and say, I am safe; I may sleep or wake as I please. He says, I am safe; but this only makes me doubly vigilant that I may not dishonor him who has saved me; and even though I may not finally fall away, I know not how much I may lose by one day's slothfulness or how much I may gain by maintaining that watchful attitude to which, as the expectant of an absent Lord, I am called. "Blessed is he that watches," and even though I could not see the reason for this, I will act upon it that I may realize the promised blessedness. He who has called me to vigilance can make me partaker of its joy. He can make my watchtower, lonely and dark as it may seem, none other than the house of God and the very gate of Heaven.

He does not make election his opiate and say, I am safe; I may sleep or wake as I please. He says, I am safe; but this only makes me doubly vigilant that I may not dishonor him who has saved me.

Justification by
Faith Alone

Charles Hodge

Foreword

THE Trinity Foundation is to be commended for placing once again in print – and within one volume – the chapter on justification from Charles Hodge's *The Way of Life: A Handbook of Christian Belief and Practice* (1841), written at the request of the American Sunday School Union that it might be used by "intelligent and educated young persons, either to arouse their attention, or to guide their steps in the WAY OF LIFE," and the chapter on justification excerpted from the third volume of his famous *Systematic Theology* (1872-1873).

This Trinity Foundation publication is a timely one, given the recent publication of the programmatic statement, "Evangelicals and Catholics Together: The Christian Mission in the Third Millennium," which appeared in *First Things* (May 1994) – a statement composed by eight Protestants (led by Charles Colson) and seven Roman Catholics (led by Richard John Neuhaus) and endorsed by twelve other Protestants and thirteen other Roman Catholics. While its call for co-belligerence against the rampant moral degeneracy in our nation's political, legal, medical, educational, and cultural life and for cooperation against social injustice and economic poverty is appropriate enough (Section IV), the statement's marginalizing of many of the stark theological differences which exist between Protestant Christianity and Roman Catholicism is inexcusable when its authors affirm their agreement on the Apostles Creed and on the proposition

I am disappointed that Dr. James I. Packer, one of the statement's Protestant endorsers, lends the prestige of his name and his leadership position among evangelicals to this ecumenical statement.

that "we are justified by grace through faith because of Christ" (Section 1) and then on this "confessional" basis call for an end to proselytizing each other's communicants and for a missiological ecumenism which cooperates together in evangelism and spiritual nurture (Section V).[1]

The word "alone" after the word "faith" in the statement's proposition on justification is thundering by its absence. As written, the statement is a capitulation to Rome's unscriptural understanding of justification, for never in the debate between Rome and the first Protestant Reformers did anyone on either side deny that sinners must be justified by faith. The whole controversy in the sixteenth century in this doctrinal area turned on whether sinners were justified by faith *alone* (*sola fide*) or by faith *and* good works which earned merit before God. The Protestant Reformers, following Paul's teaching on justification in *Romans* and *Galatians*, affirmed the former and denied the latter; Rome denied the former

As a member priest within and an advocate of the Anglican prelacy, Packer has lived within that communion and cooperated with it even though it tolerates and receives as "seminal thinkers" those whom the Bible clearly declares to be theological apostates.

1. I am disappointed that Dr. James I. Packer, one of the statement's Protestant endorsers, lends the prestige of his name and his leadership position among evangelicals to this ecumenical statement, even though he acknowledges (1) that Rome's claim to be the only institution that can without qualification be called the church of Christ is theologically and historically flawed; (2) that Rome's teaching on the Mass and on merit cuts across Paul's doctrine of justification in and through Christ by faith; (3) that all of Rome's forms of the Mary cult, its invoking of saints, its belief in purgatory, and its continuing disbursement of indulgences, to say the least, "damp down the full assurance to which, according to Scripture, justification should lead through the ministry of the Holy Spirit"; and (4) that Rome's claim of infallibility for all conciliar and some papal pronouncements and its insistence that Christians should take their beliefs from the church rather than from the Bible make self-correction virtually impossible (compare Packer's article, "Why I Signed It," *Christianity Today*, December 12, 1994, 34-37.

I say I am disappointed by Packer, but I am not surprised, since Packer's ecclesiology in the area of ecclesiastical separation from unbelief has been suspect for years. As a member priest within and an advocate of the Anglican prelacy, Packer has lived within that communion and cooperated with it even though it tolerates and receives as "seminal thinkers" those whom the Bible clearly declares to be theological apostates. His willingness to evangelize and nurture converts with Roman Catholics is simply a further extension of this lapse in his understanding of Biblical separation from unbelief.

and affirmed the latter. And the Protestant Reformers, again following Paul (compare his entire argument in *Galatians*), maintained that the path the sinner follows here leads either to Heaven or to Hell. The Protestant Reformers clearly saw – over against Rome's doctrine of salvation which was (and still is) essential to the maintenance of its priestcraft and thus its economic fortunes – (1) that saving faith is to be directed to the doing and dying of *Christ alone* and not to the good works or inner experience of the believer; (2) that the Christian's righteousness before God is *in Heaven* at the right hand of God in Jesus Christ and *not on Earth* within the believer; (3) that the ground of our justification is the vicarious work of Christ *for* us and not the gracious work of the Spirit *in* us; and (4) that the faith-righteousness of justification is not personal but vicarious, not infused but imputed, not experiential but judicial, not psychological but legal, not our own but alien to us, and not earned but graciously given through faith in Jesus Christ, which faith is itself a gift of grace. Hodge's two treatises on justification provide the Biblical ground and argumentation for these great teachings and drive home once again for the benefit of our theologically illiterate generation the reason why Luther called this doctrine the mark of a standing or falling church.

Before I close, a word about Charles Hodge the man is in order for those readers who may know little or nothing about him. Hodge (1797-1878) was the most influential American Presbyterian theologian of the nineteenth century, teaching at Princeton Theological Seminary from 1822 almost to his death in 1878 and editing the *Biblical Repertory and Princeton Review* from its inception in 1825 until 1871. During his teaching career more than three thousand ministerial students sat at his feet, most of whom became ministers in the Presbyterian church. Many of his writings – among them his commentaries on *Romans*, *1* and *2 Corinthians*, and *Ephesians*, and his *magnum opus*, his three-volume *Systematic Theology* – still stand on evangelical preachers' shelves and are regularly consulted by them. I commend this worthy old Presbyterian stalwart to

The faith-righteousness of justification is not personal but vicarious, not infused but imputed, not experiential but judicial, not psychological but legal, not our own but alien to us, and not earned but graciously given through faith in Jesus Christ, which faith is itself a gift of grace.

The Trinity Foundation readership as a trustworthy teacher and guide.

Robert L. Reymond
Professor of Systematic Theology
Knox Theological Seminary
January 1995

*I commend
this worthy old
Presbyterian
stalwart to
The Trinity
Foundation
readership as
a trustworthy
teacher and guide.*

Introduction

IN HIS letter to the churches in Galatia, Paul emphasizes the idea of justification by faith alone. In this letter Paul does not follow his usual pattern in writing to the churches: He does not praise the Galatians first and then reprimand them for their errors in later chapters; his rebuke begins in chapter 1. Paul writes:

> I marvel that you are turning away so soon from him who called you in the grace of Christ to a different gospel – which is not another – but there are some who trouble you and want to pervert the Gospel of Christ. But even if we or an angel from Heaven preach any other gospel to you than what we have preached to you, let him be accursed. As we have said before, so now I say again, if anyone preaches any other gospel to you than what you have received, let him be accursed.

"If anyone preaches any other gospel to you than what you have received, let him be accursed."
– Galatians 1

The Gospel of justification by faith alone is obviously very important, so important that anyone – including Paul himself and angels from Heaven – who teaches a different gospel is cursed by God. Paul illustrates both the meaning and the importance of justification by faith alone in chapter 2 of *Galatians*:

> But when Peter had come to Antioch, I withstood him to his face, because he was to be blamed. For before certain men came from James, he would eat with the Gentiles, but when they came, he withdrew and separated himself, fearing those who were of the circumcision. And the rest of the Jews also

played the hypocrite with him, so that even Barnabas was carried away with their hypocrisy. But when I saw that they were not straightforward about the truth of the Gospel, I said to Peter before them all, "If you, being a Jew, live in the manner of Gentiles and not as the Jews, why do you compel Gentiles to live as Jews? We who are Jews by nature and not sinners of the Gentiles, knowing that a man is not justified by the works of the law but by faith in Jesus Christ – even we have believed in Christ Jesus that we might be justified by faith in Christ and not by the works of the law, for by the works of the law no flesh shall be justified.… I do not set aside the grace of God, for if righteousness comes through the law, then Christ died in vain.

Almost all so-called Protestant churches in America – as well as the Roman Catholic Church – do not believe and even deny the doctrine of justification at the beginning of the twenty-first century.

The meaning – the heart of the Gospel – is justification by faith alone. It was the most important doctrine of the first century, and it was the most important doctrine of the Christian Reformation in the sixteenth century. Almost all so-called Protestant churches in America – as well as the Roman Catholic Church – do not believe and even deny the doctrine of justification at the beginning of the twenty-first century.

The importance Paul placed on justification by faith alone may be seen in his actions against Peter. Consider Peter: Peter was both an apostle and a disciple. His name had been given to him by Christ himself. Peter was an older man than Paul. He had lived and traveled with Jesus for three years. Peter had preached at Pentecost, opening the kingdom of God to all. The Roman Catholic Church – but not the Bible – claims that Peter was the first pope, and as such, infallible. Yet Paul withstood Peter to his face, rebuking him publicly for his errors.

Consider also Paul: He was an apostle as well, though not a disciple. Younger than Peter, he had been a student of the Pharisees while Peter was a disciple of Christ. By the grace of God, Paul had become a Christian while on his way to Damascus to persecute Christians. As a Christian who understood that salvation could not come from the law, Paul understood clearly that the doctrine of which Christians must be most jealous – for it is the heart of the Gospel – is justification by faith alone.

Consider what provoked Paul's vehement reaction to Peter: Peter had not preached a sermon against justification by faith alone; there is no suggestion that Peter made any false statements. Peter had simply withdrawn from eating with Gentile Christians, out of fear of the Jews, because the Old Testament law forbade eating with Gentiles. His actions, and those of Barnabas and the rest of the Jews, suggested that they thought that justification was not by faith alone, but by observation of the Mosaic law. For this error Paul – the same Paul who repeatedly tells Christians to "be at peace among yourselves" – rebukes the apostle Peter publicly and disrupts the peace of the church at Antioch. Paul breaks the peace and publicly, not privately, corrects Peter for his hypocrisy that seems to cast doubt on the truth of justification by faith alone.

It was this doctrine – justification by faith alone – believed and preached by the Christians of the first century that turned the world upside down. It was this doctrine – justification by faith alone – that ended the dark millennium of Roman Catholic religious superstition in Europe in the sixteenth century when God caused the Reformers to believe and preach it again. And it is the doctrine of justification by faith alone that will turn the world upside down again when God causes his people to believe and preach it once more.

Justification by faith alone is the heart of the Gospel, and the Gospel is the power of God for salvation. If the world is to be saved in any sense, temporal or eternal, it will not be saved through our keeping of the law, but only through belief of the Gospel of Jesus Christ. Before Christ – except for the land of Israel, which had the revelation of God – there was nothing but pagan darkness and superstition throughout the world. After Christ, the Gospel was suppressed by wicked ecclesiastical and political powers – by spiritual wickedness in high places – and the world was again plunged into spiritual darkness.

Since the brilliant light of the Christian Reformation enlightened the world five centuries ago, its brilliance has dimmed and the Gospel has been suppressed, Christians have been persecuted by secular and religious powers, and

It was this doctrine – justification by faith alone – believed and preached by the Christians of the first century that turned the world upside down.

Christian doctrines perverted. If God wishes his light and his truth to shine forth again in this present evil age, it will shine first and most brilliantly in a recovery of the doctrine of justification by faith alone.

John W. Robbins
September 2005

If God wishes his light and his truth to shine forth again in this present evil age, it will shine first and most brilliantly in a recovery of the doctrine of justification by faith alone.

1

The Meaning of Justification

How can a man be just with God? The answer given to this question decides the character of our religion, and, if practically adopted, our future destiny. To give a wrong answer is to mistake the way to Heaven. It is to err where error is fatal, because it cannot be corrected. If God requires one thing, and we present another, how can we be saved? If he has revealed a method in which he can be just and yet justify the sinner, and if we reject that method and insist upon pursuing a different way, how can we hope to be accepted? The answer, therefore, which is given to the above question should be seriously pondered by all who assume the office of religious teachers and by all who rely upon their instructions. As we are not to be judged by proxy, but every man must answer for himself, so every man should be satisfied for himself what the Bible teaches on this subject. All that religious teachers can do is to endeavor to aid the investigations of those who are anxious to learn the way of life. And in doing this, the safest method is to adhere strictly to the instructions of the Scriptures and to exhibit the subject as it is there presented. The substance and the form of this all-important doctrine are so intimately connected that those who attempt to separate them can hardly fail to err. What one discards as belonging merely to the form, another considers as belonging to its substance. All certainty and security are

To give a wrong answer is to mistake the way to Heaven. It is to err where error is fatal, because it cannot be corrected.

149

lost as soon as this method is adopted, and it becomes a matter to be decided exclusively by our own views of right and wrong what is to be retained and what rejected from the Scriptural representations. Our only security, therefore, is to take the language of the Bible in its obvious meaning and put upon it the construction which the persons to whom it was addressed must have given, and which, consequently, the sacred writers intended it should bear.

It is one of the primary doctrines of the Bible, everywhere either asserted or assumed, that we are under the law of God. This is true of all classes of men, whether they enjoy a divine revelation or not.

As the doctrine of justification is not only frequently stated in the sacred Scriptures but formally taught and vindicated, all that will be attempted in this chapter is to give as faithfully as possible a representation of what the inspired writers inculcate on this subject; that is, to state what positions they assume, by what arguments they sustain those positions, how they answer the objections to their doctrine, and what application they make of it to the hearts and consciences of their readers.

It is one of the primary doctrines of the Bible, everywhere either asserted or assumed, that we are under the law of God. This is true of all classes of men, whether they enjoy a divine revelation or not. Everything which God has revealed as a rule of duty enters into the constitution of the law which binds those to whom that revelation is given and by which they are to be ultimately judged. Those who have not received any external revelation of the divine will are a law unto themselves. The knowledge of right and wrong, written upon their hearts, is of the nature of a divine law, having its authority and sanction, and by it the heathen are to be judged in the last day.

God has seen fit to annex the promise of life to obedience to his law, "The man who does those things shall live by them" (*Romans* 10:5) is the language of Scripture on this subject. To the lawyer who admitted that the law required love to God and man, our Savior said, "You have answered right: This do, and you shall live" (*Luke* 10:28). And to one who asked him, "What good things shall I do, that I may have eternal life?" he said, "If you will enter into life, keep the commandments" (*Matthew* 19:17). On the other hand, the law denounces death as the penalty of transgression: "The wages of sin is death" (*Romans* 6:23). Such is the uniform declaration of Scripture on this subject.

The obedience which the law demands is called righteousness, and those who render that obedience are called righteous. To ascribe righteousness to anyone, or to pronounce him righteous, is the Scriptural meaning of the word "to justify." The word never means to make good in a moral sense, but always to pronounce just or righteous. Thus God says, "I will not justify the wicked" (*Exodus* 23:7). Judges are commanded to justify the righteous and to condemn the wicked (*Deuteronomy* 25:1). Woe is pronounced on those who "justify the wicked for reward" (*Isaiah* 5:23). In the New Testament it is said, "By the deeds of the law there shall no flesh be justified in his sight" (*Romans* 3:20). "It is God that justifies. Who is he that condemns?" (*Romans* 8:33, 34). There is scarcely a word in the Bible the meaning of which is less open to doubt. There is no passage in the New Testament in which it is used out of its ordinary and obvious sense![1] When God justifies a man he declares him to be righteous. *To justify* never means *to render* one holy. It is said to be sinful to justify the wicked, but it could never be sinful to render the wicked holy. And as the law demands righteousness, to impute or ascribe righteousness to anyone, is, in Scriptural language, to justify. To make (or constitute) righteous is another equivalent form of expression. Hence, to be righteous before God and to be justified mean the same thing as in the following passage: "Not the hearers of the law are just before God, but the doers of the law shall be justified" (*Romans* 2:13).

The attentive and especially the anxious reader of the Bible cannot fail to observe that these various expressions – *to be righteous in the sight of God, to impute righteousness, to constitute righteous, to justify*, and others of similar import – are so interchanged as to explain each other and to make it clear that to justify a man is to ascribe or impute to him righteousness. The great question then is, How is this righteousness to be

To ascribe righteousness to anyone, or to pronounce him righteous, is the Scriptural meaning of the word "to justify." The word never means to make good in a moral sense.

1. *Revelation* 22:11 is probably no exception to this remark, as the text in that passage is uncertain.

obtained? We have reason to be thankful that the answer which the Bible gives to this question is so perfectly plain.

In the first place, that the righteousness by which we are to be justified before God is not of works is not only asserted, but proved. The apostle's first argument on this point is derived from the consideration that the law demands a perfect righteousness. If the law were satisfied by an imperfect obedience, or by a routine of external duties, or by any service which men are competent to render, then indeed justification would be by works. But since the law demands perfect obedience, justification by works is, for sinners, absolutely impossible. It is thus the apostle reasons, "As many as are of the works of the law are under the curse: For it is written, Cursed is every one that continues not in all things which are written in the book of the law to do them" (*Galatians* 3:10). As the law pronounces its curse upon every man who continues not to do all that it commands, and as no man can pretend to this perfect obedience, it follows that all who look to the law for justification must be condemned. To the same effect, in a following verse, he says, "The law is not of faith: but, the man that does them shall live by them." That is, the law is not satisfied by any single grace or imperfect obedience. It knows and can know no other ground of justification than complete compliance with its demands. Hence, in the same chapter Paul says, "If there had been a law given which could have given life, truly righteousness should have been by the law." Could the law pronounce righteous, and thus give a title to the promised life to those who had broken its commands, there would have been no necessity of any other provision for the salvation of men; but as the law cannot thus lower its demands, justification by the law is impossible. The same truth is taught in a different form when it is said, "If righteousness *come* by the law, then Christ is dead in vain" (*Galatians* 2:21). There would have been no necessity for the death of Christ if it had been possible to satisfy the law by the imperfect obedience which we can render. Paul therefore warns all those who look to works for justification that they are debtors to do the whole law (*Galatians* 5:3). It knows

Since the law demands perfect obedience, justification by works is, for sinners, absolutely impossible.

no compromise; it cannot demand less than what is right, and perfect obedience is right. Therefore its only language is as before, "Cursed is every one that continues not in all things which are written in the book of the law to do them" (*Galatians* 3:10); and, "The man which does those things shall live by them" (*Romans* 10:5). Every man, therefore, who expects justification by works must see to it, not that he is better than other men, or that he is very exact and does many things, or that he fasts twice in the week and gives tithes of all he possesses, but that he is *sinless.*

That the law of God is thus strict in its demands is a truth which lies at the foundation of all Paul's reasoning in reference to the method of justification. He proves that the Gentiles have sinned against the law written on their hearts, and that the Jews have broken the law revealed in their Scriptures; both Jews and Gentiles, therefore, are under sin, and the whole world is guilty before God. Hence, he infers, by the deeds of the law there shall no flesh be justified in his sight. There is, however, no force in this reasoning, except on the assumption that the law demands perfect obedience. How many men, who freely acknowledge that they are sinners, depend upon their works for acceptance with God! They see no inconsistency between the acknowledgment of sin and the expectation of justification by works. The reason is that they proceed upon a very different principle from that adopted by the apostle. They suppose that the law may be satisfied by very imperfect obedience. Paul assumes that God demands perfect conformity to his will, that his wrath is revealed against all ungodliness and unrighteousness of men. With him, therefore, it is enough that men have sinned to prove that they cannot be justified by works. It is not a question of degrees, more or less, for as to this point there is no difference, since "all have sinned, and come short of the glory of God" (*Romans* 3:23).

This doctrine, though so plainly taught in Scripture, men are disposed to think very severe. They imagine that their good deeds will be compared with their evil deeds, and that they will be rewarded or punished as the one or the other

That the law of God is thus strict in its demands is a truth which lies at the foundation of all Paul's reasoning in reference to the method of justification.

preponderates; or that the sins of one part of life may be atoned for by the good works of another; or that they can escape by mere confession and repentance. They could not entertain such expectations if they believed themselves to be under a law. No human law is administered as men seem to hope the law of God will be. He who steals or murders, though it be but once, though he confesses and repents, though he does any number of acts of charity, is not less a thief or murderer. The law cannot take cognizance of his repentance and reformation. If he steals or murders, the law condemns him. Justification by the law is for him impossible. The law of God extends to the most secret exercises of the heart. It condemns whatever is in its nature evil. If a man violate this perfect rule of right, there is an end of justification by the law; he has failed to comply with its conditions, and the law can only condemn him. To justify him would be to say that he had not transgressed.

Men, however, think that they are not to be dealt with on the principles of strict law. Here is their fatal mistake. It is here that they are in most direct conflict with the Scriptures.

Men, however, think that they are not to be dealt with on the principles of strict law. Here is their fatal mistake. It is here that they are in most direct conflict with the Scriptures, which proceed upon the uniform assumption of our subjection to the law. Under the government of God, strict law is nothing but perfect excellence; it is the steady exercise of moral rectitude. Even conscience, when duly enlightened and roused, is as strict as the law of God. It refuses to be appeased by repentance, reformation, or penance. It enforces every command and every denunciation of our Supreme Ruler, and teaches – as plainly as do the Scriptures themselves – that justification by an imperfect obedience is impossible. As conscience, however, is fallible, no reliance on this subject is placed on her testimony. The appeal is to the Word of God, which clearly teaches that it is impossible a sinner can be justified by works, because the law demands perfect obedience.

The apostle's second argument to show that justification is not by works is the testimony of the Scriptures of the Old Testament. This testimony is urged in various forms. In the first place, as the apostle proceeds upon the principle that the law demands perfect obedience, all those passages which assert the universal sinfulness of men are so many declarations that they cannot be justified by works. He therefore quotes such passages as the following: "There is none righteous, no, not one; there is none that understands, there is none that seeks after God. They are all gone out of the way; they are together become unprofitable; there is none that does good, no, not one" (*Romans* 3:10-12). The Old Testament, by teaching that all men are sinners, does, in the apostle's view, thereby teach that they can never be accepted before God on the ground of their own righteousness. To say that a man is a sinner is to say that the law condemns him – and of course it cannot justify him. As the ancient Scriptures are full of declarations of the sinfulness of men, so they are full of proof that justification is not by works.

But in the second place, Paul cites their direct affirmative testimony in support of his doctrine. In the *Psalms* it is said, "Enter not into judgment with your servants, for in your sight shall no man living be justified" (*Psalm* 143:2). This passage he often quotes, and to the same class belong all those passages which speak of the insufficiency or worthlessness of human righteousness in the sight of God.

In the third place, the apostle refers to those passages which imply the doctrine for which he contends; that is, to those which speak of the acceptance of men with God as a matter of grace, as something which they do not deserve, and for which they can urge no claim founded upon their own merit. It is with this view that he refers to the language of David: "Blessed are they whose iniquities are forgiven and whose sins are covered. Blessed is the man to whom the Lord will not impute sin" (*Romans* 4:7, 8). The fact that a man is forgiven implies that he is guilty, and the fact that he is guilty implies that his justification cannot rest upon his own character or conduct. It need hardly be remarked, that, in this view, the whole Scriptures, from the beginning to the end, are crowded with condemnations of the doctrine of justification by works. Every penitent confession, every appeal to God's mercy is a renunciation of all personal merit, a declaration that the

The fact that a man is forgiven implies that he is guilty, and the fact that he is guilty implies that his justification cannot rest upon his own character or conduct.

penitent's hope was not founded on anything in himself. Such confessions and appeals are indeed often made by those who still rely upon their good works or inherent righteousness for acceptance with God. This, however, does not invalidate the apostle's argument. It only shows that such persons have a different view of what is necessary for justification from that entertained by the apostle. They suppose that the demands of the law are so low that although they are sinners and need to be forgiven, they can still do what the law demands. Paul proceeds on the assumption that the law requires perfect obedience, and therefore every confession of sin or appeal for mercy involves a renunciation of justification by the law.

The law requires perfect obedience, and therefore every confession of sin or appeal for mercy involves a renunciation of justification by the law.

Again, the apostle represents the Old Testament Scriptures as teaching that justification is not by works by showing that they inculcate a different method of obtaining acceptance with God. This they do by the doctrine which they teach concerning the Messiah as a Redeemer from sin. Hence, Paul says that the method of justification without works (not founded upon works) was testified by *The Law and the Prophets*; that is, by the whole of the Old Testament. The two methods of acceptance with God – the one by works, the other by a propitiation for sin – are incompatible. And as the ancient Scriptures teach the latter method, they repudiate the former. They, moreover, in express terms assert that "the just shall live by faith." The law knows nothing of faith; its language is, "The man that does them shall live in them" (*Galatians* 3:11, 12). The law knows nothing of anything but obedience as the ground of acceptance. If the Scriptures say we are accepted through faith, they thereby say that we are not accepted on the ground of obedience.

Again: The examples of justification given in the Old Testament show that it was not by works. The apostle appeals particularly to the case of Abraham and asks whether he attained justification by works. He answers, No, for if he were justified by works he had whereof to glory; but he had no ground of glorying before God, and therefore he was not justified by works. And the Scriptures expressly assert, "Abraham believed God, and it was counted unto him for righteousness" (*Romans* 4:3). His acceptance, therefore, was by faith, and not by works.

In all these various ways does the apostle make the authority of the Old Testament sustain his doctrine that justification is not by works. This authority is as decisive for us as it was for the ancient Jewish Christians. We also believe the Old Testament to be the Word of God, and its truths come to us explained and enforced by Christ and his apostles. We have the great advantage of an infallible interpretation of these early oracles of truth, and the argumentative manner in which their authority is cited and applied prevents all obscurity as to the real intentions of the sacred writers. That by the deeds of the law no flesh shall be justified before God is taught so clearly and so frequently in the New Testament, it is so often asserted, so formally proved, so variously assumed, that no one can doubt that such is indeed the doctrine of the Word of God. The only point on which the serious inquirer can even raise a question, is, What kind of works do the Scriptures mean to exclude as the foundation for acceptance with God? Does the apostle mean works in the widest sense, or does he merely intend ceremonial observances or works of mere formality, performed without any real love to God?

Those who attend to the nature of his assertions and to the course of his argument will find that there is no room for doubt on this subject. The primary principle on which his argument rests precludes all ground for mistaking his meaning. He assumes that the law demands perfect obedience, and as no man can render that obedience, he infers that no man can be justified by the law. He does not argue that because the law is spiritual it cannot be satisfied by mere ceremonies or by works flowing from an impure motive. He nowhere says that though we cannot be justified by external rites, or by works having the mere form of goodness, we are justified by our sincere, though imperfect, obedience.

On the contrary, he constantly teaches that since we are sinners, and since the law condemns all sin, it condemns us, and justification by the law is, therefore, impossible. This argument he applies to the Jews and the Gentiles without

Paul does not argue that because the law is spiritual it cannot be satisfied by mere ceremonies or by works flowing from an impure motive. He nowhere says that though we cannot be justified by external rites, or by works having the mere form of goodness, we are justified by our sincere, though imperfect, obedience.

distinction – to the whole world, whether they knew anything of the Jewish Scriptures or not. It was the moral law, the law which he pronounced holy, just, and good, which says, "You shall not covet"; it is this law, however revealed – whether in the writings of Moses, or in the human heart – of which he constantly asserts that it cannot give life, or teach the way of acceptance with God.

Paul never contrasts one class of works with another, but he constantly contrasts works and faith, excluding all classes of the former, works of righteousness as well as those of mere formality.

As most of those to whom he wrote had enjoyed a divine revelation – and as that revelation included the law of Moses and all its rites – he of course included that law in his statement and often specially refers to it, but never in its limited sense (as a code of religious ceremonies) but always in its widest scope, as including the highest rule of moral duty made known to men. Hence he never contrasts one class of works with another, but he constantly contrasts works and faith, excluding all classes of the former, works of righteousness as well as those of mere formality. "Not by works of righteousness which we have done, but according to his mercy he saved us" (*Titus* 3:5). "Who has saved us – not according to our works" (*2 Timothy* 1:9). We are saved by faith, not by works (*Ephesians* 2:9). Men are said to be justified without works, to be in themselves ungodly when justified; and it is not until they are justified that they perform any real, good works. It is only when united to Christ that we bring forth fruit unto God. Hence, we are said to be "his workmanship, created in Christ Jesus unto good works" (*Ephesians* 2:10). All the inward excellence of the Christian and the fruits of the Spirit are the consequences – and not the causes – of his reconciliation and acceptance with God. They are the robe of beauty, the white garment, with which Christ arrays those who come to him poor, and blind, and naked. It is, then, the plain doctrine of the Word of God that our justification is not founded upon our own obedience to the law. Nothing done by us or wrought in us can for a moment stand the test of a rule of righteousness which pronounces a curse upon all those who continue not in all things written in the book of the law to do them.

2

Christ's Satisfaction of the Law

WE HAVE seen that the Scriptures teach, first, that all men are naturally under the law as prescribing the terms of their acceptance with God; and, second, that no obedience which sinners can render is sufficient to satisfy the demands of that law. It follows, then, that unless we are freed from the law, not as a rule of duty, but as prescribing the conditions of acceptance with God, justification is for us impossible. It is, therefore, the third great point of Scriptural doctrine on this subject that believers are free from the law in the sense just stated. "You are not under the law," says the apostle, "but under grace" (*Romans* 6:14). To illustrate this declaration, he refers to the case of a woman who is bound to her husband as long as he lives; but when he is dead, she is free from her obligation to him, and is at liberty to marry another man. So we are delivered from the law as a rule of justification and are at liberty to embrace a different method of obtaining acceptance with God (*Romans* 7:1-6). Paul says of himself that he had died to the law; that is, become free from it (*Galatians* 2:19). And the same is said of all believers (*Romans* 7:6).

He insists upon this freedom as essential not only to justification, but to sanctification. For while under the law, the motions of sins, which were by the law, brought forth fruit unto death; but now we are delivered from the law that we may serve God in newness of spirit (*Romans* 7:5, 6).

Unless we are freed from the law, not as a rule of duty, but as prescribing the conditions of acceptance with God, justification is for us impossible.

159

Before faith came we were kept under the law, which he compares to a schoolmaster, but now we are no longer under a schoolmaster (*Galatians* 3:24, 25). He regards the desire to be subject to the law as the greatest infatuation. "Tell me," he says, "you that desire to be under the law, do you not hear the law?" and then shows that those who are under the demands of a legal system are in the condition of slaves and not of sons and heirs. "Stand fast therefore," he exhorts, "in the liberty wherewith Christ has made us free. Behold, I, Paul, say unto you, that if you be circumcised, Christ shall profit you nothing. For I testify again to every man that is circumcised that he is a debtor to do the whole law. Christ is become of no effect unto you, whosoever of you are justified by the law; you are fallen from grace (*Galatians* 4:21-31; 5:1-4).

This infatuation Paul considered madness, and exclaims, "O foolish Galatians, who has bewitched you that you should not obey the truth, before whose eyes Jesus Christ has been evidently set forth crucified among you? This only would I learn of you. Did you receive the Spirit by the works of the law or by the hearing of faith?" (*Galatians* 3:1-2). This apostasy was so fatal, the substitution of legal obedience for the work of Christ as the ground of justification was so destructive, that Paul pronounces accursed any man or angel who should preach such a doctrine for the Gospel of the grace of God.

It was to the law, as revealed in the books of Moses, that the fickle Galatians were disposed to look for justification. Their apostasy, however, consisted in going back to the law, no matter in what form revealed – to works, no matter of what kind, as the ground of justification.

It was to the law, as revealed in the books of Moses, that the fickle Galatians were disposed to look for justification. Their apostasy, however, consisted in going back to the law, no matter in what form revealed – to works, no matter of what kind, as the ground of justification. The apostle's arguments and denunciations, therefore, are so framed as to apply to the adoption of any form of legal obedience, instead of the work of Christ, as the ground of our confidence toward God. To suppose that all he says relates exclusively to a relapse into Judaism is to suppose that we Gentiles have no part in the redemption of Christ. If it was only from the bondage of the Jewish economy that he redeemed his people, then those who were never subject to that bondage have no interest in his work. And of course Paul was strangely infatuated in preaching Christ crucified to the Gentiles. We find, however, that what he taught in the epistle to the Galatians, in special reference to the law of Moses, he teaches in the epistle to the Romans in reference to that law which is holy, just, and good, and which condemns the most secret sins of the heart.

The nature of the apostle's doctrine is, if possible, even more clear from the manner in which he vindicates it than from his direct assertions. "What then?" he asks, "Shall we sin, because we are not under the law, but under grace? God forbid" (*Romans* 6:15). Had Paul taught that we are freed from the ceremonial, in order to be subject to the moral law, there could have been no room for such an objection. But if he taught that the moral law itself could not give life – that we must be freed from its demands as the condition of acceptance with God – then, indeed, to the wise of this world, it might seem that he was loosing the bands of moral obligation and opening the door to the greatest licentiousness. Hence the frequency and earnestness with which he repels the objection and shows that, so far from legal bondage being necessary to holiness, it must cease before holiness can exist; that it is not until the curse of the law is removed and the soul reconciled to God that holy affections rise in the heart and the fruits of holiness appear in the life. "Do we then make void the law through faith? God forbid: We establish the law" (*Romans* 3:31).

It is then clearly the doctrine of the Bible that believers are freed from the law as prescribing the conditions of their acceptance with God; it is no longer incumbent upon them, in order to justification, to fulfill its demand of perfect obedience, or to satisfy its penal exactions. But how is this deliverance effected? How is it that rational and accountable beings are exempted from the obligations of that holy and just law, which was originally imposed upon their race as the rule of justification? The answer to this question includes the fourth great truth respecting the way of salvation taught in the Scriptures. It is not by the abrogation of the law, either as to its precepts or penalty; it is not by lowering its demands, and accommodating them to the altered capacities or inclinations of men. We have seen how constantly the

"What then?" he asks, "Shall we sin, because we are not under the law, but under grace? God forbid" (Romans 6:15). Had Paul taught that we are freed from the ceremonial, in order to be subject to the moral law, there could have been no room for such an objection.

apostle teaches that the law still demands perfect obedience, and that they are debtors to do the whole law who seek justification at its hands. He no less clearly teaches that death is as much the wages of sin in our case as it was in that of Adam. If it is neither by abrogation nor relaxation that we are freed from the demands of the law, how has this deliverance been effected? By the mystery of vicarious obedience and suffering. This is the Gospel of the grace of God. This is what was a scandal to the Jews and foolishness to the Greeks; but to those that are called, the power of God and the wisdom of God (1 *Corinthians* 1:23, 24).

The Scriptures teach us that the Son of God – the brightness of the Father's glory and the express image of his person, who thought it not robbery to be equal with God – became flesh and subjected himself to the very law to which we were bound; that he perfectly obeyed that law and suffered its penalty, and thus, by satisfying its demands, delivered us from its bondage and introduced us into the glorious liberty of the sons of God. It is thus that the doctrine of redemption is presented in the Scriptures. "God," says the apostle, "sent forth his Son, made of a woman, made under the law, to redeem those that were under the law" (*Galatians* 4:4, 5). Being made under the law, we know that he obeyed it perfectly, brought in everlasting righteousness, and is therefore declared to be "the Lord our righteousness" (*Jeremiah* 23:6), since, by his obedience, many are constituted righteous (*Romans* 5:19). He, therefore, is said to be made righteousness unto us (1 *Corinthians* 1:30). And those who are in him are said to be righteous before God, not having their own righteousness, but that which is through the faith of Christ (*Philippians* 3:9).

That we are redeemed from the curse of the law by Christ's enduring that curse in our place is taught in every variety of form from the beginning to the end of the Bible. There was the more need that this point should be clearly and variously presented, because it is the one on which an enlightened conscience immediately fastens. The desert of death begets the fear of death. And this fear of death cannot be allayed until it is seen how, in consistency with divine justice, we are

That we are redeemed from the curse of the law by Christ's enduring that curse in our place is taught in every variety of form from the beginning to the end of the Bible.

162

freed from the righteous penalty of the law. How this is done, the Scriptures teach in the most explicit manner. "Christ has redeemed us from the curse of the law, being made a curse for us" (*Galatians* 3:13). Paul has just said, "As many as are of the works of the law are under the curse." But all men are naturally under the law, and therefore all are under the curse. How are we redeemed from it? By Christ's being made a curse for us. Such is the simple and sufficient answer to this most important of all questions.

The doctrine so plainly taught in *Galatians* 3:13 – that Christ has redeemed us from the curse of the law by bearing it in our stead – is no less clearly presented in *2 Corinthians* 5:21: "He has made him who knew no sin to be sin for us, that we might be made the righteousness of God in him." This is represented as the only ground on which men are authorized to preach the Gospel. "We are ambassadors from Christ," says the apostle, "as though God did beseech you by us: We pray you in Christ's stead, be reconciled to God" (*2 Corinthians* 5:20). Then follows a statement of the ground upon which this offer of reconciliation is presented. God has made effectual provision for the pardon of sin by making Christ – though holy, harmless, and separate from sinners – sin for us, that we might be made righteous in him. The iniquities of us all were laid on him; he was treated as a sinner in our place in order that we might be treated as righteous in him.

The iniquities of us all were laid on him; he was treated as a sinner in our place in order that we might be treated as righteous in him.

The same great truth is taught in all those passages in which Christ is said to bear our sins. The expression, "to bear sin," is one which is clearly explained by its frequent occurrence in the sacred Scriptures. It means to bear the punishments due to sin. In *Leviticus* 20:17, it is said that he that marries his sister "shall bear his iniquity." Again, "Whoever curses his God shall bear his sin" (*Leviticus* 24:15). Of him that failed to keep the passover it was said, "That man shall bear his sin" (*Numbers* 9:13). If a man sin, he shall bear his iniquity.

It is used in the same sense when one man is spoken of as bearing the sin of another: "Your children shall wander in the wilderness forty years and bear your whoredoms" (*Numbers* 14:33). "Our fathers have sinned and are not; and we have borne their iniquities" (*Lamentations* 5:7). And when, in *Ezekiel* 18:20, it is said that "the son shall not bear the iniquity of the father," it is obviously meant that the son shall not be punished for the sins of the father. The meaning of this expression being thus definite, of course there can be no doubt as to the manner in which it is to be understood when used in reference to the Redeemer. The prophet says, "The Lord has laid on him the iniquity of us all. My righteous servant shall justify many, for he shall bear their iniquities. He was numbered with the transgressors, and he bore the sin of many" (*Isaiah* 53:6, 11, 12). Language more explicit could not be used. This whole chapter is designed to teach one great truth: that our sins were to be laid on the Messiah that we might be freed from the punishment which our sins deserved. It is therefore said, "He was wounded for our transgressions, he was bruised for our iniquities; the chastisement of our peace was upon him…. For the transgression of my people was he stricken." In the New Testament, the same doctrine is taught in the same terms. "Who his own self bore our sins in his own body on the tree" (1 *Peter* 2:24). "Christ was once offered to bear the sins of many" (*Hebrews* 9:28). "You know that he was manifested to take away [to bear] our sins" (1 *John* 3:5). According to all these representations, Christ saves us from the punishment due to our sins by bearing the curse of the law in our stead.

Intimately associated with the passages just referred to are those which describe the Redeemer as a sacrifice or propitiation. The essential idea of a sin offering is propitiation by means of vicarious punishment. That this is the Scriptural idea of a sacrifice is plain from the laws of their institution, from the effects ascribed to them, and from the illustrative declarations of the sacred writers. The law prescribed that the offender should bring the victim to the altar, lay his hands upon its head, make confession of his crime; and that the animal should then be slain and its blood sprinkled upon the altar. Thus, it is said, "He shall put his hand upon the head of the burnt offering, and it shall be accepted from him to make atonement for him" (*Leviticus* 1:4). "And he brought

"He was wounded for our transgressions, he was bruised for our iniquities; the chastisement of our peace was upon him…. For the transgression of my people was he stricken."
– Isaiah 53

the bullock for the sin offering; and Aaron and his sons laid their hands upon the head of the bullock for the sin offering" (*Leviticus* 8:14).

The import of this imposition of hands is clearly taught in the following passage: "And Aaron shall lay both his hands upon the head of the live goat and confess over him all the iniquities of the children of Israel and all their transgressions in all their sins, putting them upon the head of the goat.... And the goat shall bear upon him all their iniquities unto a land not inhabited" (*Leviticus* 16:21, 22). The imposition of hands, therefore, was designed to express symbolically the ideas of substitution and transfer of the liability to punishment. In the case just referred to, in order to convey more clearly the idea of the removal of the liability to punishment, the goat on whose head the sins of the people were imposed was sent into the wilderness, but another goat was slain and consumed in its stead.

They were intended to prefigure and predict the true atoning sacrifice which was to be offered when the fulness of time should come.

The nature of these offerings is further obvious from the effects attributed to them. They were commanded in order to make atonement, to propitiate, to make reconciliation, to secure the forgiveness of sins. And this effect they actually secured. In the case of every Jewish offender, some penalty connected with the theocratical constitution under which he lived was removed by the presentation and acceptance of the appointed sacrifice. This was all the effect, in the way of securing pardon, that the blood of bulls and of goats could produce. Their efficacy was confined to the purifying of the flesh and to securing, for those who offered them, the advantages of the external theocracy. Besides, however, this efficacy – which, by divine appointment, belonged to them considered in themselves – they were intended to prefigure and predict the true atoning sacrifice which was to be offered when the fulness of time should come. Nothing, however, can more clearly illustrate the Scriptural doctrine of sacrifices than the expressions employed by the sacred writers to convey the same idea as that intended by the term, "sin offering." Thus, all that Isaiah taught by saying of the Messiah that the chastisement of our peace was upon him; that with his stripes we are healed; that he was stricken for the transgression of the people; that on him was laid the iniquity of us all; and that he bore the sins of many, he taught by saying, "he made his soul an offering for sin." And in the epistle to the Hebrews it is said, he "was once offered [as a sacrifice] to bear the sins of many" (*Hebrews* 9:28). The same idea, therefore, is expressed by saying either he bore our sins or he was made an offering for sin. But to bear the sins of anyone means to bear the punishment of those sins; and, therefore, to be a sin offering conveys the same meaning.

Such being the idea of a sacrifice which pervades the whole Jewish Scriptures, it is obvious that the sacred writers could not teach more distinctly and intelligibly the manner in which Christ secures the pardon of sin than by saying he was made an offering for sin. With this mode of pardon all the early readers of the Scriptures were familiar. They had been accustomed to it from their earliest years. Not one of them could recall the time when the altar, the victim, and the blood were unknown to him. His first lessons in religion contained the ideas of confession of sin, substitution, and vicarious sufferings and death. When, therefore, the inspired penmen told men imbued with these ideas that Christ was a propitiation for sin, that he was offered as a sacrifice to make reconciliation, they told them, in the plainest of all terms, that he secures the pardon of our sins by suffering in our stead. Jews could understand such language in no other way; and, therefore, we may be sure it was intended to convey no other meaning. And, in point of fact, it has been so understood by the Christian church from its first organization to the present day.

If it were merely in the way of casual allusion that Christ was declared to be a sacrifice, we should not be authorized to infer from it the method of redemption. But this is far from being the case. This doctrine is presented in the most didactic form. It is exhibited in every possible mode. It is asserted, illustrated, vindicated. It is made the central point of all divine institutions and instructions. It is urged as the foundation of hope, as the source of consolation, the motive to obedience.

When, therefore, the inspired penmen told men imbued with these ideas that Christ was a propitiation for sin, that he was offered as a sacrifice to make reconciliation, they told them, in the plainest of all terms, that he secures the pardon of our sins by suffering in our stead.

It is, in fact, *the Gospel*. It would be vain to attempt a reference to all the passages in which this great doctrine is taught. We are told that God set forth Jesus Christ as a propitiation for our sins through faith in his blood (*Romans* 3:25). Again, he is declared to be a "propitiation for our sins, and not for ours only: but also for the sins of the whole world" (*1 John* 2:2). He is called "the Lamb of God, which takes away [bears] the sin of the world" (*John* 1:29). "You were not redeemed," says the Apostle Peter, "with corruptible things, as silver and gold, from your vain conversation received by tradition from your fathers; but with the precious blood of Christ, as of a lamb without blemish and without spot" (*1 Peter* 1:18, 19).

In the epistle to the Hebrews, this doctrine is more fully exhibited than in any other portion of Scripture. Christ is not only repeatedly called a sacrifice, but an elaborate comparison is made between the offering which he presented and the sacrifices which were offered under the old dispensation. "If the blood of bulls and of goats," says the apostle, "and the ashes of an heifer sprinkling the unclean sanctified to the purifying of the flesh, how much more shall the blood of Christ, who through the eternal Spirit [possessing an eternal spirit] offered himself without spot to God, purge your conscience from dead works to serve the living God?" (*Hebrews* 9:13, 14). The ancient sacrifices in themselves could only remove ceremonial uncleanness. They could not purge the conscience or reconcile the soul to God. They were mere shadows of the true sacrifice for sins. Hence, they were offered daily.

Christ's sacrifice, being really efficacious, was offered but once. It was because the ancient sacrifices were ineffectual that Christ said, when he came into the world, "Sacrifice and offering you do not want, but a body you have prepared me: in burnt offerings and sacrifices for sin you have had no pleasure. Then said I, Lo, I come to do your will, O God." "By which will," adds the apostle, that is, by accomplishing the purpose of God, "we are sanctified [or atoned for] through the offering of the body of Jesus Christ once for all"; and by that "one offering he has perfected for ever them that are

The ancient sacrifices in themselves could only remove ceremonial uncleanness. They could not purge the conscience or reconcile the soul to God. They were mere shadows of the true sacrifice for sins. Hence, they were offered daily.

sanctified," and of all this, he adds, the Holy Ghost is witness (*Hebrews* 10:5-15).

The Scriptures, therefore, clearly teach that Jesus Christ delivers us from the punishment of our sins by offering himself as a sacrifice in our behalf. As under the old dispensation the penalties attached to the violations of the theocratical covenant were removed by the substitution and sacrifice of bulls and of goats, so under the spiritual theocracy, in the living temple of the living God, the punishment of sin is removed by the substitution and death of the Son of God. As no ancient Israelite, when by transgression he had forfeited his liberty of access to the earthly sanctuary, was ignorant of the mode of atonement and reconciliation; so now no conscience-stricken sinner, who knows that he is unworthy to draw near to God, need be ignorant of that new and living way which Christ has consecrated for us, through his flesh, so that we have boldness to enter into the holiest by the blood of Jesus.

In all the forms of expression hitherto mentioned – Christ was made a curse for us; he was made sin for us; he bore our sins; he was made a sin offering – there is the idea of substitution. Christ took our place, he suffered in our stead, he acted as our representative. But as the act of a substitute is in effect the act of the principal, all that Christ did and suffered in that character every believer is regarded as having done and suffered. The attentive and pious reader of the Bible will recognize this idea in some of the most common forms of Scriptural expression. Believers are those who are in Christ. This is their great distinction and most familiar designation. They are so united to him that what he did in their behalf they are declared to have done. When he died, they died; when he rose, they rose; as he lives, they shall live also. The passages in which believers are said to have died in Christ are very numerous. "If one died for all," says the apostle, "then all died" (not, "were all dead" as rendered in the *King James Version*) (*2 Corinthians* 5:14). He that died with Christ is justified from sin, that is, freed from its condemnation and power; and if we died with Christ, we believe that we shall

Christ took our place, he suffered in our stead, he acted as our representative. But as the act of a substitute is in effect the act of the principal, all that Christ did and suffered in that character every believer is regarded as having done and suffered.

live with him (*Romans* 6:7, 8). As a woman is freed by death from her husband, so believers are freed from the law by the body (the death) of Christ, because his death is in effect their death (*Romans* 7:3). And in the following verse, he says, having died (in Christ) we are freed from the law. Every believer, therefore, may say with Paul, I was crucified with Christ (*Galatians* 2:20).

In like manner, the resurrection of Christ secures both the spiritual life and future resurrection of all his people. If we have been united to him in his death, we shall be in his resurrection. If we died with him, we shall live with him (*Romans* 6:5, 8). "God," says the apostle, "has quickened us together with Christ; and has raised us up together and made us sit together in heavenly places in Christ Jesus" (*Ephesians* 2:4-6). That is, God has quickened, raised, and exalted us together with Christ.[1] It is on this ground, also, that Paul says that Christ rose as the firstfruits of the dead not merely the first in order, but the earnest and security of the resurrection of his people. "For as in Adam all die, even so in Christ shall all be made alive" (*1 Corinthians* 15:20, 22). As our union with Adam secures our death, union with Christ secures our resurrection. Adam is a type of him who was to come – that is, Christ, inasmuch as the relation in which Adam stood to the whole race is analogous to that in which Christ stands to his own people. As Adam was our natural head, the poison of sin flows in all our veins. As Christ is our spiritual head, eternal life which is in him descends to all his members. It is not they who live, but Christ who lives in them (*Galatians* 2:20). This doctrine of the representative and vital union of Christ and believers pervades the New Testament. It is the source of the humility, the joy, the confidence which the sacred writers so often express. In themselves they were nothing and deserved nothing, but in him they possessed all things. Hence, they counted all things but loss that they might be found in him.

> This doctrine of the representative and vital union of Christ and believers pervades the New Testament.

1. There is no separate word in the original to answer to the word *together*, which is not to be understood of the union of believers with one another in the participation of these blessings. It is their union with Christ that the passage asserts.

Hence, they determined to know nothing, to preach nothing, to glory in nothing, but Christ and him crucified.

The great doctrine of the vicarious sufferings and death of Jesus Christ is further taught in those numerous passages which refer our salvation to his blood, his death, or his cross. Viewed in connection with the passages already mentioned, those now referred to not only teach the fact that the death of Christ secures the pardon of sin, but how it does it. To this class belong such declarations as the following: "The blood of Jesus Christ cleanses us from all sin" (*1 John* 1:7). "We have redemption through his blood" (*Ephesians* 1:7). He has "made peace through the blood of his cross" (*Colossians* 1:20). "Being now justified by his blood" (*Romans* 5:9). You "are made nigh by the blood of Christ" (*Ephesians* 2:13). "You are come to the blood of sprinkling" (*Hebrews* 12:22, 24). "Elect unto obedience and sprinkling of the blood of Jesus Christ" (*1 Peter* 1:2). "Unto him that loved us, and washed us from our sins in his own blood" (*Revelation* 1:5). "He has redeemed us unto God by his blood" (*Revelation* 5:9). "This cup," said the Son of God himself, "is the new testament in my blood, which is shed for many for the remission of sins" (*Matthew* 26:28, and *Luke* 22:20). The sacrificial character of the death of Christ is taught in all these passages. Blood was the means of atonement, and without the shedding of blood there was no remission; and, therefore, when our salvation is so often ascribed to the blood of the Savior, it is declared that he died as a propitiation for our sins.

The same remark may be made in reference to those passages which ascribe our redemption to the death, the cross, the flesh of Christ: These terms are interchanged as being of the same import. We are "reconciled to God by the death of his Son" (*Romans* 5:10). We are reconciled by his cross (*Ephesians* 2:16). We are "reconciled in the body of his flesh through death" (*Colossians* 1:21, 22). We are delivered from the law "by the body of Christ" (*Romans* 7:4); he abolished the law in his flesh (*Ephesians* 2:15); he took away the handwriting which was against us, nailing it to his cross (*Colossians* 2:14). The more general expressions

The sacrificial character of the death of Christ is taught in all these passages. Blood was the means of atonement, and without the shedding of blood there was no remission.

respecting Christ's dying for us receive a definite meaning from their connection with the more specific passages above mentioned. Everyone, therefore, knows what is meant when it is said that "Christ died for the ungodly" (*Romans* 5:6); that he gave himself "a ransom for many" (*Matthew* 20:28); that he died "the just for the unjust, that he might bring us to God" (*1 Peter* 3:18). Not less plain is the meaning of the Holy Spirit when he said, God "spared not his own Son, but delivered him up for us all" (*Romans* 8:32); that he "was delivered for our offenses" (*Romans* 4:25); that he "gave himself for our sins" (*Galatians* 1:4).

Seeing, then, that we owe everything to the expiatory sufferings of the blessed Savior, we cease to wonder that the cross is rendered so prominent in the exhibition of the plan of salvation. We are not surprised at Paul's anxiety lest the cross of Christ should be made of no effect; or that he should call the preaching of the Gospel the preaching of the cross; or that he should preach Christ crucified, both to Jews and Greeks, as the wisdom of God and the power of God; or that he should determine to glory in nothing save the cross of Christ.

As there is no truth more necessary to be known, so there is none more variously or plainly taught than the method of escaping the wrath of God due to us for sin. Besides all the clear exhibitions of Christ as bearing our sins, as dying in our stead, as making his soul an offering for sin, as redeeming us by his blood, the Scriptures set him forth in the character of a priest, in order that we might more fully understand how it is that he effects our salvation. It was predicted, long before his advent, that the Messiah was to be a priest. "You are a priest forever after the order of Melchizedek," was the declaration of the Holy Spirit by the mouth of David (*Psalm* 110:4). Zechariah predicted that he should sit as "a priest upon his throne" (*Zechariah* 6:13). The apostle defines a priest to be a man "ordained for men in things pertaining to God, that he may offer both gifts and sacrifices for sins" (*Hebrews* 5:1).

Jesus Christ is the only real priest in the universe. All others were either pretenders or the shadow of the great high priest of our profession. For this office he had every

Seeing, then, that we owe everything to the expiatory sufferings of the blessed Savior, we cease to wonder that the cross is rendered so prominent in the exhibition of the plan of salvation. We are not surprised at Paul's anxiety lest the cross of Christ should be made of no effect.

necessary qualification. He was a man: "For inasmuch as the children were partakers of flesh and blood, he also took part of the same, in order that he might be a merciful and faithful high priest – one who can be touched with a sense of our infirmities, seeing he was tempted in all points like as we are, yet without sin." He was sinless: "For such an high priest became us, who was holy, harmless, and separate from sinners." He was the Son of God. The law made men, having infirmity, priests. But God declared his Son to be a priest who is consecrated forevermore (*Hebrews* 7:28).

The sense in which Christ is declared to be the Son of God is explained in the first chapter of the epistle to the Hebrews. It is there said that he is the express image of God; that he upholds all things by the word of his power; that all the angels are commanded to worship him; that his throne is an everlasting throne; that in the beginning he laid the foundations of the Earth; that he is from everlasting, and that his years fail not. It is from the dignity of his person, as possessing this divine nature, that the apostle deduces the efficacy of his sacrifice (*Hebrews* 9:14), the perpetuity of his priesthood (*Hebrews* 7:16), and his ability to save to the uttermost all who come unto God by him (*Hebrews* 7:25). He was duly constituted a priest. He glorified not himself to be made a high priest; but he that said unto him, "You are my Son," said also, "You are a priest forever."

He is the only real priest, and therefore his advent superseded all others, and put an immediate end to all their lawful ministrations by abolishing the typical dispensation with which they were connected. For the priesthood being changed, there was of necessity a change of the law. There was an annulling of the former commandment for the weakness and unprofitableness thereof, and there was the introduction of a better hope (*Hebrews* 7:12, 18, 19). He has an appropriate offering to present. As every high priest is appointed to offer sacrifices, it was necessary that this man should have something to offer. This sacrifice was not the blood of goats or of calves, but his own blood; it was himself he offered unto God to purge our conscience from dead works (*Hebrews* 9:12,

It is from the dignity of his person, as possessing this divine nature, that the apostle deduces the efficacy of his sacrifice (Hebrews 9:14), the perpetuity of his priesthood (Hebrews 7:16), and his ability to save to the uttermost all who come unto God by him (Hebrews 7:25).

14). He has "put away sin by the sacrifice of himself," which was accomplished when he was "once offered to bear the sins of many" (*Hebrews* 9:26, 28). He has passed into the heavens. As the high priest was required to enter into the most holy place with the blood of atonement, so Christ has entered not into the holy places made with hands, "but into Heaven itself, now to appear in the presence of God for us" (*Hebrews* 9:24), and where "he ever lives to make intercession for us" (*Hebrews* 7:25).

Seeing then we have a great high priest that is passed into the heavens, Jesus the Son of God (let the reader remember what that means), who has sat down on the right hand of the Majesty on high, having by himself purged our sins and made reconciliation for the sins of the people, every humble believer who commits his soul into the hands of this high priest may come with boldness to the throne of grace, assured that he shall find mercy and grace to help in time of need.

We have a great high priest that is passed into the heavens, Jesus the Son of God, who has sat down on the right hand of the Majesty on high, having by himself purged our sins and made reconciliation for the sins of the people.

3
The Righteousness of Christ

The Bible, as we have seen, teaches, first, that we are under a law which demands perfect obedience and which threatens death in case of transgression; second, that all men have failed in rendering that obedience, and therefore are subject to the threatened penalty; third, that Christ has redeemed us from the law by being made under it, and in our place satisfying its demands. It only remains to be shown that this perfect righteousness of Christ is presented as the ground of our justification before God.

In Scriptural language, condemnation is a sentence of death pronounced upon sin; justification is a sentence of life pronounced upon righteousness. As this righteousness is not our own, as we are sinners – ungodly, without works – it must be the righteousness of another, even of him who is our righteousness. Hence we find so constantly the distinction between our own righteousness and that which God gives. The Jews, the apostle says, being ignorant of God's righteousness and going about to establish their own righteousness, would not submit themselves unto the righteousness of God (*Romans* 10:3). This was the rock on which they shattered. They knew that justification required a righteousness; they insisted on urging their own, imperfect as it was, and would not accept that which God had provided in the merits of

The Bible… teaches, first, that we are under a law which demands perfect obedience and which threatens death in case of transgression; second, that all men have failed in rendering that obedience…; third, that Christ has redeemed us from the law by being made under it, and in our place satisfying its demands.

174

his Son, who is the end of the law for righteousness to everyone that believes.

The same idea is presented in *Romans* 9:30-32, where Paul sums up the case of the rejection of the Jews and the acceptance of believers. The Gentiles have attained righteousness, even the righteousness which is of faith. But Israel has not attained it. Why? Because they sought it not by faith, but as it were by the works of the law. The Jews would not receive and confide in the righteousness which God had provided, but endeavored, by works, to prepare a righteousness of their own. This was the cause of their ruin.

In direct contrast to the course pursued by the majority of his kinsmen, we find Paul renouncing all dependence upon his own righteousness, and thankfully receiving that which God had provided. Though he had every advantage and every temptation to trust in himself that any man could have, for he was one of the favored people of God, circumcised on the eighth day and touching the righteousness which is in the law, blameless; yet all these things Paul counted but loss, that he might win Christ and be found in him, not having his own righteousness, which is of the law, but that which is through the faith of Christ, the righteousness which is of God by faith (*Philippians* 3:4-9). Here the two righteousnesses are brought distinctly into view. The one was his own, consisting in obedience to the law; this Paul rejects as inadequate and unworthy of acceptance. The other is of God, and received by faith; this Paul accepts and glories in as all-sufficient and as alone sufficient. This is the righteousness which the apostle says God imputes to those without works. Hence it is called a gift, a free gift, a gift by grace, and believers are described as those who receive this gift of righteousness (*Romans* 5:17). Hence we are never said to be justified by anything done by us or wrought in us, but by what Christ has done for us. We are justified through the redemption that is in him (*Romans* 3:24). We are justified by his blood (*Romans* 5:9). We are justified by his obedience (*Romans* 5:19). We are justified by him from all things (*Acts* 13:39). He is our righteousness (*1 Corinthians* 1:30). We are

We are never said to be justified by anything done by us or wrought in us, but by what Christ has done for us.

made the righteousness of God in him (*2 Corinthians* 5:21). We are justified in his name (*1 Corinthians* 6:11). There is no condemnation to those who are in him (*Romans* 8:1). Justification is, therefore, by faith in Christ, because faith is receiving and trusting to him as our Savior, as having done all that is required to secure our acceptance before God.

It is thus, then, the Scriptures answer the question, How can a man be just with God? When the soul is burdened with a sense of sin, when it sees how reasonable and holy is that law which demands perfect obedience and threatens death as the penalty of transgression, when it feels the absolute impossibility of ever satisfying these just demands by its own obedience and sufferings, it is then that the revelation of Jesus Christ as our righteousness is felt to be the wisdom and power of God unto salvation. Destitute of all righteousness in ourselves, we have our righteousness in him. What we could not do, he has done for us. The righteousness, therefore – on the ground of which the sentence of justification is passed upon the believing sinner – is not his own, but that of Jesus Christ.

It is one of the strongest evidences of the divine origin of the Scriptures that they are suited to the nature and circumstances of man. If their doctrines were believed and their precepts obeyed, men would stand in their true relation to God and the different classes of men to each other. Parents and children, husbands and wives, rulers and subjects would be found in their proper sphere and would attain the highest possible degree of excellence and happiness. Truth is in order to holiness. And all truth is known to be truth by its tendency to promote holiness. As this test, when applied to the Scriptures generally, evidences their divine perfection, so when applied to the cardinal doctrine of justification by faith in Jesus Christ, it shows that doctrine to be worthy of all acceptation. On this ground it is commended by the sacred writers. They declare it to be in the highest degree honorable to God and beneficial to man. They assert that it is so arranged as to display the wisdom, justice, holiness, and love of God, while it secures the pardon, peace, and holiness of men. If it

The righteousness, therefore – on the ground of which the sentence of justification is passed upon the believing sinner – is not his own, but that of Jesus Christ.

failed in either of these objects, if it were not suited to the divine character or to our nature and necessities, it could not answer the end for which it was designed.

It will be readily admitted that the glory of God in the exhibition or revelation of the divine perfections is the highest conceivable end of creation and redemption; and consequently that any doctrine which is suited to make such an exhibition is, on that account, worthy of being universally received and gloried in. Now, the inspired writers teach us that it is peculiarly in the plan of redemption that the divine perfections are revealed; that it was designed to show unto principalities and powers the manifold wisdom of God; that Christ was set forth as a propitiatory sacrifice to exhibit his righteousness or justice; and especially that in the ages to come he might show forth the exceeding riches of his grace in his kindness toward us in Christ Jesus. It is the love of God – the breadth, length, depth, and height of which pass knowledge – that is here most conspicuously displayed. Some men strangely imagine that the death of Christ procured for us the love of God, but it was the effect and not the cause of that love. Christ did not die that God might love us; he died because God loved us. "God commends his love toward us in that, while we were yet sinners, Christ died for us" (*Romans* 5:8). He "so loved the world, that he gave his only begotten Son, that whoever believes in him should not perish, but have everlasting life" (*John* 3:16). "In this was manifested the love of God toward us, because God sent his only begotten Son into the world that we might live through him. Herein is love, not that we loved God, but that he loved us and sent his Son to be the propitiation for our sins" (*1 John* 4:9, 10).

As this love of God is manifested toward the unworthy, it is called grace, and this it is which the Scriptures dwell upon with such peculiar frequency and earnestness. The mystery of redemption is that a Being of infinite holiness and justice should manifest such wonderful love to sinners. Hence the sacred writers so earnestly denounce everything that obscures this peculiar feature of the Gospel – everything which represents men as worthy, as meriting, or, in any way

Some men strangely imagine that the death of Christ procured for us the love of God, but it was the effect and not the cause of that love. Christ did not die that God might love us; he died because God loved us.

by their own goodness securing the exercise of this love of God. It is of grace, lest any man should boast. We are justified by grace; we are saved by grace; and if of grace, it is no more of works, otherwise grace is no more grace (*Ephesians* 2:8, 9; *Romans* 11:6). The apostle teaches us not only that the plan of salvation had its origin in the unmerited kindness of God, and that our acceptance with him is in no way or degree founded in our own worthiness; but, moreover, that the actual administration of the economy of mercy is so conducted as to magnify this attribute of the divine character. God chooses the foolish, the base, the weak – those who are nothing – in order that no flesh should glory in his presence. Christ is made everything to us, that those who glory should glory only in the Lord (*1 Corinthians* 1:27-31).

God chooses the foolish, the base, the weak – those who are nothing – in order that no flesh should glory in his presence. Christ is made everything to us, that those who glory should glory only in the Lord.

It cannot fail to occur to every reader that unless he sincerely rejoices in this feature of the plan of redemption, unless he is glad that the whole glory of his salvation belongs to God, his heart cannot be in accordance with the Gospel. If he believes that the ground of his acceptance is in himself, or even wishes that it were so, he is not prepared to join in those grateful songs of acknowledgment to him who has saved us and called us with an holy calling, not according to our works, but according to his own purpose and grace, which it is the delight of the redeemed to offer unto him that loved them and gave himself for them. It is most obvious that the sacred writers are abundant in the confession of their unworthiness in the sight of God. They acknowledged that they were unworthy absolutely, and unworthy comparatively. It was of grace that any man was saved, and it was of grace that they were saved rather than others. It is, therefore, all of grace, that God may be exalted and glorified in all them that believe.

The doctrine of the gratuitous justification of sinners by faith in Jesus Christ not only displays the infinite love of God, but it is declared to be peculiarly honorable to him, or peculiarly consistent with his attributes, because it is adapted to all men. "Is he the God of the Jews only? Is he not also of the Gentiles? Yes, of the Gentiles also: Seeing it is one God who shall justify the circumcision by faith and uncircumcision through faith," (*Romans* 3:29, 30). "For the same Lord over all is rich unto all that call upon him. For *whoever* shall call upon the name of the Lord shall be saved" (*Romans* 10:12, 13). This is no narrow, national, or sectarian doctrine. It is as broad as the Earth. Wherever men, the creatures of God, can be found, there the mercy of God in Christ Jesus may be preached. The apostle greatly exults in this feature of the plan of redemption as worthy of God and as making the Gospel the foundation of a religion for all nations and ages. In revealing a salvation sufficient for all and suited for all, it discloses God in his true character, as the God and Father of all.

The Scriptures, however, represent this great doctrine as not less suited to meet the necessities of man than it is to promote the glory of God. If it exalts God, it humbles man. If it renders it manifest that he is a Being of infinite holiness, justice, and love, it makes us feel that we are destitute of all merit, and more, are most ill-deserving; that we are without strength; that our salvation is an undeserved favor. As nothing is more true than the guilt and helplessness of men, no plan of redemption which does not recognize these facts could ever be in harmony with our inward experience, or command the full acquiescence of the penitent soul. The ascription of merit which we are conscious we do not deserve produces of itself severe distress; and if this false estimate of our deserts is the ground of the exhibition of special kindness toward us, it destroys the happiness such kindness would otherwise produce. To a soul, therefore, sensible of its pollution and guilt in the sight of God, the doctrine that it is saved on account of its own goodness, or because it is better than other men, is discordant and destructive of its peace. Nothing but an absolutely gratuitous salvation can suit a soul sensible of its ill desert. Nothing else suits its views of truth or its sense of right. The opposite doctrine involves a falsehood and a moral impropriety in which neither the reason nor conscience can acquiesce.

The Scriptural doctrine, which assumes what we know to be true – namely, our guilt and helplessness – places us in our

This is no narrow, national, or sectarian doctrine. It is as broad as the Earth. Wherever men, the creatures of God, can be found, there the mercy of God in Christ Jesus may be preached.

proper relation to God – that relation which accords with the truth, with our sense of right, with our inward experience, and with every proper desire of our hearts. This is one of the reasons why the Scriptures represent peace as the consequence of justification by faith. There can be no peace while the soul is not in harmony with God, and there can be no such harmony until it willingly occupies its true position in relation to God. So long as it does not acknowledge its true character, so long as it acts on the assumption of its ability to merit or to earn the divine favor, it is in a false position. Its feelings toward God are wrong, and there is no manifestation of approbation or favor on the part of God toward the soul. But when we take our true place and feel our ill desert and look upon pardoning mercy as a mere gratuity, we find access to God; and his love is shed abroad in our hearts, producing that peace which passes all understanding. The soul ceases from its legal strivings; it gives over the vain attempt to make itself worthy, or to work out a righteousness wherewith to appear before God. It is contented to be accepted as unworthy, and to receive as a gift a righteousness which can bear the scrutiny of God. Peace, therefore, is not the result of the assurance of mere pardon, but of pardon founded upon a righteousness which illustrates the character of God; which magnifies the law and makes it honorable; which satisfies the justice of God while it displays the infinite riches of divine tenderness and love. The soul can find no objection to such a method of forgiveness. It is not pained by the ascription of merit to itself which is felt to be undeserved. Its utter unworthiness is not only recognized but openly declared. Nor is it harassed by the anxious doubt whether God can, consistently with his justice, forgive sin. For justice is as clearly revealed in the cross of Christ as love. The whole soul, therefore – however enlightened, or however sensitive – acquiesces with humility and delight in a plan of mercy which thus honors God, and which, while it secures the salvation of the sinner, permits him to hide himself in the radiance which surrounds his Savior.

The apostles, moreover, urge on men the doctrine of justification by faith with peculiar earnestness, because

The apostles, moreover, urge on men the doctrine of justification by faith with peculiar earnestness, because it presents the only method of deliverance from sin.

it presents the only method of deliverance from sin. So long as men are under the condemnation of the law, and feel themselves bound by its demands of obedience as the condition and ground of their acceptance with God, they do and must feel that he is unreconciled, that his perfections are arrayed against them. Their whole object is to propitiate him by means which they know to be inadequate. Their spirit is servile, their religion a bondage, their God a hard Master. To men in such a state, true love, true obedience, and real peace are alike impossible. But when they are brought to see that God, through his infinite love, has set forth Jesus Christ as a propitiation for our sins, that he might be just and yet justify those that believe – that it is not by works of righteousness which we have done, but according to his mercy he saves us – they are emancipated from their former bondage and made the sons of God. God is no longer a hard Master, but a kind Father. Obedience is no longer a task to be done for a reward; it is the joyful expression of filial love. The whole relation of the soul to God is changed, and all our feelings and conduct change with it. Though we have no works to perform in order to justification, we have everything to do in order to manifest our gratitude and love. "Do we then make void the law through faith? God forbid: We establish the law" (*Romans* 3:31). There is no such thing as real, acceptable obedience until we are thus delivered from the bondage of the law as the rule of justification and are reconciled to God by the death of his Son. Till then we are slaves and enemies, and have the feelings of slaves. When we have accepted the terms of reconciliation, we are the sons of God, and have the feelings of sons.

Though we have no works to perform in order to justification, we have everything to do in order to manifest our gratitude and love.

It must not, however, be supposed that the filial obedience rendered by the children of God is the effect of the mere moral influence arising from a sense of his favor. Though, perhaps, the strongest influence which any external consideration can exert, it is far from being the source of the holiness which always follows faith. The very act by which we become interested in the redemption of Christ from the condemnation of the law makes us partakers of his Spirit. It is not mere pardon or any other isolated blessing that is offered to us in the Gospel, but complete redemption, deliverance from evil, and restoration to the love and life of God. Those, therefore, who believe, are not merely forgiven, but are so united to Christ that they derive from and through him the Holy Spirit. This is his great gift, bestowed upon all who come to him and confide in him. This is the reason why he says, "Without me you can do nothing. As the branch cannot bear fruit of itself, except it abide in the vine; no more can you, except you abide in me. I am the vine, you are the branches: He that abides in me, and I in him, the same brings forth much fruit" (*John* 15:4, 5).

"He that believes not is condemned already, because he has not believed in the name of the only begotten Son of God."

– John 3

The Gospel method of salvation, therefore, is worthy of all acceptation. It reveals the divine perfections in the clearest and most affecting light, and it is in every way suited to the character and necessities of men. It places us in our true position as undeserving sinners; and it secures pardon, peace of conscience, and holiness of life. It is the wisdom and the power of God unto salvation. It cannot be a matter of surprise that the Scriptures represent the rejection of this method of redemption as the prominent ground of the condemnation of those who perish under the sound of the Gospel. That the plan should be so clearly revealed and yet men should insist upon adopting some other, better suited to their inclinations, is the height of folly and disobedience. That the Son of God should come into the world, die the just for the unjust, and offer us eternal life, and yet we should reject his proffered mercy, proves such an insensibility to his excellence and love, such a love of sin, such a disregard to the approbation and enjoyment of God, that – could all other grounds of condemnation be removed – this alone would be sufficient. "He that believes not is condemned already, because he has not believed in the name of the only begotten Son of God" (*John* 3:18).

4
Confessional Statements
of the Doctrine

The Westminster Standards

J USTIFICATION is defined in the *Westminster Shorter Catechism*: "An act of God's free grace, wherein he pardons all our sins, and accepts us as righteous in his sight, only for the righteousness of Christ imputed to us, and received by faith alone."

The Heidelberg Catechism

The *Heidelberg Catechism* in answer to the question, "How do you become righteous before God," answers,

> Only by faith in Jesus Christ. My conscience accuses me as far as it can, that I have gravely sinned against all of God's orders, and I have not observed any of them, that until now I have been inclined to every evil; but nevertheless (provided that I embrace these true benefits of the Spirit with confidence), Christ's perfect satisfaction, righteousness, and sanctity is reckoned and given to me without any merit of my own, out of God's pure mercy; just as if I had not committed any sin, and as if no disgrace were clinging to me; indeed, just as if I myself had perfectly shown that compliance, which Christ has manifested for me.[1]

"Justification is an act of God's free grace, wherein he pardons all our sins, and accepts us as righteous in his sight, only for the righteousness of Christ imputed to us, and received by faith alone."

— Westminster Shorter Catechism

1. "Sola fide in Jesum Christum, adeo ut licet mea me conscientia accuset, quod adversus omnia mandata Dei graviter peccaverim, nec

And in answer to the question, Why does faith alone justify? it says: "Not because I please God with the worth of my faith, but because only Christ's satisfaction, righteousness, and sanctity are my justice in the presence of God. But I am able to be near this justice by no other method than by embracing faith."[2]

The Second Helvetic Confession

The *Second Helvetic Confession*, chapter 15, says,

> To justify, to the apostle in debate about justification, means to forgive sins, to absolve from blame and punishment, to accept into grace, and to declare righteous. For indeed, as the apostle says to the Romans, "God is he who justifies; who is he who condemns?" Justification and condemnation are opposites.... For indeed, Christ accepted the sins of the world into himself and removed them, and he made amends to divine justice. Therefore, God is gracious to our sins only because of Christ's suffering and resurrection, and he does not impute these sins to us; moreover, he reckons Christ's righteousness for us: so that now we are not only cleansed of our sins and purified, or virtuous, but also granted the righteousness of Christ and even absolved from sins, death, or condemnation; in short, we are suitable and proper for eternal life. Therefore, strictly speaking, God alone justifies us, and he justifies only because of Christ, not ascribing our sins to us but giving us his righteousness.[3]

"God alone justifies us, and he justifies only because of Christ, not ascribing our sins to us but giving us his righteousness."
– Second Helvetic Confession

---

ullum eorum servaverim, adhæc etiamnum ad omne malum propensus sim, nihilominus tamen (modo hæc beneficia vera animi fiducia amplectar), sine ullo meo merito, ex mera Dei misericordia, mihi perfecta satisfactio, justitia, et sanctitas Christi, imputetur ac donetur; perinde ac si nec ullum ipse peccatum admisissem, nec ulla mihi labes inhæreret imo vero quasi eam obedientiam, quam pro me Christus præstitit ipse perfecte præstitissem." (All English translations are provided by the editor.)

2. "Non quod dignitate meæ fidei Deo placeam, sed quod sola satisfactio, justitia ac sanctitas Christi, mea justitia sit coram Deo. Ego vero eam non alia ratione, quam fide amplecti, et mihi applicare queam."

3. "Justificare significat Apostolo in disputatione de justificatione, peccata remittere, a culpa et pœna absolvere, in gratiam recipere, et justum pronunciare. Etenim ad Romanos dicit apostolus, "Deus est, qui justificat, quis ille, qui condemnet?" opponuntur justificare et condemnare.... Etenim Christus peccata mundi in se recepit et sustulit, divinæque justitiæ satisfecit. Deus ergo propter solum Christum passum et resuscitatum, propitius est

These are the most generally received and authoritative standards of the Reformed churches, with which all other Reformed symbols agree.

The Lutheran confessions teach precisely the same doctrine on this subject.[4]

> Agreeing unanimously, we teach and we make known... that man the sinner is justified in the presence of God, that is, he is absolved from all his own sins and from the judgment of a very justified condemnation, and he is adopted into the number of God's sons and appointed to eternal life, without any of our own deserving or worth, and without any of our own labors, past, present, or future – out of pure grace, only and just because of one unique merit: the most perfect obedience, the bitterest suffering, the death and resurrection of our Lord Jesus Christ, whose obedience is imputed to us for righteousness.[5]

The Lutheran confessions teach precisely the same doctrine on this subject.

Again,

> We believe, we teach, and we make known that this itself is our justice in the presence of God, because the Lord has remitted our sins for us out of pure grace, without any regard for our own past, present, or future labors, for our own merit, or for our own worth. For he has reckoned and given to us the righteousness of Christ's compliance; because

---

peccatis nostris, nec illa nobis imputat, imputat autem justitiam Christi pro nostra: ita ut jam simus non solum mundati a peccatis et purgati, vel sancti, sed etiam donati justitia Christi, adeoque absoluti a peccatis, morte vel condemnatione, justi denique ac, hæredes vitæ æternæ Proprie ergo loquendo, Deus solus nos justificat, et duntaxat propter Christum justificat, non imputans nobis peccata, sed imputans ejus nobis justitiam." (See Niemeyer, *Collectio Confessionum*, Leipzig, 1840.)

4. The main passages are *Augsburg Confession*, Part 1, Article IV; the *Apology* for that *Confession*, Article III; and the *Formula of Concord*, Article III.

5. "Unanimi consensu, docemus et confitemur...quod homo peccator coram Deo justificetur, hoc est, absolvatur ab omnibus suis peccatis et ajudicio justissimæ condemnationis, et adoptetur in numerum filiorum Dei atque hæres æternæ vitæ scribatur, sine ullis nostris meritis, aut dignitate, et absque ullis præcedentibus præsentibus aut sequentibus nostris operibus, ex mera gratia, tantummodo propter unicum meritum, perfectissimam obedientiam, passionem acerbissimam, mortem et resurrectionem Domini nostri, Jesu Christi, cujus obedientia nobis ad justitiam imputatum" (*Formula of Concord*, III, 9).

of this righteousness, we are accepted in grace by God and we are considered perfect.[6]

To be justified here means not that a perfect man is produced from a godless one, but that he is pronounced perfect by a judicial exercise.[7]

And "Justification in this passage [*Romans* 5:1] by judicial custom means to absolve the defendant and pronounce him perfect, but because of someone else's righteousness, namely Christ's, which alien righteousness is communicated to us through faith."[8]

So also: "The term *justification* in this matter means to pronounce perfect, to absolve from sins and from the eternal punishments of sins, because of Christ's righteousness, which is imputed by God through faith."[9]

Hase[10] concisely states the Lutheran doctrine on this subject in these words: "Justification is a judicial act, by which God, led by grace alone, imputes Christ's righteousness to the sinner because of Christ's merit, which is acquired by means of faith; he forgives sins, and reconciles the sinner with himself."[11]

> *"Justification is a judicial act, by which God, led by grace alone, imputes Christ's righteousness to the sinner because of Christ's merit, which is acquired by means of faith."*
>
> *– Hase*

---

6. "Credimus, docemus, et confitemur, hoc ipsum nostram, esse coram Deo justitiam, quod Dominus nobis peccata remittit, ex mera gratia, absque ullo respectu præcedentium præsentium aut consequentium nostrorum operum, dignitatis, aut meriti. Ille enim donat atque imputat nobis justitiam obedientiæ Christi; propter eam justitiam a Deo in gratiam recipimur et justi reputamur" (*Formula of Concord, Epitome*, III, 4).

7. "Justificari significat hic non ex impio justum effici, sed usu forensi justum pronuntiari."

8. "Justificare hoc loco [*Romans* 5:1] forensi consuetudine significat reum absolvere et pronuntiare justum, sed propter alienam justitiam, videlicet Christi, quæ aliena justitia communicatur nobis per fidem" (*Apology for the Augsburg Confession*, Article III, 131, 184).

9. "Vocabulum justificationis in hoc negotio significant justum pronuntiare, a peccatis et æternis peccatorum suppliciis absolvere, propter justitiam Christi, quæ a Deo fidei imputatur." (*Formula of Concord*, III, 17. See Hase, *Libri Symbolici*, 3rd edition, Leipzig, 1836).

10. *Hutterus Redivivus*, § 109, 6th edition, Leipzig, 1845, 274.

11. "Justificatio est actus forensis, quo Deus, sola gratia ductus, peccatori, propter Christi meritum fide apprehensum, justitiam Christi imputat, peccata remittit, eumque sibi reconciliat."

The *Formula of Concord* says,

> This article, concerning the righteousness of faith, is extraordinary (as the *Apologia* says) in the entire Christian doctrine, without which troubled consciences can never have true and firm consolation or properly understand the riches of Christ's grace. Luther also confirmed this with his own testimony when he said: If this one unique point remains uncorrupt, the Christian church will also remain uncorrupt, harmonious, and without all possible divisions; but if it is weakened, it is impossible for one mistaken or frenzied spirit to be properly corrected.[12]

The Lutheran theologians, therefore, speak of it as the "ἀκρόπολυς of the whole Christian religion, and the connection by which all the limbs of the body of Christian doctrine are held together, and by which they are exempt from breaking."[13]

Jonathan Edwards

This statement of the doctrine of justification has retained confessional authority in the Lutheran and Reformed churches to the present day. President Edwards, who is regarded as having initiated certain departures from some points of the Reformed faith, was firm in his adherence to this view of justification, which he held to be of vital importance. In his discourse on "Justification by Faith Alone," he thus defines justification:

> A person is said to be justified when he is approved of God as free from the guilt of sin and its deserved punishment; and as having that righteousness belonging to him that entitles

This statement of the doctrine of justification has retained confessional authority in the Lutheran and Reformed churches to the present day.

---

12. "Hic articulus, de justitia fidei, præcipuus est (ut Apologia loquitur) in tota doctrina Christiana, sine quo conscientiæ perturbatæ nullam veram et firmam consolationem habere, aut divitias gratiæ Christi recte agnoscere possunt. Id D. Luterus suo etiam testimonio confirmavit, cum inquit: Si unicus his articulus sincerus permanserit, etiam Christiana Ecclesia sincera, concors et sine omnibus sectis permanet: sin vero corrumpitur, impossibile est, ut uni errori aut fanatico spiritui recte obviam iri posit" (III, 6).

13. "ἀκρόπολυς totius Christianæ religionis, ac nexus, quo omnia corporis doctrinæ Christianæ membra continentur, quoque rupto solvuntur" (Quenstedt).

to the reward of life. That we should take the word in such a sense and understand it as the judge's accepting a person as having both a negative and positive righteousness belonging to him, and looking on him therefore as not only quit or free from any obligation to punishment, but also as just and righteous, and so entitled to a positive reward, is not only most agreeable to the etymology and natural import of the word, which signifies to make righteous, or to pass one for righteous in judgment, but also manifestly agreeable to the force of the word as used in Scripture.

We are justified "by faith alone, without any manner of virtue or goodness of our own."
– Jonathan Edwards

He then shows how it is, or why faith alone justifies. It is not on account of any virtue or goodness in faith, but as it unites us to Christ and involves the acceptance of him as our righteousness. Thus it is we are justified "by faith alone, without any manner of virtue or goodness of our own."

The ground of justification is the righteousness of Christ imputed to the believer. "By that righteousness being imputed to us," says Edwards,

is meant no other than this, that that righteousness of Christ is accepted for us and admitted instead of that perfect inherent righteousness that ought to be in ourselves: Christ's perfect obedience shall be reckoned to our account so that we shall have the benefit of it, as though we had performed it ourselves. And so we suppose that a title to eternal life is given us as the reward of this righteousness.... The opposers of this doctrine suppose that there is an absurdity in it: They say that to suppose that God imputes Christ's obedience to us is to suppose that God is mistaken and thinks that we performed that obedience that Christ performed. But why cannot that righteousness be reckoned to our account and be accepted for us without any such absurdity? Why is there any more absurdity in it than in a merchant's transferring debt or credit from one man's account to another when one man pays a price for another, so that it shall be accepted, as if that other had paid it? Why is there any more absurdity in supposing that Christ's obedience is imputed to us than that his satisfaction is imputed? If Christ has suffered the penalty of the law for us and in our stead, then it will follow that his suffering that penalty is imputed to us, that is, that it is accepted for us and in our stead, and is reckoned to our account as through we had suffered it. But why may not his obeying the law of God be as rationally reckoned to our account as his suffering the penalty of the law?[14]

Points Included in the Above Statements of the Doctrine

According to the above statements, justification is

1. An act, and not, as sanctification, a continued and progressive work.

2. It is an act of grace to the sinner. In himself he deserves condemnation when God justifies him.

3. As to the nature of the act, it is, in the first place, not an efficient act, or an act of power. It does not produce any subjective change in the person justified. It does not effect a change of character, making those good who were bad, those holy who were unholy. That is done in regeneration and sanctification. In the second place, it is not a mere executive act, as when a sovereign pardons a criminal and thereby restores him to his civil rights or to his former status in the commonwealth. In the third place, it is a forensic or judicial act, the act of a judge, not of a sovereign. That is, in the case of the sinner, or, *in foro Dei*, it is an act of God not in his character of sovereign, but in his character of judge. It is a declarative act in which God pronounces the sinner just or righteous, that is, declares that the claims of justice, so far as the sinner is concerned, are satisfied, so that he cannot be justly condemned, but is in justice entitled to the reward promised or due to perfect righteousness.

4. The meritorious ground of justification is not faith; we are not justified on account of our faith, considered as a virtuous or holy act or state of mind. Nor are our works of any kind the ground of justification. Nothing done by us or wrought in us satisfies the demands of justice or can be the ground or reason of the declaration that justice as far as it concerns us is satisfied. The ground of justification is the righteousness of Christ, active and passive, that is, including his perfect obedience to the law as a covenant, and his enduring the penalty of the law in our stead and on our behalf.

> *The ground of justification is the righteousness of Christ, active and passive, that is, including his perfect obedience to the law as a covenant, and his enduring the penalty of the law in our stead and on our behalf.*

14. *Works of President Edwards*, New York, 1868, Volume IV, 66, 91, 92.

5. The righteousness of Christ is in justification imputed to the believer. That is, it is set to his account, so that he is entitled to plead it at the bar of God as though it were personally and inherently his own.

6. Faith is the instrument of justification. That is, God imputes the righteousness of Christ to the sinner when he (through grace) receives and rests on Christ alone for his salvation.

That such is the doctrine of the Reformed and Lutheran churches on this important doctrine cannot be disputed. The statements of the standards of those churches are so numerous, explicit, and discriminating as to preclude all reasonable doubt on this subject. That such is the doctrine of the Word of God appears from the following consideration.

It will not be necessary to discuss all the points above specified separately, as some of them are necessarily included in others. The following propositions include all the essential points of the doctrine.

That such is the doctrine of the Reformed and Lutheran churches on this important doctrine cannot be disputed. The statements of the standards of those churches are so numerous, explicit, and discriminating as to preclude all reasonable doubt.

5

Justification Is a Forensic Act

B Y THIS the Reformers intended, in the first place, to deny the Romish doctrine of subjective justification; that is, that justification consists in an act or agency of God making the sinner subjectively holy. Romanists confound or unite justification and sanctification. They define justification as "the remission of sin and infusion of new habits of grace." By remission of sin they mean not simply pardon, but the removal of everything of the nature of sin from the soul. Justification, therefore, with them, is purely subjective, consisting in the destruction of sin and the infusion of holiness. In opposition to this doctrine, the Reformers maintained that by *justification* the Scriptures mean something different from sanctification; that the two gifts, although inseparable, are distinct; and that justification, instead of being an efficient act changing the inward character of the sinner, is a declarative act announcing and determining his relation to the law and justice of God.

Romanists confound or unite justification and sanctification. They define justification as "the remission of sin and infusion of new habits of grace."

In the second place, the confessions of the Reformation no less explicitly teach that justification is not simply pardon and restoration. It includes pardon, but it also includes a declaration that the believer is just or righteous in the sight of the law. He has a right to plead a righteousness which completely satisfies its demands.

And, therefore, in the third place, affirmatively, those confessions teach that justification is a judicial or forensic act, that is, an act of God as judge proceeding according to law declaring that the sinner is just, that is, that the law no longer condemns him, but acquits and pronounces him to be entitled to eternal life.

Here, as so often in other cases, the ambiguity of words is apt to create embarrassment. The Greek word δίκαιος and the English word *righteous* have two distinct senses. They sometimes express moral character. When we say that God is righteous, we mean that he is right. He is free from any moral imperfection. So when we say that a man is righteous, we generally mean that he is upright and honest; that he is and does what he ought to be and do. In this sense the word expresses the relation which a man sustains to the rule of moral conduct. At other times, however, these words express, not moral character, but the relation which a man sustains to justice. In this sense a man is just with regard to whom justice is satisfied or against whom justice has no demands. The lexicons, therefore, tell us that δίκαιος sometimes means *leges observans*; at others, *insons, culpa vacans* (free from guilt or obligation to punishment) – *judicio Dei insons*. Pilate (*Matthew* 27:24) said, "I am innocent of the blood of this just person"; that is, of this person who is free from guilt; free from anything which justifies his condemnation to death. "Christ, also," says the apostle, "has once suffered for sins, the just for the unjust"; the innocent for the guilty (1 *Peter* 3:18). See *Romans* 2:13; 5:19. "As by one man's disobedience many were made sinners, so by the obedience of one shall many be made righteous."

> As the predicate of *judicandus* in his relation to the judge, "righteousness" expresses, not a positive virtue, but a judicial negative freedom from *reatus*. In the presence of his judge, he is צַדִּיק who stands free from guilt and desert of punishment (*straflos*), either because he has contracted no guilt (as, *e.g.*, Christ), or, because in the way demanded by the judge (under the Old Testament by expiatory sacrifice) he has expiated the guilt contracted.[1]

1. *Christliche Dogmatik*, Johannes Heinrich August Ebrard. § 402 Königsberg edition, 1852), Volume II, 163.

The confessions of the Reformation teach that justification is a judicial or forensic act, that is, an act of God as judge proceeding according to law declaring that the sinner is just, that is, that the law no longer condemns him, but acquits and pronounces him to be entitled to eternal life.

If, therefore, we take the word *righteous* in the former of the two senses above mentioned, when it expresses moral character, it would be a contradiction to say that God pronounces the sinner righteous. This would be equivalent to saying that God pronounces the sinner to be not a sinner, the wicked to be good, the unholy to be holy. But if we take the word in the sense in which the Scriptures so often use it, as expressing relation to justice, then when God pronounces the sinner righteous or just, he simply declares that his guilt is expiated, that justice is satisfied, that he has the righteousness which justice demands. This is precisely what Paul says when he says that God "justifies the ungodly" (*Romans* 4:5). God does not pronounce the ungodly to be godly; he declares that notwithstanding the sinner's personal sinfulness and unworthiness, he is accepted as righteous on the ground of what Christ has done for him.

Proof of the Doctrine Just Stated

That *to justify* means neither simply *to pardon*, nor *to make inherently righteous* or *good*, is proved by the uniform usage of the word *to justify* in Scripture. It is never used in either of those senses, but always *to declare* or *pronounce just*. It is unnecessary to cite passages in proof of a usage which is uniform. The few following examples are enough. *Deuteronomy* 25:1: "If there be a controversy between men, and they come into judgment, that the judges may judge them; then they shall justify the righteous, and condemn the wicked." *Exodus* 23:7: "I will not justify the wicked." *Isaiah* 5:23: "Which justify the wicked for reward." *Proverbs* 17:15: "He that justifies the wicked" is "abomination to the Lord." *Luke* 10:29: "He willing to justify himself." *Luke* 16:15: "You are they which justify yourselves before men." *Matthew* 11:19: "Wisdom is justified by her children." *Galatians* 2:16: "A man is not justified by the works of the law." *Galatians* 5:4: "Whosoever of you are justified by the law; you are fallen from grace." Thus men are said to justify God. *Job* 32:2: "Because he justified himself, rather than God." *Psalm* 51:4: "That you might be justified when you speak." Luke 7:29: "All the people

That to justify means neither simply to pardon, nor to make inherently righteous or good, is proved by the uniform usage of the word to justify in Scripture. It is never used in either of those senses, but always to declare or pronounce just.

that heard him, and the publicans, justified God." The only passage in the New Testament where the word δικαιωθήτω ἔτι seems to be used in a different sense is *Revelation* 22:11: ὁ δίκαιος δικαιωθήτω ἔτι, "He that is righteous, let him be righteous still." Here the first aorist passive appears to be used in a middle sense: "Let him show himself righteous, or continue righteous." Even if the reading in this passage were undoubted, this single case would have no force against the established usage of the word. The reading, however, is not merely doubtful, but it is, in the judgment of the majority of the critical editors, Tischendorf among the rest, incorrect. They give, as the true text, δικαιοσύνην ποιησάτω ἔτι. Even if this latter reading be, as De Wette thinks, a gloss, it shows that ὁ δίκαιος δικαιωθήτω ἔτι was as intolerable to a Greek ear as the expression, "He that is righteous, let him justify himself still" would be to us.

> *Condemnation is not the opposite either of pardon or of reformation. To condemn is to pronounce guilty or worthy of punishment. To justify is to declare not guilty.*

The usage of common life as to this word is just as uniform as that of the Bible. It would be a perfect solecism to say of a criminal whom the executive had pardoned that he was justified; or that a reformed drunkard or thief was justified. The word always expresses a judgment, whether of the mind, as when one man justifies another for his conduct, or officially of a judge. If such be the established meaning of the word, it ought to settle all controversy as to the nature of justification. We are bound to take the words of Scripture in their true established sense. And, therefore, when the Bible says, "God justifies the believer," we are not at liberty to say that it means that he pardons, or that he sanctifies him. It means, and can mean only, that he pronounces him just.

Justification the Opposite of Condemnation

This is still further evident from the antithesis between condemnation and justification. Condemnation is not the opposite either of pardon or of reformation. *To condemn* is to *pronounce guilty* or worthy of punishment. *To justify* is *to declare not guilty*, or that justice does not demand punishment, or that the person concerned cannot justly be condemned. When, therefore, the apostle says (*Romans* 8:1), "There is, therefore, now no condemnation to them which are in Christ Jesus," he declares that they are absolved from guilt; that the penalty of the law cannot justly be inflicted upon them. "Who," he asks, "shall lay anything to the charge of God's elect? God who justifies? Who is he that condemns? Christ who died?" (33, 34). Against the elect in Christ no ground of condemnation can be presented. God pronounces them just, and therefore no one can pronounce them guilty.

This passage is certainly decisive against the doctrine of subjective justification in any form. This opposition between condemnation and justification is familiar both in Scripture and in common life. *Job* 9:20: "If I justify myself, my own mouth shall condemn me." *Job* 34:17: "And will you condemn him that is most just?" If *to condemn* does not mean to make wicked, *to justify* does not mean to make good. And if condemnation is a judicial as opposed to an executive act, so is justification. In condemnation it is a judge who pronounces sentence on the guilty. In justification it is a judge who pronounces or who declares the person arraigned free from guilt and entitled to be treated as righteous.

In condemnation it is a judge who pronounces sentence on the guilty. In justification it is a judge who pronounces or who declares the person arraigned free from guilt.

Argument from Equivalent Forms of Expression

The forms of expression which are used as equivalents of the word *justify* clearly determine the nature of the act. Thus Paul speaks of "the blessedness of the man unto whom God imputes righteousness without works" (*Romans* 4:6). *To impute righteousness* is not to pardon; neither is it to sanctify. It means to justify, that is, to attribute righteousness. The negative form in which justification is described is equally significant. "Blessed are they whose iniquities are forgiven, and whose sins are covered. Blessed is the man to whom the Lord will not impute sin" (*Romans* 4:7-8). As *to impute sin* never means and cannot mean to make wicked; so the negative statement *not to impute sin* cannot mean to sanctify. And as *to impute sin* does mean to lay sin to one's account and to treat him accordingly; so *to justify* means to lay righteousness to one's account and treat him accordingly. "God sent not his Son into the world to condemn the world…. He that believes on him is not condemned; but he that believes not is condemned already" (*John* 3:17, 18).

For "as by the offense of one, judgment came upon all men to condemnation; even so by the righteousness of one the free gift came upon all men unto justification of life" (*Romans* 5:18). It was κρῖμα a judicial sentence, which came on men for the offense of Adam, and it is a judicial sentence (justification, a δικαίωσις which comes for the righteousness of Christ; or, as is said in verse 16 of the same chapter, it was a κρῖμα εἰς κατάκριμα, a condemnatory sentence that came for one offense; and a χάρισμα εἰς δικαίωμα, a sentence of gratuitous justification from many offenses. Language cannot be plainer. If a sentence of condemnation is a judicial act, then justification is a judicial act.

Argument from the Statement of the Doctrine

The question is not, How can a man become holy? but, How can he become just? How can he satisfy the claims which justice has against him?

The judicial character of justification is involved in the mode in which the doctrine is presented in the Bible. The Scriptures speak of law, of its demands, of its penalty, of sinners as arraigned at the bar of God, of the day of judgment. The question is, How shall man be just with God? The answer to this question determines the whole method of salvation. The question is not, How can a man become holy? but, How can he become just? How can he satisfy the claims which justice has against him?

It is obvious that if there is no such attribute as justice in God, if what we call justice is only benevolence, then there is no pertinency in this question. In that case, man is not required to be just in order to be saved. There would be no claims of justice to be satisfied. Repentance is all that would need to be rendered as the condition of restoration to the favor of God. Or, any didactic declaration or exhibition of God's disapprobation of sin would open the way for the safe pardon of sinners. Or, if the demands of justice were easily satisfied – if partial, imperfect obedience and fatherly chastisements, or self-inflicted penances, would suffice to satisfy its claims – then the sinner need not be just with God in order to be saved. But the human soul knows intuitively that these are refuges of lies. It knows that there is such an attribute as justice. It knows that the demands thereof are inexorable because they are righteous. It knows that it cannot be saved unless it be justified, and it knows that it cannot be declared just unless the demands of justice are fully satisfied. Low views of the evil of sin and of the justice of God lie at the foundation of all false views of this great doctrine.

The Apostle's Argument in the Epistle to the Romans

The apostle begins the discussion of this subject by assuming that the justice of God, his purpose to punish all sin, to demand perfect conformity to his law, is revealed from Heaven, that is, so revealed that no man, whether Jew or Gentile, can deny it (*Romans* 1:18). Men, even the most degraded pagans, know the righteous judgment of God that those who sin are worthy of death (verse 32). He next proves that all men are sinners and, being sinners, are under condemnation. The whole world is "guilty before God" (*Romans* 3:19). From this he infers, as intuitively certain (because plainly included in the premises), that no flesh living can be justified before God "by the deeds of the law," that is, on the ground of his own character and conduct. If guilty he cannot be pronounced not guilty, or just. In Paul's argument, *to justify* is to pronounce just. Δίκαιος is the opposite of ὑπόδικος (that is, "reus, satisfactionem alteri debens"). That is, *righteous* is the opposite of *guilty*. *To pronounce guilty* is to condemn. *To pronounce righteous*, that is, not guilty, is to justify. If a man denies the authority of Scripture, or if he feels at liberty (while holding what he considers the substance of Scripture doctrines) to reject the form, it is conceivable that he may deny that justification is a judicial act; but it seems impossible that any one should deny that it is so represented in the Bible. Some men, professing to believe the Bible, deny that there is anything supernatural in the work of regeneration and sanctification. "Being born of the Spirit"; "quickened by the mighty power of God"; "created anew in Christ Jesus" are only, they say, strong oriental expressions for a self-wrought reformation. By a similar process it is easy to

Low views of the evil of sin and of the justice of God lie at the foundation of all false views of this great doctrine.

get rid, not only of the doctrine of justification as a judicial act, but of all other distinguishing doctrines of the Scriptures. This, however, is not to interpret, but to pervert.

The apostle, having taught that God is just, that is, that he demands the satisfaction of justice, and that men are sinners and can render no such satisfaction themselves, announces that such a righteousness has been provided and is revealed in the Gospel. It is not our own righteousness, which is of the law, but the righteousness of Christ, and, therefore, the righteousness of God, in virtue of which and on the ground of which God can be just and yet justify the sinner who believes in Christ. As long as the Bible stands, this must stand as a simple statement of what Paul teaches as to the method of salvation. Men may dispute as to what he means, but this is surely what he says.

Justification cannot be mere pardon. Pardon does not proceed on the ground of a satisfaction.

Argument from the Ground of Justification

The nature of justification is determined by its ground. This indeed is an anticipation of another part of the subject, but it is in point here. If the Bible teaches that the ground of justification – the reason why God remits to us the penalty of the law and accepts us as righteous in his sight – is something out of ourselves, something done for us and not what we do or experience, then it of necessity follows that justification is not subjective. It does not consist in the infusion of righteousness or in making the person justified personally holy. If the "formal cause" of our justification be our goodness, then we are justified for what we are. The Bible, however, teaches that no man living can be justified for what he is. He is condemned for what he is and for what he does. He is justified for what Christ has done for him.

Justification Not Mere Pardon

For the same reason, justification cannot be mere pardon. Pardon does not proceed on the ground of a satisfaction. A prisoner delivered by a ransom is not pardoned. A debtor whose obligations have been cancelled by a friend becomes entitled to freedom from the claims of his creditor. When a sovereign pardons a criminal, it is not an act of justice. It is not on the ground of satisfaction to the law. The Bible, therefore, in teaching that justification is on the ground of an atonement or satisfaction; that the sinner's guilt is expiated; that he is redeemed by the precious blood of Christ; and that judgment is pronounced upon him as righteous, does thereby teach that justification is neither pardon nor infusion of righteousness.

Argument from the Immutability of the Law

The doctrine that justification consists simply in pardon and consequent restoration assumes that the divine law is imperfect and mutable. In human governments it is often expedient and right that men justly condemned to suffer the penalty of the law should be pardoned. Human laws must be general. They cannot take in all the circumstances of each particular case. Their execution would often work hardship or injustice. Human judgments may therefore often be set aside. It is not so with the divine law. The law of the Lord is perfect. And being perfect it cannot be disregarded. It demands nothing which ought not to be demanded. It threatens nothing which ought not to be inflicted. It is in fact its own executioner. Sin is death (*Romans* 8:6). The justice of God makes punishment as inseparable from sin as life is from holiness. The penalty of the law is immutable and as little capable of being set aside as the precept. Accordingly, the Scriptures everywhere teach that in the justification of the sinner there is no relaxation of the penalty. There is no setting aside or disregarding the demands of the law. We are delivered from the law, not by its abrogation, but by its execution (*Galatians* 2:19). We are freed from the law by the body of Christ (*Romans* 7:4). Christ, having taken our place, bore our sins in his own body on the tree (*1 Peter* 2:24). The handwriting which was against us, he took out of the way, nailing it to his cross (*Colossians* 2:14). We are therefore not under the law, but under grace (*Romans* 6:14). Such representations are inconsistent with the theory which supposes that the law may be dispensed with; that the restoration of sinners to the favor and fellowship of God

We are delivered from the law, not by its abrogation, but by its execution (Galatians 2:19).

requires no satisfaction to its demands; that the believer is pardoned and restored to fellowship with God, just as a thief or forger is pardoned and restored to his civil rights by the executive in human governments. This is against the Scriptures. God is just in justifying the sinner. He acts according to justice.

It will be seen that everything in this discussion turns on the question: Is there such an attribute in God as justice? If justice be only "benevolence guided by wisdom," then there is no justification. What evangelical Christians so regard is only pardon or sanctification. But if God, as the Scriptures and conscience teach, be a just God – as immutable in his justice as in his goodness and truth – then there can be no remission of the penalty of sin except on the ground of expiation, and no justification except on the ground of the satisfaction of justice; and therefore justification must be a judicial act, and neither simply pardon nor the infusion of righteousness. These doctrines sustain each other. What the Bible teaches of the justice of God proves that justification is a judicial declaration that justice is satisfied. And what the Bible teaches of the nature of justification proves that justice in God is something more than benevolence. It is thus that all the great doctrines of the Bible are concatenated.

Everything in this discussion turns on the question: Is there such an attribute in God as justice? If justice be only "benevolence guided by wisdom," then there is no justification.

Argument from the Nature of Our Union with Christ

The theory which reduces justification to pardon and its consequences is inconsistent with what is revealed concerning our union with Christ. That union is mystical, supernatural, representative, and vital. We were in him before the foundation of the world (*Ephesians* 1:4); we are in him as we were in Adam (*Romans* 5:12, 21; *1 Corinthians* 15:22); we are in him as the members of the body are in the head (*Ephesians* 1:23, 4:16; *1 Corinthians* 12:12, 27); we are in him as the branches are in the vine (*John* 15:1-12). We are in him in such a sense that his death is our death, we were crucified with him (*Galatians* 2:20; *Romans* 6:1-8); we are so united with him that we rose with him and sit with him in heavenly places (*Ephesians* 2:1-6). In virtue of this union we are (in our measure) what he is. We are the sons of God in him. And what he did, we did. His righteousness is our righteousness. His life is our life. His exaltation is our exaltation. Such is the pervading representation of the Scriptures.

All this is overlooked by the advocates of the opposite theory. According to that view, Christ is no more united to his people (except in sentiment) than to other men. He has simply done what renders it consistent with the character of God and the interests of his kingdom to pardon any and every man who repents and believes. His relation is purely external. He is not so united to his people that his merit becomes their merit and his life their life. Christ is not in them the hope of glory (*Colossians* 1:27). He is not of God made unto them wisdom, righteousness, sanctification, and redemption (*1 Corinthians* 1:30). They are not so in him that, in virtue of that union, they are filled with all the fulness of God (*Colossians* 2:10; and *Ephesians* 3:19). On the other hand, the Protestant doctrine of justification harmonizes with all these representations. If we are so united to Christ as to be made partakers of his life, we are also partakers of his righteousness. What he did in obeying and suffering he did for his people. One essential element of his redeeming work was to satisfy the demands of justice in their behalf, so that in him and for his sake they are entitled to pardon and eternal life.

There can be no satisfaction to the mind until there is satisfaction of justice.

Arguments from the Effects Ascribed to Justification

The consequences attributed to justification are inconsistent with the assumption that it consists either in pardon or in the infusion of righteousness. Those consequences are peace, reconciliation, and a title to eternal life. "Being justified by faith," says the apostle, "we have peace with God" (*Romans* 5:1). But pardon does not produce peace. It leaves the conscience unsatisfied. A pardoned criminal is not only just as much a criminal as he was before, but his sense of guilt and remorse of conscience are in no degree lessened. Pardon can remove only the outward and arbitrary penalty. The sting of sin remains. There can be no satisfaction to the mind until there is satisfaction of justice.

Justification secures peace, not merely because it includes pardon, but because that pardon is dispensed on the ground of a full satisfaction of justice. What satisfies the justice of God satisfies the conscience of the sinner. The blood of Jesus Christ cleanses from all sin (*1 John* 1:7) by removing guilt and thus producing a peace which passes all understanding. When the soul sees that Christ bore his sins upon the cross and endured the penalty which he had incurred, that all the demands of the law are fully satisfied, that God is more honored in his pardon than in his condemnation, that all the ends of punishment are accomplished by the work of Christ in a far higher degree than they could be by the death of the sinner, and that he has a right to plead the infinite merit of the Son of God at the bar of divine justice, then he is satisfied. Then he has peace. He is humble; he does not lose his sense of personal demerit, but the conscience ceases to demand satisfaction. Criminals have often been known to give themselves up to justice. They could not rest until they were punished. The infliction of the penalty incurred gave them peace. This is an element in Christian experience. The convinced sinner never finds peace until he lays his burden of sin on the Lamb of God; until he apprehends that his sins have been punished, as the apostle says (*Romans* 8:3), in Christ.

Again, we are said to be reconciled to God by the death of his Son (*Romans* 5:10). But pardon does not produce reconciliation. A pardoned criminal may be restored to his civil rights, so far as the penalty remitted involved their forfeiture, but he is not reconciled to society. He is not restored to its favor. Justification, however, does secure a restoration to the favor and fellowship of God. We become the sons of God by faith in Jesus Christ (*Galatians* 3:26). No one can read the eighth chapter of the epistle to the Romans without being convinced that in Paul's apprehension a justified believer is something more than a pardoned criminal. He is a man whose salvation is secure because he is free from the law and all its demands; because the righteousness of the law (that is, all its righteous requirements) has been fulfilled in him, because thereby he is so united to Christ as to become a partaker of his

A justified believer is something more than a pardoned criminal. He is a man whose salvation is secure because he is free from the law and all its demands.

life, because no one can lay anything to the charge of those for whom Christ died and whom God has justified, and because such believers being justified are revealed as the objects of the mysterious, immutable, and infinite love of God.

Again, justification includes or conveys a title to eternal life. Pardon is purely negative. It simply removes a penalty. It confers no title to benefits not previously enjoyed. Eternal life, however, is suspended on the positive condition of perfect obedience. The merely pardoned sinner has no such obedience. He is destitute of what, by the immutable principles of the divine government, is the indispensable condition of eternal life. He has no title to the inheritance promised to the righteous. This is not the condition of the believer. The merit of Christ is entitled to the reward. And the believer, being partaker of that merit, shares in that title. This is constantly recognized in the Scriptures. By faith in Christ we become the sons of God. But sonship involves heirship, and heirship involves a title to the inheritance. "If children, then heirs; heirs of God, and joint heirs with Christ" (*Romans* 8:17). This is the doctrine taught in *Romans* 5:12-21. For the offense of one, judgment passed on all men to condemnation. For the righteousness of one, the sentence of justification of life has passed on all; that is, of a justification which entitles to life. As the sin of Adam was the judicial ground of our condemnation (that is, was the ground on which justice demanded condemnation), so the righteousness of Christ is the judicial ground of justification. That is, it is the ground on which the life promised to the righteous should in justice be granted to the believer. The church in all ages has recognized this truth. Believers have always felt that they had a title to eternal life. For this they have praised God in the loftiest strains. They have ever regarded it as intuitively true that Heaven must be merited. The only question was whether that merit was in them or in Christ. Being in Christ, it was a free gift to them; and thus righteousness and peace kissed each other. Grace and justice unite in placing the crown of righteousness on the believer's head.

It is no less certain that the consequences attributed to justification do not flow from the infusion of righteousness.

The consequences attributed to justification do not flow from the infusion of righteousness. The amount of holiness possessed by the believer does not give him peace. Even perfect holiness would not remove guilt.

The amount of holiness possessed by the believer does not give him peace. Even perfect holiness would not remove guilt. Repentance does not atone for the crime of murder. It does not still the murderer's conscience, nor does it satisfy the sense of justice in the public mind. It is the πρῶτον ψεῦδος of Romanism, and of every theory of subjective justification, that they make nothing of guilt, or reduce it to a minimum. If there were no guilt, then infusion of righteousness would be all that is necessary for salvation. But if there be justice in God, then no amount of holiness can atone for sin, and justification cannot consist in making the sinner holy.

If there were no guilt, then infusion of righteousness would be all that is necessary for salvation. But if there be justice in God, then no amount of holiness can atone for sin, and justification cannot consist in making the sinner holy.

Besides this, even admitting that the past could be ignored – that the guilt which burdens the soul could be overlooked or so easily removed – subjective righteousness, or holiness, is so imperfect that it could never give the believer peace. Let the holiest of men look within himself and say whether what he sees there satisfies his own conscience. If not, how can it satisfy God? He is greater than our hearts, and knows all things. No man, therefore, can have peace with God founded on what he is or on what he does. Romanists admit that nothing short of perfect holiness justifies or gives peace to the soul. In answer to the Protestant argument founded on that admission, Bellarmin says:

> This argument, if it proves anything, proves that actual justice is not perfect; however, it does not prove that habitual justice, because of which we are formally complete…is not so perfect that we are called, and are, absolutely, simply, and properly complete. For we are not formally complete by means of our labor but by God's labor, who at the same time scours the blemishes of our sins and instills the condition of faith, hope, and charity. Moreover, God's labors are perfect…. Whence very young children are baptized, they are truly complete, although they have done no labor.[2]

2. "Hoc argumentum, si quid probat, probat justitiam actualem non esse perfectam: non autem probat, justitiam habitualem, qua formaliter justi sumus…. non esse ita perfectam, ut absolute, simpliciter, et proprie justi nominemur, et simus. Non enim formaliter justi sumus opere nostro, sed opere Dei, qui simul maculas peccatorum tergit, et habitum fidei, spei, et caritatis infundit. Dei autem perfecta sunt opera…. Unde parvuli baptizati, vere justi sunt, quamvis nihil operis fecerint."

Again,

> For actual justice, although it is by all means imperfect because of a mixture of venal faults, and although it is without a daily remission of sin, nevertheless it does not as a result of this necessarily cease to be true justice, and even perfect in its own certain way.[3]

No provision is made in this system for guilt. If the soul is made holy by the infusion of habits, or principles, of grace, it is just in the sight of God. No guilt or desert of punishment remains. "The state of being accused," says Bellarmin, "…is relative,"[4] but if the thing of which it is a relation be taken away, where is the relation? It is impossible that such a view of justification can give peace. It makes no provision for the satisfaction of justice, and places all our hopes upon what is within, which our conscience and the Scripture testify cannot meet the just requirements of God.

Neither can the theory of subjective justification account for reconciliation with God, and for the same reasons. What is infused, the degree of holiness imparted, does not render us the objects of divine complacency and love. His love to us is of the nature of grace: love for the unlovely. We are reconciled to God by the death of his Son. That removes the obstacle arising from justice to the outflow toward us of the mysterious, unmerited love of God. We are accepted in the beloved. We are not in ourselves fit for fellowship with God. And if driven to depend on what is within, on our subjective righteousness, instead of peace we should have despair.

Again, justification according to the Scriptures gives a title to eternal life. For this our own righteousness is utterly inadequate. So far from anything in us being meritorious or entitled to reward, the inward state and the exercises of the holiest of men come so far short of perfection as to merit

Justification according to the Scriptures gives a title to eternal life. For this our own righteousness is utterly inadequate. So far from anything in us being meritorious or entitled to reward, the inward state and the exercises of the holiest of men come so far short of perfection as to merit condemnation.

3. "Justitia enim actualis, quamvis aliquo modo sit imperfecta, propter admixtionem venalium delictorum, et egeat quotidiana remissione peccati, tamen non propterea desinit esse vera justitia, et suo etiam quodam modo perfecta." Thus we see the absurdity of a justice which is "by all means imperfect" and "even perfect in its own certain way." — *Editor*

4. "Reatus," says Bellarmin, "… est relatio."

condemnation. In us there is no good thing. When we would do good, evil is present with us. There is ever a law in our members warring against the law of the mind. Indwelling sin remains. It forced even Paul to cry out, "O wretched man that I am! Who shall deliver me from the body of this death?" (*Romans* 7:24). "No labor of a pious man has ever appeared which, if it were considered by God's stern judgment, would not be able to be condemned."[5] Ignoring the plain truth of Scripture and of Christian experience expressing itself in daily and hourly confession, humiliation, and prayers for forgiveness, the doctrine of subjective justification assumes that there is no sin in the believer – or no sin which merits the condemnation of God – but on the contrary that there is in him what merits eternal life. The Romanists make a distinction between a first and second justification. The first they admit to be gratuitous, and to be founded on the merit of Christ, or rather, to be gratuitously bestowed for Christ's sake. This consists in the infusion of habitual grace (that is, regeneration). This justifies in rendering the soul subjectively just or holy. The second justification is not a matter of grace. It is founded on the merit of good works, the fruits of regeneration. But if these fruits are, as our consciousness and the Scripture testify, defiled by sin, how can they merit eternal life? How can they cancel the handwriting which is against us? How can they be the ground of Paul's confident challenge, "Who shall lay anything to the charge of God's elect?" It is not what is within us, but what is without us; not what we are or do, but what Christ is and has done that is the ground of confidence and of our title to eternal life. This is the admitted doctrine of the Protestant Reformation.

> Among theologians of the Augustinian confession it has been regarded beyond dispute that our entire righteousness resides beyond us, and beyond the merits, labors, virtues, and sought-after worth of all men, and that it resides only in our Lord Jesus Christ.[6]

5. "Nullum unquam exstitisse pii hominis opus, quod, si severo Dei judicio examinaretur, non esset damnabile" (Calvin, *Institutio*, III, xiv, 11; Berlin edition, 1834, part II, 38).

It is not what is within us, but what is without us; not what we are or do, but what Christ is and has done that is the ground of confidence and of our title to eternal life.

As high as the heavens are above the Earth, so high is a hope founded on the work of Christ for us, above a hope founded on the merit of anything wrought in us. Calvin teaches the same doctrine as Luther.[7] He quotes Lombard as saying that our justification in Christ may be interpreted in two ways:

> First, the death of Christ justifies us, while through that death love is aroused in our hearts, by which we are made complete; then, because through that same death sin is obliterated, whereby the devil divides us as captives, so that now he does not have that with which he condemns us.[8]

To which Calvin replies,

> However, the Scripture, which speaks about the justice of faith, leads us far in another direction: to be sure, so that we, having been turned away from consideration of our labors, depend so much on God's mercy and Christ's perfection.... This is the knowledge of faith, through which the sinner comes into possession of his own salvation, while he understands from the Evangelical doctrine that he has been reconciled to God: because when he has obtained remission of his sins, and Christ's righteousness has intervened, he is justified: and although reborn in the Spirit of God, he thinks that eternal righteousness is in store for him, not in the good labors to which he applies himself, but because of Christ's justice alone.[9]

Calvin teaches the same doctrine as Luther.

---

6. "Apud theologos Augustanæ confessionis extra controversiam positum est totam justitiam nostram extra nos, et extra omnium hominum merita, opera, virtutes, atque dignitatem quærendam eamque in solo Domino nostro, Jesu Christo consistere." (*Solida Declaratio*, III, 55; Hase, *Libri Symbolici*, third edition, Leipzig, 1846, 695).

7. *Institutio*, III, xi, 15, 16; *ut supra*, 17.

8. "Primum, mors Christi nos justificat, dum per eam excitatur caritas in cordibus nostris, qua justi efficimur: deinde quod per eandem exstinctum est peccatum; quo nos captivos distinebat diabolus, ut jam non habeat unde nos damnet."

9. "Scriptura autem, quem de fidei justitia loquitur, longe alio nos ducit: nempe ut ab intuitu operum nostrorum aversi, in Dei misericordiam ac Christi perfectionem, tantum respiciamus.... Hic est fidei sensus, per quem peccator in possessionem venit suæ salutis, dum ex Evangelii

Summary

That justification is not merely pardon, and that it is not the infusion of righteousness whereby the sinner is made inherently just or holy, but a judgment on the part of God that the demands of the law in regard to the believer are satisfied, and that he has a right to a righteousness which entitles him to eternal life has been argued:

(1) From the uniform usage of Scripture both in the Old and New Testament.

(2) From the constant opposition between justification and condemnation.

(3) From equivalent forms of expression.

(4) From the whole design and drift of the apostle's argument in his epistles to the Romans and to the Galatians.

(5) From the ground of justification, namely, the righteousness of Christ.

(6) From the immutability of the law and the justice of God.

(7) From the nature of our union with Christ.

(8) From the fact that peace, reconciliation with God, and a title to eternal life which, according to Scripture, are the consequences of justification, do not flow either from mere pardon, or from subjective righteousness, or from sanctification.

That this is the doctrine of Protestants, both Lutheran and Reformed, cannot with any show of reason be disputed.

That this is the doctrine of Protestants, both Lutheran and Reformed, cannot with any show of reason be disputed.

Calvin's Doctrine

It is true indeed that by the earlier Reformers, and especially by Calvin, justification is often said to consist in the pardon of sin. But that statement was not intended as a denial of the judicial character of justification, or as excluding the imputation of the righteousness of Christ by

doctrina agnoscit Deo se reconciliatum: quod intercedente Christi justitia, impetrata peccatorum remissione, justificatus sit: et quanquam Spiritu Dei regeneratus, non in bonis operibus, quibus incumbit, sed sola Christi justitia repositam sibi perpetuam justitiam cogitat."

which the believer is counted just in the sight of the law. This is obvious from the nature of the controversy in which those Reformers were engaged. The question between them and the Romanists was, Does justification consist in the act of God making the sinner inherently just or holy? or, Does it express the judgment of God by which the believer is pronounced just? What Calvin denied was that justification is a making holy. What he affirmed was that it was delivering the believer from the condemnation of the law and introducing him into a state of favor with God. The Romanists expressed their doctrine by saying that justification consists in the remission of sin and the infusion of charity or righteousness. But by *the remission* of sin they meant the removal of sin, the putting off the old man. In other words, justification with them consisted (to use the Scholastic language then in vogue) in the removal of the habits of sin and the infusion of habits of grace. In those justified, therefore, there was no sin, and, therefore, nothing to punish. Pardon, therefore, followed as a necessary consequence. It was a mere accessory. This view of the matter makes nothing of guilt, nothing of the demands of justice.

Calvin, therefore, insisted that besides the subjective renovation connected with the sinner's conversion, his justification concerned the removal of guilt, the satisfaction of justice, which in the order of nature – although not of time – must precede the communication of the life of God to the soul. That Calvin did not differ from the other Reformers and the whole body of the Reformed church on this subject appears from his own explicit declarations and from the perfectly unambiguous statements of the confessions to which he gave his assent. Thus he says,

> Further, so that we not block the entrance itself (which happens if we begin a debate about an unknown matter), first let us explain what those expressions signify, that man is justified in the presence of God, that he is justified either by faith or by works. He who is both considered just in God's judgment and accepted on account of his righteousness is said to be justified in the presence of God. As iniquity is

That Calvin did not differ from the other Reformers and the whole body of the Reformed church on this subject appears from his own explicit declarations and from the perfectly unambiguous statements of the confessions to which he gave his assent.

hateful to God, so is a sinner unable to find grace in his eyes, insofar as he is a sinner, and as long as he is considered such. Consequently, wherever there is sin, there also the anger and vengeance of God reveals itself. However, he is justified who is held in a position not of sin but of righteousness, and in that name he stands in the presence of God's tribunal, where all sinners are thrown down. In this manner, if an innocent defendant is led to the tribunal of a just judge, he is said to be justified in the presence of the judge. So is he, who has been freed from the number of sinners, justified before God; he has God as a witness and protector of his righteousness. Therefore, he will be said to be justified, by reason of works, in whose life will be found that purity and sanctity which merits the proof of justice at God's throne: or he who can answer with the righteousness of his own works and prove them sufficiently to his judge. On the other hand, that man who, having been excluded from the righteousness of his works, seizes the righteousness of Christ through his faith, he will be justified by means of faith, as far as he appears in the sight of God clothed not as a sinner but just as if perfect. Thus we interpret *justification* simply as acceptance, whereby God considers us perfect when we have been received in grace. And we say that this grace has been offered because of the remission of sins and the imputation of Christ's righteousness.[10]

> "That man who, having been excluded from the righteousness of his works, seizes the righteousness of Christ through his faith, he will be justified by means of faith."
> – John Calvin

10. "Porro ne impingamus in ipso limine (quod fieret si de re incognita disputationem ingrediremur) primum explicemus quid sibi velint istæ loquutiones, Hominem coram Deo justificari, Fide justificari, vel operibus. Justificari coram Deo dicitur qui judicio Dei et censetur justus, et acceptus est ob suam justitiam: siqui dem ut Deo abominabilis est iniquitas, ita nec peccator in ejus oculis potest invenire gratiam, quatenus est peccator, et quamdiu talis censetur. Proinde ubicunque peccatum est, illic etiam se profert ira et ultio Dei. Justificatur autem qui non loco peccatoris, sed justi habetur, eoque nomine consistit coram Dei tribunali, ubi peccatores omnes corruunt. Quemadmodum si reus innocens ad tribunal æqui judicis adducatur, ubi secundum innocentiam ejus judicatum fuerit, justificatus apud judicem dicitur: sic apud Deum justificatur, qui numero peccatorum exemptus, Deum habet sum suæ justitiæ testem et assertorem. Justificari, ergo, operibus ea ratione dicetur, in cujus vita reperietur ea puritas ac sanctitas quæ testimonium justitiæ apud Dei thronum mereatur: seu qui operum suorum integritate respondere et satisfacere illius judicio queat. Contra, justificabitur ille fide, qui operum justitia exclusus, Christi justitiam per fidem apprehendit, qua vestitus in Dei conspectu non ut peccator, sed tanquam justus apparet. Ita nos justificationem simpliciter

This passage is decisive as to the views of Calvin: for it is professedly a formal statement of the "Status Quæstionis" given with the utmost clearness and precision. Justification consists "in the remission of sins and the imputation of the righteousness of Christ." "He is justified in the sight of God who is taken from the class of sinners and has God for the witness and assertor of his righteousness."

> "He is justified in the sight of God who is taken from the class of sinners and has God for the witness and assertor of his righteousness."
> – John Calvin

interpretamur acceptionem, qua nos Deus in gratiam receptos pro justos habet. Eamque in peccatorum remissione ac justitiæ Christi imputatione positam esse dicimus." (*Institutio*, III, xi, 2, *ut supra*, 6).

6

Works Not the Ground of Justification

What is meant by works of the law? To this question the following answers have been given: First, that by works of the law are meant works prescribed in the Jewish law.

I{N REFERENCE} to men since the Fall the assertion is so explicit and so often that justification is not of works, that that proposition has never been called into question by anyone professing to receive the Scriptures as the Word of God. It being expressly asserted that the whole world is guilty before God, that by the works of the law no flesh living can be justified, the only question open for discussion is, What is meant by *works of the law*?

To this question the following answers have been given: First, that by *works of the law* are meant works prescribed in the Jewish law. It is assumed that as Paul's controversy was with those who taught that unless men were circumcised and kept the law of Moses, they could not be saved (*Acts* 15:1, 24), all he intended to teach was the reverse of that proposition. He is to be understood as saying that the observance of Jewish rites and ceremonies is not essential to salvation; that men are not made righteous or good by external ceremonial works, but by works morally good. This is the ground taken by Pelagians and by most of the modern Rationalists.

It is only a modification of this view that men are not justified, that is, that their character before God is not determined, so much by their particular acts or works as by their general disposition and controlling principles. To be justified by faith, therefore, is to be justified on the ground

212

of our trust or pious confidence in God and truth. Thus Wegscheider says:

> Men are found truly good by God not by being properly engaged in certain discrete deeds and works nor because of certain worth attributed to them, but only by true faith: that is, by adapting their spirit to Christ's example and his commands, and by directing their spirit to God both most holy and most kind, so that all thoughts and actions answer to God and his most holy will; and they are steeped, having complete faith in God's benevolence, with hope for future blessedness for the most certain moral worth granted to them.[1]

Steudlin expresses the same view. "All true reformation, every good act," he says, "must spring from faith, provided we understand by faith the conviction that something is right, a conviction of general moral and religious principles."[2] Kant says that Christ in a religious aspect is the ideal of humanity. When a man so regards him and endeavors to conform his heart and life to that ideal, he is justified by faith.[3] According to all these views, mere ceremonial works are excluded, and the ground of justification is made to be our own natural moral character and conduct.

Kant says that Christ in a religious aspect is the ideal of humanity. When a man so regards him and endeavors to conform his heart and life to that ideal, he is justified by faith.

Roman Catholic Doctrine

The doctrine of Romanists on this subject is much higher. Romanism retains the supernatural element of Christianity throughout.[4] On the matter of justification the Romish

---

1. "Homines non singulis quibusdam recte factis operibusque operatis, nec propter meritum quoddam iis attribuendum, sed sola vera fide, *i.e.,* animo ad Christi exemplum ejusdemque præcepta composito et ad Deum et sanctissimum et benignissimum converso, ita, ut omnia cogitata et facta ad Deum ejusque voluntatem sanctissimam pie referant, Deo vere probantur et benevolentæ Dei confisi spe beatitatis futuræ pro dignitate ipsorum morali iis concedendæ certissima imbuuntur" (*Institutiones Theologiæ*, III, iii, §155, 5th edition, Halle, 1826, 476).

2. *Dogmatik*, Zweiter Theil, §134, B, g, h; Göttingen, 1800, 783, 784.

3. See Strauss, *Dogmatik*, Tübingen and Stuttgart, 1841, Volume II, 493, 494.

4. Hodge errs when he writes: "Indeed it is a matter of devout thankfulness to God that underneath the numerous grievous and

According to this Roman Catholic view, we are not justified by works done before regeneration, but we are justified for gracious works, that is, for works which spring from the principle of divine life infused into the heart.

theologians have marred and defaced the truth as they have almost all other doctrines pertaining to the mode in which the merits of Christ are made available to our salvation. They admit, indeed, that there is no good in fallen man; that he can merit nothing and claim nothing on the ground of anything he is or can do of himself. He is by nature dead in sin; and until made partaker of a new life by the supernatural power of the Holy Ghost, he can do nothing but sin. For Christ's sake, and only through his merits, as a matter of grace, this new life is imparted to the soul in regeneration (that is, as Romanists teach, in baptism). As life expels death; as light banishes darkness, so the entrance of this new divine life into the soul expels sin (that is, sinful habits) and brings forth the fruits of righteousness. Works done after regeneration have real merit, "meritum condigni [condign merit]," and are the ground of the second justification; the first justification consisting in making the soul inherently just by the infusion of righteousness. According to this view, we are not justified by works done before regeneration, but we are justified for gracious works, that is, for works which spring from the principle of divine life infused into the heart. The whole ground of our acceptance with God is thus made to be what we are and what we do.

---

destructive errors of the Romish Church, the great truths of the Gospel are preserved. The Trinity, the true divinity of Christ, the true doctrine concerning his person as God and man in two distinct natures and one person forever, salvation though his blood, regeneration and sanctification through the almighty power of the Spirit, the resurrection of the body, and eternal life, are doctrines on which the people of God in that communion live, and which have produced such saintly men as St. Bernard, Fénélon, and doubtless thousands of others who are of the number of God's elect. Every true worshipper of Christ must in his heart recognize as a Christian brother, wherever he may be found, anyone who loves, worships, and trusts the Lord Jesus Christ as God manifest in the flesh and the only Saviour of men." Hodge errs because any man or church which denies justification by faith alone cannot be said to preserve the great truths of the Gospel. Furthermore, Rome, while retaining the Biblical words, changes the meaning of the words. Modernism was not the first movement in the church to equivocate and thereby deny the truth. – Editor.

Arminian Doctrine

According to the Remonstrants or Arminians the works which are excluded from our justification are works of the law as distinguished from works of the Gospel. In the covenant made with Adam God demanded perfect obedience as the condition of life. For Christ's sake, God in the Gospel has entered into a new covenant with men, promising them salvation on the condition of evangelical obedience. This is expressed in different forms. Sometimes it is said that we are justified on account of faith. Faith is accepted in place of that perfect righteousness demanded by the Adamic law. But by faith is not meant the act of receiving and resting upon Christ alone for salvation. It is regarded as a permanent and controlling state of mind. And therefore it is often said that we are justified by a "fides obsequiosa," an obedient faith; a faith which includes obedience. At other times, it is said that we are justified by evangelical obedience, that is, that kind and measure of obedience which the Gospel requires, and which men since the Fall, in the proper use of "sufficient grace" granted to all men, are able to render. Limborch says, "It must be known that when we say that we are justified by means of faith, we do not exclude works that faith demands, just as a fruitful mother brings forth; but we include them."[5]

And again,

> And so it [faith] is such an act, which although having been seen is by no means perfect in itself, but failing in many things, nevertheless is accepted as full and complete by God, because of his favorable and very unrestrained will, and because of which God graciously wishes to attribute to man remission of sins and the reward of eternal life.[6]

But by faith Arminians do not mean the act of receiving and resting upon Christ alone for salvation. It is regarded as a permanent and controlling state of mind. And therefore it is often said that we are justified by a "fides obsequiosa," an obedient faith; a faith which includes obedience.

5. "Sciendum, quando dicimus, nos fide justificari, nos non excludere opera, quæ fides exigit et tanquam fœcunda mater producit; sed ea includere."

6. "Est itaque [fides] talis actus, qui, licet in se spectatus perfectus nequaquam sit, sed in multis deficiens, tamen a Deo, gratiosa et liberrima voluntate, pro pleno et perfecto acceptatur, et propter quem Deus homini gratiose remissionem peccatorum et vitæ æternæ premium conferre vult."

Again, God, he says, demands, "The obedience of faith; that is, not strict and equal obedience from all, just as the law demands, but only as much as faith, that is, a certain conviction about divine promises, can produce in each man."[7]

Therefore justification, he says, "is a favorable valuation, or rather acceptance of our imperfect righteousness as perfect, because of Jesus Christ."[8]

Protestant Doctrine

According to the doctrine of the Lutherans and Reformed, the works excluded from the ground of our justification are not only ritual or ceremonial works, nor merely works done before regeneration, nor the perfect obedience required by the law given to Adam, but works of all kinds, everything done by us or wrought in us. That this is the doctrine of the Bible is plain because the language of Scripture is unlimited. The declaration is that we are not justified "by works." No specific kind of works is designated to the exclusion of all others. But it is "works"; what we do; anything and everything we do. It is, therefore, without authority that any man limits these general declarations to any particular class of works.

The word *law* is used in a comprehensive sense. It includes all revelations of the will of God as the rule of man's obedience; and, therefore, by "works of the law" must be intended all kinds of works. As νόμος means that which binds, it is used for the law of nature, or the law written on the heart (*Romans* 2:14-15), for the Decalogue, for the law of Moses, for the whole of the Old Testament Scriptures (*Romans* 3:19). Sometimes one and sometimes another of these aspects of the law is specially referred to. Paul assures the Jews that they could not be justified by the works of the law, which was especially

According to the doctrine of the Lutherans and Reformed, the works excluded from the ground of our justification are not only ritual or ceremonial works, nor merely works done before regeneration, nor the perfect obedience required by the law given to Adam, but works of all kinds.

7. "Obedientiam fidei, hoc est, non rigidam et ab omnibus æqualem prout exigebat lex; sed tantam, quantam fides, id est, certa de divinis promissionibus persuasio, in unoquoque efficere potest." (*Theologia Christiana*, VI, iv, 32, 31, 37; Amsterdam edition, 1725, 705b, a, 706a).

8. "Est gratiosa tstimatio, seu potius acceptatio justitiæ nostræ imperfectæ pro perfecta propter Jesum Christum" (Limborch, VI, vi, 18; *ut supra*, 703, 1).

binding on them. He assures the Gentiles that they could not be justified by the law written on their hearts. He assures believers under the Gospel that they cannot be justified by works of the law binding on them. The reason given includes all possible works. That reason is that all human obedience is imperfect; all men are sinners; and the law demands perfect obedience (*Galatians* 3:10). Therefore, it is that "by the deeds of the law there shall no flesh be justified" (*Romans* 3:20).

The law of which Paul speaks is the law which says, "You shall not covet" (*Romans* 7:7); the law which is spiritual (verse 14); which is "holy, and just, and good" (verse 12); the law of which the great command is, You shall love the Lord your God with all your heart, and your neighbor as yourself. Besides, what are called works of the law are in *Titus* 3:5 called "works of righteousness." Higher works than these there cannot be. The apostle repudiates any ground of confidence in his "own righteousness" (*Philippians* 3:9), that is, own excellence, whether habitual or actual. He censures the Jews because they went about to establish their own righteousness and would not submit to the righteousness of God (*Romans* 10:3). From these and many similar passages it is clear that it is not any one or more specific kinds of work which are excluded from the ground of justification, but all works, all personal excellence of every kind.

This is still further evident from the contrast constantly presented between faith and works. We are not justified by works, but by faith in Jesus Christ (*Galatians* 2:16, and often elsewhere). It is not one kind of works as opposed to another; legal as opposed to evangelical; natural as opposed to gracious; moral as opposed to ritual; but works of every kind as opposed to faith.

The same is evident from what is taught of the gratuitous nature of our justification. Grace and works are antithetical. "To him that works the reward is not reckoned of grace, but of debt" (*Romans* 4:4). "If by grace, then is it no more of works: otherwise grace is no more grace" (*Romans* 11:6). Grace of necessity excludes works of every kind, and more especially those of the highest kind, which might have some show of

It is clear that it is not any one or more specific kinds of work which are excluded from the ground of justification, but all works, all personal excellence of every kind.

merit. But merit of any degree is of necessity excluded, if our salvation be by grace.

When the positive ground of justification is stated, it is always declared to be not anything done by us or wrought in us, but what was done for us. It is ever represented as something external to ourselves. We are justified by the blood of Christ (*Romans* 5:9); by his obedience (*Romans* 5:19); by his righteousness (verse 18). This is involved in the whole method of salvation. Christ saves us as a priest, but a priest does not save by making those who come to him good. He does not work *in* them, but *for* them. Christ saves us by a sacrifice; but a sacrifice is effectual, not because of its subjective effect upon the offerer, but as an expiation, or satisfaction to justice. Christ is our Redeemer; he gave himself as a ransom for many. But a ransom does not infuse righteousness. It is the payment of a price. It is the satisfaction of the claims of the captor upon the captive. The whole plan of salvation, therefore – as presented in the Bible and as it is the life of the Church – is changed, if the ground of our acceptance with God be transferred from what Christ has done for us to what is wrought in us or done by us. The Romish theologians do not agree exactly as to whether habitual or actual righteousness is the ground of justification. Bellarmin says it is the former.[9] He says,

> It is only through habitual righteousness that we are called formally perfect, and we are: but actual righteousness, that is, truly just labors, does indeed justify, as Saint James says when he says in chapter 2 that man is justified from his labors, but deservedly, not formally.[10]

This he says is clearly the doctrine of the Council of Trent, which teaches, "The formal condition of justification is righteousness, or charity, which God administers to each

Christ saves us as a priest, but a priest does not save by making those who come to him good. He does not work in them, but for them.

9. *De Justificatione*, 11, 15; *Disputationes*, Paris edition, 1608, Volume IV, 820a.

10. "Solam esse habitualem justitiam, per quam formaliter justi nominamur, et sumus: justitiam vero actualem, id est, opera vere justa justificare quidem, ut sanctus Jacobus loquitur, cum ait cap. 2 ex operibus hominem justificari, sed meritorie, non formaliter."

man as his own, following a measure of arrangements, and which cleaves to the hearts of the righteous."[11]

This follows also, he argues, from the fact that the sacraments justify "by the instrumental means of the infusion of habitual justice."[12] This, however, only amounts to the distinction, already referred to, between the first and second justification. The infusion of righteousness renders the soul inherently righteous; then good works merit salvation. The one is the formal, the other the meritorious cause of the sinner's justification. But according to the Scriptures, both habitual and actual righteousness, both inherent grace and its fruits, are excluded from any share in the ground of our justification.

That justification is by faith alone still further and most decisively appears from the grand objection to his doctrine which Paul was constantly called upon to answer. That objection was that if our personal goodness or moral excellence is not the ground of our acceptance with God, then all necessity of being good is denied, and all motive to good works is removed. We may continue in sin that grace may abound. This objection has been reiterated a thousand times since it was urged against the apostles. It seems so unreasonable and so demoralizing to say, as Paul says in *Romans* 3:22, that, so far as justification is concerned, there is no difference between Jew and Gentile, between a worshiper of the true God and a worshiper of demons, between the greatest sinner and the most moral man in the world, that men have ever felt that they were doing God service in denouncing this doctrine as a soul-destroying heresy.

Had Paul taught that men are justified for their good moral works as the Pelagians and Rationalists say; or for their evangelical obedience as the Arminians say; or for their inherent righteousness and subsequent good works as the Romanists say, there would have been no room for this

Had Paul taught that men are justified for their good moral works as the Pelagians and Rationalists say; or for their evangelical obedience as the Arminians say; or for their inherent righteousness and subsequent good works as the Romanists say, there would have been no room for this formidable objection.

---

11. "Causam formalem justificationis esse justitiam, sive caritatem, quam Deus unicuique propriam infundit, secundum mensuram dispositionum, et quæ in cordibus justificatorum inhæret" (see Session vi, cap. 7).

12. "per modum instrumenti ad infusionem justitæ habitualis" (Bellarmin, *ut supra*, 820b).

formidable objection. Or, if through any misapprehension of his teaching the objection had been urged, how easy had it been for the apostle to set it aside. How obvious would have been the answer, "I do not deny that really good works are the ground of our acceptance with God. I only say that ritual works have no worth in his sight, that he looks on the heart"; or, that "works done before regeneration have no real excellence or merit"; or, that "God is more lenient now than in his dealing with Adam"; that "he does not demand perfect obedience, but accepts our imperfect, well-meant endeavors to keep his holy commandments." How reasonable and satisfactory would such answers have been.

Our own personal moral excellence has nothing to do with our justification; God justifies the ungodly; he receives the chief of sinners.

Paul, however, does not make them. He adheres to his doctrine that our own personal moral excellence has nothing to do with our justification; that God justifies the ungodly; that he receives the chief of sinners. He answers the objection indeed, and answers it effectually; but his answer supposes him to teach just what Protestants teach, that we are justified without works, not for our own righteousness, but gratuitously, without money and without price, solely on the ground of what Christ has done for us. His answer is that so far from its being true that we must be good before we can be justified, we must be justified before we can be good; that so long as we are under the curse of the law we bring forth fruit unto death; that it is not until reconciled unto God by the death of his Son that we bring forth fruit unto righteousness; that when justified by the righteousness of Christ we are made partakers of his Spirit; being justified we are sanctified; that union with Christ by faith secures not only the imputation of his righteousness to our justification, but the participation of his life unto our sanctification; so that as surely as he lives and lives unto God, so they that believe on him shall live unto God; and that none is a partaker of the merit of his death who does not become a partaker of the power of his life. We do not, therefore, he says, make void the law of God. Yea, we establish the law. We teach the only true way to become holy, although that way appears foolishness unto the wise of this world, whose wisdom is folly in the sight of God.

7

The Righteousness of Christ the Ground of Justification

Tʜᴇ imperative question remains, How shall a man be just with God? If our moral excellence be not the ground on which God pronounces us just, what is that ground? The grand reason why such different answers are given to this question is that it is understood in different senses. The Scriptural and Protestant answer is absurd, if the question means what Romanists and others understand it to mean. If *just* means *good*, that is, if the word be taken in its moral, and not in its judicial sense, then it is absurd to say that a man can be good with the goodness of another, or to say that God can pronounce a man to be good who is not good. Bellarmin says an Ethiopian clothed in a white garment is not white. Curcellæus the Arminian, says, "A man can no more be just with the justice of another than he can be white with the whiteness of another." Moehler says it is impossible that anything should appear to God other than it really is, that an unjust man should appear to him or be pronounced by him just.[1] All this is true in the sense intended by these writers, "The judgment of God is according to truth" (*Romans* 2:2). Every man is truly just whom he justifies or declares to be just. It is in vain to dispute until the *status quæstionis* be clearly determined.

The imperative question remains, How shall a man be just with God? If our moral excellence be not the ground on which God pronounces us just, what is that ground?

---

1. *Symbolik*, § 14, 6ᵗʰ edition, Mainz, 1843, 139.

The word δίκαιος "righteous," or "just," has two distinct senses, as above stated. It has a moral, and also a legal, forensic, or judicial sense. It sometimes expresses moral character, sometimes simply a relation to law and justice. In one sense, to pronounce a man just is to declare that he is morally good. In another sense, it is to declare that the claims of justice against him are satisfied, and that he is entitled to the reward promised to the righteous. When God justifies the ungodly, he does not declare that he is godly in himself, but that his sins are expiated, and that he has a title founded in justice to eternal life. In this there is no contradiction and no absurdity. If a man under attainder appear before the proper tribunal and show cause why the attainder should in justice be reversed, and he be declared entitled to his rank, titles, and estates, a decision in his favor would be a justification. It would declare him just in the eye of the law, but it would declare nothing and effect nothing as to his moral character. In the like manner, when the sinner stands at the bar of God, he can show good reason why he cannot be justly condemned and why he should be declared entitled to eternal life.

Now the question is, "On what ground can God pronounce a sinner just in this legal or forensic sense?" It has been shown that *to justify*, according to uniform Scriptural usage, is to pronounce just in the sense stated, that it is not merely to pardon, and that it is not to render inherently righteous or holy. It has also been shown to be the doctrine of Scripture, what indeed is intuitively true to the conscience, that our moral excellence – habitual or actual – is not and cannot be the ground of any such judicial declaration. What then is the ground? The Bible and the people of God with one voice answer, "The righteousness of Christ." The ambiguity of words, the speculations of theologians, and misapprehensions may cause many of the people of God to deny in words that such is the proper answer, but it is nevertheless the answer rendered by every believer's heart. He relies for his acceptance with God, not on himself but on Christ, not on what he is or has done, but on what Christ is and has done for him.

When God justifies the ungodly, he does not declare that he is godly in himself, but that his sins are expiated, and that he has a title founded in justice to eternal life.

Meaning of the Terms

By *the righteousness of Christ* is meant all he became, did, and suffered to satisfy the demands of divine justice and merit for his people the forgiveness of sin and the gift of eternal life. The righteousness of Christ is commonly represented as including his active and passive obedience. This distinction is Scriptural. The Bible does teach that Christ obeyed the law in all its precepts, and that he endured its penalty, and that this was done in such sense for his people that they are said to have done it. They died in him. They were crucified with him. They were delivered from the curse of the law by his being made a curse for them. He was made under the law that he might redeem those who were under the law. We are freed from the law by the body of Christ. He was made sin that we might be made the righteousness of God in him. He is the end of the law for righteousness to all them that believe. It is by his obedience that many are made righteous (*Romans* 5:19). We obeyed in him, according to the teaching of the apostle in *Romans* 5:12-21, in the same sense in which we sinned in Adam. The active and passive obedience of Christ, however, are only different phases or aspects of the same thing. He obeyed in suffering. His highest acts of obedience were rendered in the garden and upon the cross. Hence this distinction is not so presented in Scripture as though the obedience of Christ answered one purpose and his sufferings another and a distinct purpose. We are justified by his blood. We are reconciled unto God by his death. We are freed from all the demands of the law by his body (*Romans* 7:4), and we are freed from the law by his being made under it and obeying it in our stead (*Galatians* 4:4, 5). Thus the same effect is ascribed to the death or sufferings of Christ and to his obedience, because both are forms or parts of his obedience or righteousness by which we are justified. In other words, the obedience of Christ includes all he did in satisfying the demands of the law.

> *By the righteousness of Christ is meant all he became, did, and suffered to satisfy the demands of divine justice and merit for his people the forgiveness of sin and the gift of eternal life.*

The Righteousness of Christ Is the Righteousness of God

The righteousness of Christ, on the ground of which the believer is justified, is the righteousness of God. It is so designated in Scripture not only because it was provided and is accepted by him; it is not only the righteousness which avails before God, but it is the righteousness of a divine person of God manifest in the flesh. God purchased the Church with his own blood (*Acts* 20:28). It was the Lord of glory who was crucified (*1 Corinthians* 2:8). He who was in the form of God and thought it not robbery to be equal with God became obedient unto death, even the death of the cross (*Philippians* 2:6-8). He who is the brightness of the Father's glory and the express image of his person; who upholds all things by the word of his power; whom angels worship; who is called God; who in the beginning laid the foundations of the Earth, and of whose hands the heavens are the workmanship; who is eternal and immutable, has, the apostle teaches, by death destroyed him who has the power of death and delivered those who through fear of death (that is, of the wrath of God) were all their lifetime subject to bondage. He whom Thomas recognized and avowed to be his Lord and God was the person into whose wounded side he thrust his hand. He whom John says he saw, looked upon, and handled, he declares to be the true God and eternal life. The soul, in which personality resides, does not die when the man dies; yet it is the soul that gives dignity to the man, and which renders his life of unspeakably greater value in the sight of God and man than the life of any irrational creature. So it is not the divine nature in Christ in which his personality resides, the eternal Logos, that died when Christ died. Nevertheless the hypostatic union between the Logos and the human nature of Christ makes it true that the righteousness of Christ (his obedience and sufferings) was the righteousness of God. This is the reason why it can avail before God for the salvation of the whole world. This is the reason why the believer, when arrayed in this righteousness, need fear neither death nor Hell. This is the reason why Paul challenges the universe to lay anything to the charge of God's elect.

The soul, in which personality resides, does not die when the man dies; yet it is the soul that gives dignity to the man, and which renders his life of unspeakably greater value in the sight of God and man than the life of any irrational creature.

8

Imputation of Righteousness

THE RIGHTEOUSNESS of Christ is imputed to the believer
for his justification. The word *impute* is familiar and
unambiguous. To *impute* is to *ascribe to*, to *reckon to*, to *lay to
one's charge*. When we say we impute a good or bad motive
to a man, or that a good or evil action is imputed to him, no
one misunderstands our meaning. Philemon had no doubt
what Paul meant when he told him to impute to him the
debt of Onesimus. "Let not the king impute anything unto
his servant" (*1 Samuel* 22:15). "Let not my lord impute iniquity
unto me" (*2 Samuel* 19:19). "Neither shall it be imputed unto
him that offers it" (*Leviticus* 7:18). "Blood shall be imputed
unto that man; he has shed blood" (*Leviticus* 17:4). "Blessed is
the man unto whom the Lord imputes not iniquity" (*Psalm*
32:2). "Unto whom God imputes righteousness without
works" (*Romans* 4:6). God is "in Christ not imputing their
trespasses unto them" (*2 Corinthians* 5:19).

*We use the word
impute in its
simple, admitted
sense when we
say that the
righteousness of
Christ is imputed
to the believer for
his justification.*

The meaning of these and similar passages of Scripture
has never been disputed. Everyone understands them. We
use the word *impute* in its simple, admitted sense when we
say that the righteousness of Christ is imputed to the believer
for his justification.

It seems unnecessary to remark that this does not and
cannot mean that the righteousness of Christ is infused into
the believer, or in any way so imparted to him as to change

or constitute his moral character. Imputation never changes the inward, subjective state of the person to whom the imputation is made. When sin is imputed to a man he is not made sinful; when the zeal of Phinehas was imputed to him, he was not made zealous. When you impute theft to a man, you do not make him a thief. When you impute goodness to a man, you do not make him good. So when righteousness is imputed to the believer, he does not thereby become subjectively righteous. If the righteousness be adequate, and if the imputation be made on adequate grounds and by competent authority, the person to whom the imputation is made has the right to be treated as righteous. And, therefore, in the forensic (although not in the moral or subjective sense) the imputation of the righteousness of Christ does make the sinner righteous; that is, it gives him a right to the full pardon of all his sins and a claim in justice to eternal life.

In the forensic (although not in the moral or subjective sense) the imputation of the righteousness of Christ does make the sinner righteous; that is, it gives him a right to the full pardon of all his sins and a claim in justice to eternal life.

That this is the simple and universally accepted view of the doctrine as held by all Protestants at the Reformation and by them regarded as the cornerstone of the Gospel has already been sufficiently proved by extracts from the Lutheran and Reformed confessions, and has never been disputed by any candid or competent authority. This has continued to be the doctrine of both the great branches of the Protestant church, so far as they pretend to adhere to their standards. Schmid proves this by a whole catena of quotations so far as the Lutheran church is concerned.[1] Schweizer does the same for the Reformed church.[2] A few citations, therefore, from authors of a recognized representative character will suffice as to this point.

Turretin with his characteristic precision says,

When we say that Christ's righteousness is reckoned as justification to us, and that we are complete in the presence of God through that imputed righteousness, and not through any righteousness which is inherent in us, we wish

1. *Die Dogmatik der evangelisch – lutherischen Kirche, dargestellt und aus den Quellen belegt*, third edition, Frankfort and Erlangen, 1853.
2. *Die Glaubenslehre der evangelisch-reformirten Kirche dargestellt und aus den Quellen belegt*. Zürich, 1844, 1847.

nothing other than that Christ's obedience shown to God the Father in our name be thus granted to us by God, so that it is counted as truly ours, and that it is that one and only justice because of which, and because of whose worth, we are absolved from the charge of our sins. We maintain the right to life, not that there is any righteousness in us or any good works by which we deserve such kindness that is able to bear the severe examination of divine judgment, if God wishes to deal with us according to the strictness of his own law. We are able to offer nothing to him except Christ's worth and satisfaction, the only thing in which we, frightened by the knowledge of our sins, are able to find safe refuge from divine wrath and peace for our souls.[3]

On the following page he refers to Bellarmin, who says,

If they [Protestants] wished for [this] alone, that Christ's merits be imputed to us, because they have been granted to us [by God] and we can offer them to [God] the Father in the place of our sins, since Christ has taken the burden upon himself to apologize for us and to reconcile us to God the Father, their opinion would be correct.[4]

On this Turretin remarks,

But in fact we wish for nothing else; for this causes us to wish, "Let Christ's righteousness be so imputed to us that

3. "Cum dicimus Christi justitiam ad justificationem nobis imputari, et nos per justitiam illam imputatam justos esse coram Deo, et non per justitiam ullam quæ nobis inhæreat nihil aliud volumus, quam obedien–tiam Christi Deo Patri nomine nostro præstitam ita nobis a Deo donari, ut vere nostra censeatur, eamque esse unicam et solam illam justitiam propter quam, et cujus merito, absolvamur a reatu peccatorum nostrum, et jus ad vitam obtinemus; nec ullam in nobis esse justitiam, aut ulla bona opera, quibus beneficia tanta promereamur, quæ ferre possint severum judicii divini examen, si Deus juxta legis suæ rigorem, nobiscum agere vellet; nihil nos illi posse opponere, nisi Christi meritum et satisfactionem, in qua sola, peccatorum conscientia territi, tutum adversus iram divinam perfugium, et animarum nostrarum pacem invenire possumus" (*Institutio*, XVI, iii, 9, Edinburgh, 1847, Volume 11, 570).

4. "Si [Protestantes hoc] solum vellent, nobis imputari Christi merita, quia [a Deo] nobis donata sunt, et possumus ea [Deo] Patri offere pro peccatis nostris, quoniam Christus suscepit super se onus satisfaciendi pro nobis, nosque Deo Patri reconciliandi, recta esset eorum sententia" (*De Justificatione*, ii. 7; *Disputationes*, Paris, 1608, 801b).

"If they [Protestants] wished for [this] alone, that Christ's merits be imputed to us, because they have been granted to us [by God] and we can offer them to [God] the Father in the place of our sins, since Christ has taken the burden upon himself to apologize for us and to reconcile us to God the Father, their opinion would be correct."
—Cardinal Bellarmin

through it we are called, and are, formally perfect." This he supposes false and for nothing, out of his own distorted and perverse opinion about ethical justification. But it is asked, for what is this imputation done? Whether for justification and life, as we maintain, or in truth for the infusion of internal grace and inherent righteousness, as those men wish. That is, whether Christ's merits are reckoned and shared with us in such a way that they are the sole meritorious cause of our justification, and no other justice is given that absolves us in the sight of God, which is what we want; or whether Christ's merits are in fact so reckoned that they are the conditions of the formal cause of the same inherent justification that man can be granted – for example, Christ's merits are external causes that deserve the infusion of righteousness by which man is justified. Thus it is not Christ's worth exclusively, but inherent righteousness acquired through Christ's worth that is the true and lasting cause through which man is justified; this is what those men maintain.[5]

We are not rendered inherently righteous by the righteousness of Christ.

It may be remarked in passing that according to the Protestant doctrine there is properly no "formal cause" of justification. The righteousness of Christ is the meritorious but not the formal cause of the sinner's being pronounced righteous. A formal cause is that which constitutes the inherent, subjective nature of a person or thing. The formal cause of a man's being good is goodness; of his being holy, holiness; of his being wicked, wickedness. The formal cause of a rose's being red is redness; and of a wall's being white is whiteness. As we are not rendered inherently righteous by

5. "Atqui nihil aliud volumus; Nam quod addit, nos velle 'ita imputari nobis Christi justitiam, ut per earn formaliter justi nominemur et simus,' hoc gratis et falso supponit, ex perversa et præpostera sua hypothesi de justificatione morali. Sed quæritur, Ad quid imputatio ista fiat? An ad justificationem et vitam, ut nos pertendimus, An vero tantum ad gratiæ internæ et justitiæ inhærentis infusionem, ut illi volunt; Id est, an ita imputentur et communicentur nobis merita Christi, ut sint causa meritoria sola nostræ justificationis, nec ulla alia detur justitia propter quam absolvamur in conspectu Dei; quod volumus; An vero ita. imputentur, ut sint conditiones causæ formalis, id. justitiæ inhærentis ut ea homo donari possit, vel causæ extrinsecæ, quæ mereantur infusionem justitiæ, per quam justificatur homo; ut ita non meritum Christi proprie, sed justitia inhærens per meritum Christi acquisita, sic causa propria et vera, propter quam homo justificatur; quod illi statuunt."

the righteousness of Christ, it is hardly correct to say that his righteousness is the formal cause of our being righteous. Owen and other eminent writers do indeed often use the expression referred to, but they take the word "formal" out of its ordinary Scholastic sense.

Campegius Vitringa says:

> This most certain foundation must be maintained, that justification is a legal term and that it is written in the Scripture as the act of a judge whereby he declares that someone's cause is just in court; whether he absolves someone of a crime of which he has been accused (which is the genuine and most proper meaning of the word), or whether he awards the right to this case or grants someone that matter in his sentence.
>
> 17. By the justification of sinners we understand the action of God the Father as judge whereby he declares that the believing sinner, by nature the son of wrath and not holding any right for seeking heavenly goods outside himself, is immune from every accusation and condemnation; he adopts him as his son and, out of his grace, confers upon him the right to his communion, with eternal salvation and all goods associated with it.
>
> 27. Let us remember that no flesh is able to find in itself, or to produce outside itself, the cause and the foundation of justification.
>
> 29. Therefore, we must seek beyond the sinner for that through which the sinner is justified, to the obedience of God's Son, which he showed the Father in a human nature until death, even to the cross finally, and for the purpose of showing this obedience he had bound himself to a solemn promise (*Romans* 5:19).
>
> 32. This [obedience] is imputed to the sinner by God the judge, out of his grace, just as the right of the promise that was discussed earlier.[6]

"Justification is a legal term, and it is written in the Scripture as the act of a judge whereby he declares that someone's cause is just in court."
– Vitringa

---

6. "Tenendum est certissimum hoc fundamentum, quod justificare sit vocabulum forense, notetque in Scriptura actum judicis, quo causam alicujus in judicio justam esse declarat; sive eum a crimine, cujus postulatus est, absolvat (quæ est genuina, et maxime propria vocis significatio), sive etiam jus ad hanc, vel illam rem ei sententia addicat, et adjudicet.

"17. Per justificationem peccatoris intelligimus actum Dei Patris, ut judicis, quo peccatorem credentem, natura filium iræ neque ullum jus ex se habentem bona cœlestia petendi, declarat immunem esse ab omni reatu, et condemnatione, adoptat in filium, et in eum ex gratia confert jus

Owen in his elaborate work on justification proves that the word *to justify* – "whether the act of God toward men, or of men toward God, or of men among themselves, or of one toward another be expressed thereby – is always used in a 'forensic' sense, and does not denote a physical operation, transfusion, or transmutation."[7] He thus winds up the discussion:

> Wherefore as condemnation is not the infusing of a habit of wickedness into him that is condemned, nor the making of him to be inherently wicked who was before righteous, but the passing a sentence upon a man with respect to his wickedness; no more is justification the change of a person from inherent unrighteousness to righteousness by the infusion of a principle of grace, but a sentential declaration of him to be righteous.[8]

The ground of this justification in the case of the believing sinner is the imputation of the righteousness of Christ. This is set forth at length.[9] "The judgment of the Reformed Churches herein," he says,

> is known to all and must be confessed, unless we intend by vain cavils to increase and perpetuate contentions. Especially the Church of England is in her doctrine express as to the imputation of the righteousness of Christ, both active and passive, as it is usually distinguished. This has been of late so fully manifested out of her authentic writings, that is, the "Articles of Religion" and "Books of Homilies," and other writings publicly authorized, that it is altogether needless to give any further demonstration of it.

Owen in his elaborate work on justification proves that the word to justify... is always used in a "forensic sense, and does not denote a physical operation, transfusion, or transmutation."

---

ad suam communionem, cum salute æterna, bonisque omnibus cum ea conjunctis, postulandi.

"27. Teneamus nullam carnem in se posse reperire et ex se producere causam, et fundamentum justificationis.

"29. Quærendum igitur id, propter quod peccator justificatur, extra peccatorem in obedientia Filii Dei, quam præstitit Patri in humana natura ad mortem, imo ad mortem crucis, et ad quam præstandam se obstrinxerat in sponsione (*Romans* 5:19).

"32. Hæc [obedientia] imputatur peccatori a Deo judice ex gratia juxta jus sponsionis, de quo ante dictum" (*Doctrina Christianæ Religionis*, III, xvi, 2; Leyden, 1764. Volume III, 254*ff*.)

7. *Justification* (Philadelphia, 1841), 144.

8. *Justification*, 154.

9. *Justification*, 187.

President Edwards in his sermon on justification sets forth the Protestant doctrine in all its fulness. "To suppose," he says,

> that a man is justified by his own virtue or obedience derogates from the honor of the Mediator and ascribes that to man's virtue what belongs only to the righteousness of Christ. It puts man in Christ's stead, and makes him his own savior, in a respect in which Christ only is the Savior: And so it is a doctrine contrary to the nature and design of the Gospel, which is to abase man and to ascribe all the glory of our salvation to Christ the Redeemer. It is inconsistent with the doctrine of the imputation of Christ's righteousness, which is a gospel doctrine. Here I would (1) Explain what we mean by the imputation of Christ's righteousness. (2) Prove the thing intended by it to be true. (3) Show that this doctrine is utterly inconsistent with the doctrine of our being justified by our own virtue or sincere obedience.
>
> First, I would explain what we mean by the imputation of Christ's righteousness. Sometimes the expression is taken by our divines in a larger sense, for the imputation of all that Christ did and suffered for our redemption, whereby we are free from guilt and stand righteous in the sight of God; and so implies the imputation both of Christ's satisfaction and obedience. But here I intend it in a stricter sense, for the imputation of that righteousness or moral goodness that consists in the obedience of Christ. And by that righteousness being imputed to us is meant no other than this: that that righteousness of Christ is accepted for us and admitted instead of that perfect inherent righteousness that ought to be in ourselves. Christ's perfect obedience shall be reckoned to our account so that we shall have the benefit of it as though we had performed it ourselves: And so we suppose that a title to eternal life is given us as the reward of this righteousness.

In the same connection he asks,

> Why is there any more absurdity in supposing that Christ's obedience is imputed to us than that his satisfaction is imputed? If Christ has suffered the penalty of the law for us and in our stead, then it will follow that his suffering that penalty is imputed to us, that is, that it is accepted for us, and in our stead, and is reckoned to our account as though we had suffered it. But why may not his obeying the law of God

"By that righteousness being imputed to us is meant no other than this: that that righteousness of Christ is accepted for us and admitted instead of that perfect inherent righteousness that ought to be in ourselves."
– Jonathan Edwards

be as rationally reckoned to our account as his suffering the penalty of the law?[10]

He then goes on to argue that there is the same necessity for the one as for the other.

Dr. Shedd says,

> A second difference between the Anselmic and the Protestant soteriology is seen in the formal distinction of Christ's work into his active and his passive righteousness. By his passive righteousness is meant his expiatory sufferings, by which he satisfied the claims of justice, and by his active righteousness is meant his obedience to the law as a rule of life and conduct. It was contended by those who made this distinction that the purpose of Christ as the vicarious substitute was to meet the entire demands of the law for the sinner. But the law requires present and perfect obedience, as well as satisfaction for past disobedience. The law is not completely fulfilled by the endurance of penalty only. It must also be obeyed. Christ both endured the penalty due to man for disobedience and perfectly obeyed the law for him, so that he was a vicarious substitute in reference to both the precept and the penalty of the law. By his active obedience he obeyed the law and by his passive obedience he endured the penalty. In this way his vicarious work is complete.[11]

The earlier confessions of the Reformation do not make this distinction. So far as the Lutheran church is concerned, it first appears in the *Formula of Concord* (A.D. 1576). Its statement is as follows:

> That righteousness which is imputed to faith or to believers, of mere grace, is the obedience, suffering, and resurrection of Christ, by which he satisfied the law for us and expiated our sins. For since Christ was not only man, but truly God and man in one undivided person, he was no more subject to the law than he was to suffering and death (if his person, merely, be taken into account), because he was the Lord of the law. Hence, not only that obedience to God his Father which he exhibited in his passion and death, but also that

"By his active obedience he obeyed the law and by his passive obedience he endured the penalty. In this way his vicarious work is complete."
– W. G. T. Shedd

10. Sermon IV, *Works*, New York, 1868, Volume IV, 91, 92.
11. *History of Christian Doctrine*, New York, 1863, Volume II, 341.

obedience which he exhibited in voluntarily subjecting himself to the law and fulfilling it for our sakes, is imputed to us for righteousness, so that God on account of the total obedience which Christ accomplished (*præstitit*) for our sake before his heavenly Father, both in acting and in suffering, in life and in death, may remit our sins to us, regard us as good and righteous, and give us eternal salvation.[12]

In this point the Reformed or Calvinistic standards agree.

It has already been remarked that the distinction between the active and passive obedience of Christ is, in one view, unimportant. As Christ obeyed in suffering, his sufferings were as much a part of his obedience as his observance of the precepts of the law. The Scriptures do not expressly make this distinction, as they include everything that Christ did for our redemption under the term *righteousness* or *obedience*. The distinction becomes important only when it is denied that his moral obedience is any part of the righteousness for which the believer is justified, or that his whole work in making satisfaction consisted in expiation or bearing the penalty of the law. This is contrary to Scripture and vitiates the doctrine of justification as presented in the Bible.

The distinction between the active and passive obedience of Christ becomes important only when it is denied that his moral obedience is any part of the righteousness for which the believer is justified.

12. Hase, *Libri Symbolici*, third edition, Leipzig, 1846, 684-685.

9
Proof of the Doctrine

THAT THE Protestant doctrine as above stated is the doctrine of the Word of God appears from the following considerations:

We are not at liberty to say that the righteousness of one man cannot be imputed to another; that this would involve a mistake or absurdity.

The word δικαιόω as has been shown, means to declare δίκαιος. No one can be truthfully pronounced δίκαιος to whom δικαιοσύνη cannot rightfully be ascribed. The sinner (*ex vi verbi*) has no righteousness of his own. God, therefore, imputes to him a righteousness which is not his own. The righteousness thus imputed is declared to be the righteousness of God, of Christ, the righteousness which is by faith. This is almost in so many words the declaration of the Bible on the subject. As the question, What is the method of justification? is a Biblical question, it must be decided exegetically and not by arguments drawn from assumed principles of reason. We are not at liberty to say that the righteousness of one man cannot be imputed to another; that this would involve a mistake or absurdity; that God's justice does not demand a righteousness such as the law prescribes as the condition of justification; that he may pardon and save as a father without any consideration, unless it be that of repentance; that it is inconsistent with his grace that the demands of justice should be met before justification is granted; that this view of justification makes it a sham, a calling a man just, when he is not just, etc. All this amounts to nothing. It all pertains to that wisdom which is foolishness with God. All we have to do is to determine (1) What is the meaning of the word *to justify* as used in Scripture? (2) On what ground does the Bible affirm that God pronounces the ungodly to be just? If the answer to these questions be what the church in all ages, and especially the church of the Reformation, has given, then we should rest satisfied. The apostle in express terms says that God imputes righteousness to the sinner (*Romans* 4:6, 24). By *righteousness* everyone admits is meant that which makes a man righteous, that which the law demands. It does not consist in the sinner's own obedience or moral excellence, for it is said to be "without works"; and it is declared that no man can be justified on the ground of his own character or conduct. Neither does this righteousness consist in faith; for it is "of faith," "through faith," "by faith." We are never said to be justified on account of faith. Neither is it a righteousness or form of moral excellence springing from faith or of which faith is the source or proximate cause, because it is declared to be the righteousness of God – a righteousness which is revealed, which is offered, which must be accepted as a gift (*Romans* 5:17). It is declared to be the righteousness of Christ – his obedience (*Romans* 5:19). It is, therefore, the righteousness of Christ, his perfect obedience in doing and suffering the will of God which is imputed to the believer, and on the ground of which the believer, although in himself ungodly, is pronounced righteous and therefore free from the curse of the law and entitled to eternal life.

The Apostle's Argument

All the points above stated are not only clearly affirmed by the apostle but they are also set forth in logical order and elaborately sustained and vindicated in the epistle to the Romans. The apostle begins with the declaration that the Gospel "is the power of God unto salvation." It is not thus divinely efficacious because of the purity of its moral precepts, nor because it brings immortality to light, nor because it sets before us the perfect example of our Lord Jesus Christ, nor because it assures us of the love of God, nor because of

The apostle in express terms says that God imputes righteousness to the sinner (Romans 4:6, 24). By righteousness everyone admits is meant that which makes a man righteous, that which the law demands. It does not consist in the sinner's own obedience or moral excellence.

The first and indispensable requisite to salvation is that men should be righteous before God. They are under his wrath and curse. Until justice is satisfied, until God is reconciled, there is no possibility of any moral influence being of any avail.

the elevating, sanctifying, life-giving influence by which it is attended. There is something preliminary to all this. The first and indispensable requisite to salvation is that men should be righteous before God. They are under his wrath and curse. Until justice is satisfied, until God is reconciled, there is no possibility of any moral influence being of any avail. Therefore the apostle says that the power of the Gospel is due to the fact that "therein is the righteousness of God revealed." This cannot mean the goodness of God, for such is not the meaning of the word. It cannot in this connection mean his justice, because it is a righteousness which is "of faith," because the justice of God is revealed from Heaven and to all men, because the revelation of justice terrifies and drives away from God, because what is here called the "righteousness of God" is elsewhere contrasted with our "own righteousness" (*Romans* 10:3, *Philippians* 3:9), and because it is declared to be the righteousness of Christ (*Romans* 5:18) which is (*Romans* 5:19) explained by his "obedience" and in *Romans* 5:9 and elsewhere declared to be "his blood." This righteousness of Christ is the righteousness of God because Christ is God – because God has provided, revealed, and offers it, and because it avails before God as a sufficient ground on which he can declare the believing sinner righteous. Herein lies the saving power of the Gospel. The question, How shall man be just with God? had been sounding in the ears of men from the beginning. It never had been answered. Yet it must be answered or there can be no hope of salvation. It is answered in the Gospel, and therefore the Gospel is the power of God unto salvation to everyone who believes; that is, to everyone, whether Jew or Gentile, bond or free, good or bad, who, instead of going about to establish his own righteousness, submits himself in joyful confidence to the righteousness which his God and Savior Jesus Christ has wrought out for sinners, and which is freely offered to them in the Gospel without money and without price.

This is Paul's theme, which he proceeds to unfold and establish, as has been already stated under a previous head. He begins by asserting, as indisputably true from the revelation of God in the constitution of our nature, that God is just, that he will punish sin, that he cannot pronounce him righteous who is not righteous. He then shows from experience and from Scripture – first as regards the Gentiles, then as regards the Jews – that there is none righteous, no not one, that the whole world is guilty before God. There is therefore no difference, since all have sinned.

Since the righteousness which the law requires cannot be found in the sinner nor be rendered by him, God has revealed another righteousness, "the righteousness of God" (*Romans* 3:21), granted to every one who believes. Men are not justified for what they are or for what they do, but for what Christ has done for them. God has set him forth as a propitiation for sin, in order that he might be just and yet the justifier of them that believe.

The apostle teaches that such has been the method of justification from the beginning. It was witnessed by the law and the prophets. There had never, since the Fall, been any other way of justification possible for men. As God justified Abraham because he believed in the promise of redemption through the Messiah, so he justifies those now who believe in the fulfillment of that promise (*Romans* 4:3, 9, 24). It was not Abraham's believing state of mind that was taken for righteousness. It is not faith in the believer now – not faith as a virtue or as a source of a new life which renders us righteous. It is faith in a specific promise. Righteousness, says the apostle, is imputed to us "if we believe on him that raised up Jesus our Lord from the dead" (*Romans* 4:24). Or, as he expresses it in *Romans* 10:9: "If you shall confess with your mouth the Lord Jesus and shall believe in your heart that God has raised him from the dead, you shall be saved."

The promise which Abraham believed is the promise which we believe (*Galatians* 3:14), and the relation of faith to justification, in his case, is precisely what it is in ours. He and we are justified simply because we trust in the Messiah for our salvation. Hence, as the apostle says, the Scriptures are full of thanksgiving to God for gratuitous pardon, for free justification, for the imputation of righteousness to those

There had never, since the Fall, been any other way of justification possible for men. As God justified Abraham because he believed in the promise of redemption through the Messiah, so he justifies those now who believe in the fulfillment of that promise (Romans 4:3, 9, 24).

who have no righteousness of their own. This method of justification, he goes on to show, is adapted to all mankind. God is not the God of the Jews only but also of the Gentiles. It secures peace and reconciliation with God (*Romans* 5:1-3). It renders salvation certain, for if we are saved not by what we are in ourselves, but for what Christ has done for us, we may be sure that if we are "justified by his blood, we shall be saved from wrath through him" (*Romans* 5:9). This method of justification, he further shows, and this only, secures sanctification, namely, holiness of heart and life. It is only those who are reconciled to God by the death of his Son that are "saved by his life" (verse 10). This idea he expands and vindicates in the sixth and seventh chapters of this epistle.

The Parallel Between Adam and Christ

Not content with this clear and formal statement of the truth that sinners can be justified only through the imputation of a righteousness not their own and that the righteousness thus imputed is the righteousness (active and passive if that distinction be insisted upon) of the Lord Jesus Christ, he proceeds to illustrate this doctrine by drawing a parallel between Adam and Christ. The former, he says, was a type of the latter. There is an analogy between our relation to Adam and our relation to Christ. We are so united to Adam that his first transgression was the ground of the sentence of condemnation being passed on all mankind, and on account of that condemnation we derive from him a corrupt nature so that all mankind descending from him by ordinary generation come into the world in a state of spiritual death. In like manner, we are so united to Christ when we believe that his obedience is the ground on which a sentence of justification passes upon all thus in him, and in consequence of that sentence they derive from him a new, holy, divine, and imperishable principle of spiritual life. These truths are expressed in explicit terms: "The judgment was by one [offense] to condemnation, but the free gift is of many offenses unto justification" (*Romans* 5:16). "Therefore, as by the offense of one, judgment came upon all men to

We are so united to Adam that his first transgression was the ground of the sentence of condemnation being passed on all mankind, and on account of that condemnation we derive from him a corrupt nature.

condemnation; even so by the righteousness of one the free gift came upon all men unto justification of life. For as by one man's disobedience many were made sinners, so by the obedience of one shall many be made righteous" (verses 18-19).

These two great truths, namely, the imputation of Adam's sin and the imputation of Christ's righteousness, have graven themselves on the consciousness of the church universal. They have been reviled, misrepresented, and denounced by theologians; but they have stood their ground in the faith of God's people, just as the primary truths of reason have ever retained control over the mass of men, in spite of all the speculations of philosophers. It is not meant that the truths just mentioned have always been expressed in the terms just given, but the truths themselves have been and still are held by the people of God, wherever found, among the Greeks, Latins, or Protestants. The fact that the race fell in Adam, that the evils which come upon us on account of his transgression are penal, and that men are born in a state of sin and condemnation are outstanding facts of Scripture and history and are avowed every time the sacrament of baptism is administered to an infant. No less universal is the conviction of the other great truth. It is implied in every act of saving faith which includes trust in what Christ has done for us as the ground of our acceptance with God, as opposed to anything done by us or wrought in us. As a single proof of the hold which this conviction has on the Christian consciousness, reference may be made to the ancient direction for the visitation of the sick attributed to Anselm but of doubtful authorship:

> Do you believe that you cannot be saved but by the death of Christ? The sick man answers, Yes. Then let it be said unto him, Go to, then, and while your soul abides in you, put all your confidence in this death alone, place your trust in no other thing, commit yourself wholly to this death, cover yourself wholly with this alone, cast yourself wholly on this death, wrap yourself wholly in this death. And if God would judge you, say, Lord, I place the death of our Lord Jesus Christ between me and your judgment, and otherwise I will

These two great truths, namely, the imputation of Adam's sin and the imputation of Christ's righteousness, have graven themselves on the consciousness of the church universal. They have been reviled, misrepresented, and denounced by theologians.

not contend or enter into judgment with you. And if he shall say unto you that you are a sinner, say, I place the death of our Lord Jesus Christ between me and my sins. If he shall say unto you that you have deserved damnation, say, Lord, I put the death of our Lord Jesus Christ between you and all my sins and I offer his merits for my own, which I should have, and have not. If he say that he is angry with you, say, Lord, I place the death of our Lord Jesus Christ between me and your anger.[1]

Every assertion or promise of gratuitious forgiveness of sin to be found in the Scriptures involves this doctrine.

Such being the real and only foundation of a sinner's hope toward God, it is of the last importance that it should not only be practically held by the people, but that it should also be clearly presented and maintained by the clergy. it is not what we do or are, but solely what Christ is and has done that can avail for our justification before the bar of God.

Other Passages Teaching the Same Doctrine

This doctrine of the imputation of the righteousness of Christ – or, in other words, that his righteousness is the judicial ground of the believer's justification – is not only formally and argumentatively presented as in the passages cited, but it is constantly asserted or implied in the Word of God. The apostle argues, in the fourth chapter of his epistle to the Romans, that every assertion or promise of gratuitious forgiveness of sin to be found in the Scriptures involves this doctrine. He proceeds on the assumption that God is just, that he demands a righteousness of those whom he justifies. If they have no righteousness of their own, one on just grounds must be imputed to them. If, therefore, he forgives sin, it must be that sin is covered, that justice has been satisfied. "David, also," he says, "describes the blessedness of the man unto whom God imputes righteousness without works, saying, 'Blessed are they whose iniquities are forgiven, and whose sins are covered. Blessed is the man to whom the Lord will not impute sin'" (*Romans* 4:6-8). Not to impute sin implies the imputation of righteousness.

1. See "The General Considerations," prefixed by Owen to his work on *Justification*.

In *Romans* 5:9 we are said to be "justified by his [Christ's] blood." In *Romans* 3:25 God is said to have set Christ forth as a propitiation for sin, that he (God) might be just in justifying the ungodly. As *to justify* does not mean *to pardon*, but judicially *to pronounce righteous*, this passage distinctly asserts that the work of Christ is the ground on which the sentence of justification is passed. In *Romans* 10:3-4, he says of the Jews, "They, being ignorant of God's righteousness, and going about to establish their own righteousness, have not submitted themselves unto the righteousness of God. For Christ is the end of the law for righteousness to everyone who believes." It can hardly be questioned that the word *righteousness* (δικαιοσύνη) must have the same meaning in both members of the first of these verses. If a man's "own righteousness" is that which would render him righteous, then "the righteousness of God" in this connection must be a justifying righteousness. It is called the righteousness of God, because, as said before, he is its author. It is the righteousness of Christ. It is provided, offered, and accepted of God.

Here then are two righteousnesses: the one human, the other divine; the one valueless, the other infinitely meritorious. The folly of the Jews, and of thousands since their day, consists in refusing the latter and trusting to the former. This folly the apostle makes apparent in the fourth verse. The Jews acted under the assumption that the law as a covenant, that is, as prescribing the conditions of salvation, was still in force, that men were still bound to satisfy its demands by their personal obedience in order to be saved, whereas Christ had made an end of the law. He had abolished it as a covenant in order that men might be justified by faith. Christ, however, has thus made an end of the law, not by merely setting it aside, but by satisfying its demands. He delivers us from its curse, not by mere pardon, but by being made a curse for us (*Galatians* 3:13). He redeems us from the law by being made under it (*Galatians* 4:4-5), and fulfilling all righteousness.

In *Philippians* 3:8-9 the apostle says he "suffered the loss of all things" that he might be found in Christ, not having his "own righteousness, which is of the law, but that which

The Jews acted under the assumption that the law as a covenant, that is, as prescribing the conditions of salvation, was still in force, that men were still bound to satisfy its demands by their personal obedience in order to be saved, whereas Christ had made an end of the law. He had abolished it as a covenant in order that men might be justified by faith.

is through the faith of Christ, the righteousness which is of God by faith." Here again one's own righteousness is contrasted with that which is of God. The word must have the same sense in both members. What Paul trusted to was not his own righteousness, not his own subjective goodness, but a righteousness provided for him and received by faith. De Wette (no Augustinian) on this passage says the righteousness here means "a righteousness received from God (graciously imputed) on condition of faith" ("die von Gott empfangene [aus Gnaden zugerechnete] Gerechtigkeit um des Glaubenswillen").

The apostle says (*1 Corinthians* 1:30) Christ "of God is made unto us wisdom, and righteousness, and sanctification, and redemption." In this enumeration, sanctification and righteousness are distinguished. The former renders us holy; the latter renders us just, that is, satisfies the demands of justice. As Christ is to us the source of inward spiritual life, so he is the giver of that righteousness which secures our justification. Justification is not referred to sanctification as its proximate cause and grounds. On the contrary, the gift of righteousness precedes that of sanctification. We are justified in order that we may be sanctified. The point here, however, is that righteousness is distinguished from anything and everything in us which can recommend us to the favor of God. We are accepted, justified, and saved, not for what we are, but for what he has done in our behalf. God "made him to be sin for us, who knew no sin; that we might be made the righteousness of God in him" (*2 Corinthians* 5:21). As Christ was not made sin in a moral sense, so we are not (in justification) made righteous in a moral sense. As he was made sin in that he "bore our sins...so we are made righteousness in that we bear his righteousness. Our sins were the judicial ground of his humiliation under the law and of all his sufferings; so his righteousness is the judicial ground of our justification. In other words, as our sins were imputed to him, so his righteousness is imputed to us. If imputation of sin did not render him morally corrupt, the imputation of righteousness does not make us holy or morally good.

As our sins were imputed to him, so his righteousness is imputed to us. If imputation of sin did not render him morally corrupt, the imputation of righteousness does not make us holy or morally good.

Argument from the General Teaching of the Bible

It is unnecessary to dwell upon particular passages in support of a doctrine which pervades the whole Scriptures. The question is, What is the ground of the pardon of sin and of the acceptance of the believer as righteous (in the forensic or judicial sense of the word), in the sight of God? Is it anything we do, anything experienced by us or wrought in us? Or is it what Christ has done for us? The whole revelation of God concerning the method of salvation shows that it is the latter and not the former. In the first place, this is plain from what the Scriptures teach of the covenant of redemption between the Father and the Son. That there was such covenant cannot be denied if the meaning of the words be once agreed upon. It is plain from Scripture that Christ came into the world to do a certain work, on a certain condition. The promise made to him was that a multitude, whom no man can number, of the fallen race of man should be saved. This included the promise that they should be justified, sanctified, and made partakers of eternal life. The very nature of this transaction involves the idea of vicarious substitution. It assumes that what he was to do was to be the ground of the justification, sanctification, and salvation of his people.

In the second place, this is involved in the nature of the work which he came to perform. He was to assume our nature, to be born of a woman, to take part of flesh and blood with all their infirmities, yet without sin. He was to take his place among sinners, be made subject to the law which they are bound to obey, and to endure the curse which they had incurred. If this be so, then what he did is the ground of our salvation from first to last: of our pardon, of our reconciliation with God, of the acceptance of our persons, of the indwelling of the Spirit, of our being transformed into his image, and of our admission into Heaven. "Not unto us, O Lord, not unto us, but unto your name give glory," has, therefore, been the spontaneous language of every believer from the beginning until now.

In the third place, the manner in which Christ was to execute the work assigned as described in the prophets, and the way

> *What Christ did is the ground of our salvation from first to last: of our pardon, of our reconciliation with God, of the acceptance of our persons, of the indwelling of the Spirit, of our being transformed into his image, and of our admission into Heaven.*

If Christ saves us as a sacrifice, then it is what he does for us – his objective work and nothing subjective, nothing in us – which is the ground of our salvation and of all that salvation includes. Even our sanctification is due to his death.

in which it was actually accomplished as described by himself and by his apostles, prove that what he did and suffered is the ground of our salvation. He says that he came "to give his life a ransom for many" (*Matthew* 20:28). "There is one God," says the apostle, "and one mediator between God and men, the man Christ Jesus, who gave himself a ransom for all" (*1 Timothy* 2:5-6). The deliverance effected by a ransom has no reference to the character or conduct of the redeemed. Its effects are due exclusively to the ransom paid. It is, therefore, to deny that Christ was a ransom – that we are redeemed by his blood – to affirm that the proximate ground of our deliverance from the curse of the law and of our introduction into the liberty of the sons of God is anything wrought in us or done by us. Again, from the beginning to the end of the Bible, Christ is represented as a sacrifice. From the first institution of sacrifices in the family of Adam, during the patriarchal period, in all the varied and costly ritual of the Mosaic law, in the predictions of the prophets, and in the clear didactic statements of the New Testament it is taught with a constancy, a solemnity, and an amplitude which proves it to be a fundamental and vital element of the divine plan of redemption that the Redeemer was to save his people by offering himself as a sacrifice unto God in their behalf. There is no one characteristic of the plan of salvation more deeply engraven on the hearts of Christians which more effectually determines their inward spiritual life, which so much pervades their prayers and praises, or which is so directly the foundation of their hopes as the sacrificial nature of the death of Christ. Strike from the Bible the doctrine of redemption by the blood of Christ, and what have we left? But if Christ saves us as a sacrifice, then it is what he does for us – his objective work and nothing subjective, nothing in us – which is the ground of our salvation and of all that salvation includes. Even our sanctification is due to his death. His blood cleanses from all sin (*1 John* 1:7). It cleanses from the guilt of sin by expiation and secures inward sanctification by securing the gift of the Holy Spirit.

Again, the whole Bible is full of the idea of substitution. Christ took our place; he undertook to do for us what we could not do for ourselves. This is taught in every possible way. He bore our sins. He died for us and in our place; he was made under the law for us. He was made a curse for us. He was made sin for us that we might be made the righteousness of God in him. The chastisement of our peace was laid upon him. Everything, therefore, which the Bible teaches of the method of salvation is irreconcilable with the doctrine of subjective justification in all its forms. We are always and everywhere referred to something outside of ourselves as the ground of our confidence toward God.

In the fourth place, the effects ascribed to the work of Christ (as before remarked) are such as do not flow from anything in the believer himself, but must be referred to what has been done for him. These effects are expiation of sin; propitiation; the gift and indwelling of the life-giving Spirit of God; redemption, or deliverance from all forms of evil; and a title to eternal life and actual participation in the exaltation, glory, and blessedness of the Son of God. It is out of all question that these wonderful effects should be referred to what we personally are – to our merit, to our holiness, to our participation of the life of Christ. In whatever sense these last words may be understood, they refer to what we personally are or become. His life in us is after all a form of our life. It constitutes our character. And it is self-evident to the conscience that our character is not and cannot be the ground of our pardon, of God's peculiar love, or of our eternal glory and blessedness in Heaven.

In the fifth place, the condition on which our participation in the benefits of redemption is suspended is inconsistent with any form of the doctrine of subjective justification. We are never said to be justified on account of faith, considered either as an act or as a principle, as an exercise or as a permanent state of the mind. Faith is never said to be the ground of justification. Nor are we saved by faith as the source of holiness or of spiritual life in the soul or as the organ of receiving the infused life of God. We are saved simply "by" faith, by receiving and resting upon Christ alone for salvation. The thing received is something out of

Everything, therefore, which the Bible teaches of the method of salvation is irreconcilable with the doctrine of subjective justification in all its forms. We are always and everywhere referred to something outside of ourselves as the ground of our confidence toward God.

ourselves. It is Christ, his righteousness, his obedience, the merit of his blood or death. We look to him. We flee to him. We lay hold on him. We hide ourselves in him. We are clothed in his righteousness. The Romanist indeed says that an Ethiopian in a white robe does not become white. True, but a suit of armor gives security from the sword or spear, and that is what we need before attending to the state of our complexion. We need protection from the wrath of God in the first instance. The inward transformation of the soul into his likeness is provided for by other means.

In the sixth place and finally, the fact that we are saved by grace proves that the ground of salvation is not in ourselves. The grace of God, his love for the unlovely, for the guilty and polluted, is represented in the Bible as the most mysterious of the divine perfections. It was hidden in God. It could not be discovered by reason, neither was it revealed prior to the redemption of man. The specific object of the plan of salvation is the manifestation of this most wonderful, most attractive, and most glorious attribute of the divine nature. Everything connected with our salvation, says the apostle, is intended for the "praise of the glory of his grace" (*Ephesians* 1:6). God has quickened us, he says, and raised us up, and made us sit together in heavenly places in Christ Jesus, in order "that in the ages to come, he might show the exceeding riches of this grace in his kindness toward us through Christ Jesus."

Grace and works are antithetical. The one excludes the other. What is of grace is not of works. And by works in Scripture, in relation to this subject, is meant not individual acts only, but states of mind, anything and everything internal of which moral character can be predicated.

From their nature, grace and works are antithetical. The one excludes the other. What is of grace is not of works. And by *works* in Scripture, in relation to this subject, is meant not individual acts only, but states of mind, anything and every-thing internal of which moral character can be predicated. When, therefore, it is said that salvation is of grace and not of works, it is thereby said that it is not founded upon anything in the believer himself. It was not any moral excellence in man that determined God to interpose for his redemption, while he left the apostate angels to their fate. This was a mat-ter of grace. To deny this and to make the provision of a plan of salvation for man a matter of justice is in such direct contradiction to everything in the Bible that it hardly ever has been openly asserted. The gift of his Son for the redemption of man is ever represented as the most wonderful display of unmerited love. That some and not all men are actually saved is expressly declared to be not of works, not on account of anything distinguishing favorably the one class from the other, but a matter of pure grace. When a sinner is pardoned and restored to the favor of God, this again is declared to be of grace. If of grace, it is not founded upon anything in the sinner himself. Now as the Scriptures not only teach that the plan of salvation is thus gratuitous in its inception, execution, and application, but also insist upon this characteristic of the plan as of vital importance, and even go so far as to teach that unless we consent to be saved by grace we cannot be saved at all, it of necessity follows that the doctrine of subjective justification is contrary to the whole spirit of the Bible. That doctrine in all its forms teaches that that which secures our acceptance with God is something in ourselves, something which constitutes character. If so, then salvation is not of grace; and if not of grace, it is unattainable by sinners.

The doctrine of subjective justification is contrary to the whole spirit of the Bible. That doctrine in all its forms teaches that that which secures our acceptance with God is something in ourselves, something which constitutes character. If so, then salvation is not of grace; and if not of grace, it is unattainable by sinners.

10

The Consequences of the Imputation of Righteousness

By the remission of sin, Romanists understand the removal of the pollution of sin. Their definition of justification as consisting in the remission of sin and infusion of righteousness is only a statement of the negative and positive aspects of sanctification.

IT IS frequently said that justification consists in the pardon of sin and in the imputation of righteousness. This mode of statement is commonly adopted by Lutheran theologians. This exhibition of the doctrine is founded upon the sharp distinction made in the *Formula of Concord* between the passive and active obedience of Christ. To the former is referred the remission of the penalty due to us for sin; to the latter our title to eternal life. The Scriptures, however, do not make this distinction so prominent. Our justification as a whole is sometimes referred to the blood of Christ and sometimes to his obedience. This is intelligible because the crowning act of his obedience, and that without which all else had been unavailing, was his laying down his life for us. It is, perhaps, more correct to say that the righteousness of Christ, including all he did and suffered in our stead, is imputed to the believer as the ground of his justification, and that the consequences of this imputation are, first, the remission of sin, and secondly, the acceptance of the believer as righteous. And if righteous, then he is entitled to be so regarded and treated.

By the *remission of sin*, Romanists understand the removal of the pollution of sin. Their definition of *justification* as consisting in the remission of sin and infusion of righteousness is only a statement of the negative and positive aspects of sanctification, that is, putting off the old man and putting on the new man. The effect of remission is constantly declared to be that nothing of the nature of sin remains in the soul. The Council of Trent says,

> Justification...is not only a remission of sins, but also sanctification and renewal of the inner man through the voluntary undertaking of grace and gifts.... Although no one is able to be perfect unless the merits of our Lord Jesus Christ's suffering are conferred upon him, nevertheless this happens in the justification of a godless man, while because of the worth of the same most sacred suffering, the love of God is extended to the hearts of those who are justified through the Holy Spirit, and it cleaves to them.
>
> With these words is the description of a godless man's justification introduced, so that it is a change from the condition in which man is born as the son of the first Adam, to a state of grace and by adoption the sons of God, through the second Adam, our savior Jesus Christ. Indeed, since the publication of the gospel, this change cannot happen without the washing of regeneration or his will.[1]

By *status gratiæ* in this definition is not meant a state of favor, but a state of subjective grace or holiness; because in other places and most commonly justification is said to consist in the infusion of grace. In this definition, therefore, the pardon of sin in the proper sense of the words is not included. Bellarmin says this translation into a state of adoption as sons of God,

"Justification... is not only a remission of sins, but also sanctification and renewal of the inner man through the voluntary undertaking of grace and gifts."
– Council of Trent

---

1. "Justificatio...non est sola peccatorum remissio, sed et sanctificatio, et renovatio interioris hominis per voluntariam susceptionem gratiæ et donorum.... Quanquam nemo possit esse justus, nisi cui merita passionis Domini nostri Jesu Christi communicantur: id tamen in hac impii justificatione fit, dum ejusdem sanctissimæ passionis merito per Spiritum Sanctum caritas Dei diffunditur in cordibus eorum, qui justificantur, atque ipsis inhæret.

"Quibus verbis justificationis impii descriptio insinuatur, ut sit translatio ab eo statu, in quo homo nascitur filius primi Adæ in statum gratiæ et adoptionis filiorum Dei, per secundum Adam Jesum Christum, salvatorem nostrum: quæ quidem translatio post evangelium promulgatum sine lavacro regenerationis, aut ejus voto fieri non potest" (Session VI, cap. 7, 4; Streitwolf, *Libri Symbolici*, Göttingen, 1846, 24, 25, 22).

cannot…happen, unless a man through remission of his sins ceases to be godless; and through the infusion of righteousness he begins to be pious. But just as the air ceases to be dark and begins to be bright when it is lit by the Sun through the same light which it receives, so, too, does a man cease to be imperfect through that same righteousness granted to him by the Sun of righteousness, namely, with the light of grace wiping out the shadow of sins.[2]

Guilt is either ignored or reduced to a minimum by the Romish theory of justification. There is really no satisfaction of justice in the case.

The remission of sin is therefore defined to be the removal of sin. Bellarmin argues in support of this view that guilt is removed by holiness, that guilt is a relation; the relation of sin to justice. When the thing itself is taken away, the relation itself of course ceases.[3] Hence remission of sin, even in the sense of pardon, is effected by the infusion of righteousness, as darkness is banished by the introduction of light. It is thus, as remarked above, that guilt is either ignored or reduced to a minimum by the Romish theory of justification. There is really no satisfaction of justice in the case. The merits of Christ avail to secure for man the gift of the Holy Ghost, by whose power as exercised in the sacrament of baptism the soul is made holy, and by the introduction of holiness everything of the nature of sin is banished, and all ground for the infliction of punishment is removed. A scheme so opposed to Scripture, and so inconsistent with even the natural conscience, cannot be practically adopted by the mass of the people. The conviction is too intimate that the desert of punishment is not removed by the reformation – or even by the regeneration – of the sinner to allow the conscience to be satisfied with any scheme of salvation which does not provide for the expiation of the guilt of sin by what really satisfies the justice of God.

2. "non potest…fieri, nisi homo per remissionem peccati desinat esse impius; et per infusionem justitiæ incipiat esse pius. Sed sicut aër cum illustratur a sole per idem lumen, quod recipit, desinit esse tenebrosus et incipit esse lucidus: sic etiam homo per eandem justitiam sibi a sole justitiæ donatam atque infusam desinit esse injustus, delente videlicet lumine gratiæ tenebras peccatorum" (*De Justificatione*, II, ii; *Disputationes*, Paris, 1608, Volume IV, 780, 3, 781a).

3. *De Amissione Gratiæ et Statu Peccati*, v, vii., *ibid.*, 287a, b.

In the Bible, therefore, as well as in common life, pardon is not a mere consequence of sanctification. It is exemption from the infliction of the deserved penalty of the law. Whether this exemption is a mere matter of caprice, or unworthy partiality for the offender, or for considerations of expediency, or at the promptings of compassion, or upon the ground of an adequate satisfaction to the demands of justice, makes no difference so far as the nature of pardon is concerned. It is in all cases the remission of a penalty adjudged to be deserved. It is in this sense, therefore, that justification is declared to include the pardon of sins, founded on the imputation to the believing sinner of the perfect righteousness of Christ. It is this that gives the believer peace. He sees that he is delivered from "the wrath and curse of God" due to him – not by any arbitrary exercise of executive authority – but because God, as a righteous judge, can, in virtue of the propitiation of Christ, be just and yet justify the ungodly.

The sins which are pardoned in justification include all sins – past, present, and future. It does indeed seem to be a solecism that sins should be forgiven before they are committed. Forgiveness involves remission of penalty. But how can a penalty be remitted before it is incurred? This is only an apparent difficulty arising out of the inadequacy of human language. The righteousness of Christ is a perpetual donation. It is a robe which hides, or as the Bible expresses it, covers from the eye of justice the sins of the believer. They are sins; they deserve the wrath and curse of God, but the necessity for the infliction of that curse no longer exists. The believer feels the constant necessity for confession and prayer for pardon, but the ground of pardon is ever present for him to offer and plead. So that it would perhaps be a more correct statement to say that in justification the believer receives the promise that God will not deal with him according to his transgressions, rather than to say that sins are forgiven before they are committed.

This subject is thus presented by the apostle: Believers "are not under the law but under grace" (*Romans* 6:14). They are not under a legal system administered according to the principles of retributive justice, a system which requires perfect

It would perhaps be a more correct statement to say that in justification the believer receives the promise that God will not deal with him according to his transgressions, rather than to say that sins are forgiven before they are committed.

obedience as the condition of acceptance with God, and which says, "Cursed is every one that continues not in all things which are written in the book of the law to do them." They are under grace, that is, under a system in which believers are not dealt with on the principles of justice, but on the principles of undeserved mercy in which God does not impute "their trespasses unto them" (*2 Corinthians* 5:19). There is therefore to them no condemnation. They are not condemned for their sins, not because they are not sins and do not deserve condemnation, but because Christ has already made expiation for their guilt and makes continual intercession for them.

The second consequence attributed to the imputation of Christ's righteousness is a title to eternal life. This in the older writers is often expressed by the words "adoption and heirship." Being made the children of God by faith in Christ Jesus (*Galatians* 3:26), they are heirs of God and joint heirs with Jesus Christ of a heavenly inheritance (*Romans* 8:17). The mere expiation of guilt confers no title to eternal life. The condition of the covenant under which man was placed was perfect obedience. This, from all that appears in Scripture, the perfection of God requires. As he never pardons sins unless the demands of justice be satisfied, so he never grants eternal life unless perfect obedience be rendered. Heaven is always represented as a purchased possession. In the covenant between the Father and the Son the salvation of his people was promised as the reward of his humiliation, obedience, and death. Having performed the stipulated conditions, he has a claim to the promised recompense. And this claim inures to the benefit of his people. But besides this, as the work of Christ consisted in his doing all that the law of God or covenant of works requires for the salvation of men and as that righteousness is freely offered to everyone who believes, every such believer has as valid a claim to eternal life as he would have had, had he personally done all that the law demands. Thus broad and firm is that foundation which God has laid for the hopes of his people. It is the rock of ages: Jehovah our righteousness.

As he never pardons sins unless the demands of justice be satisfied, so he never grants eternal life unless perfect obedience be rendered. Heaven is always represented as a purchased possession.

11
Relation of Faith to Justification

All who profess to be Christians admit the doctrine of justification by faith. There are different views, however, as to the relation between faith and justification, as has been already intimated.

Pelagians and Rationalists teach that faith in God's being and perfection, or in the great principles of moral and religious truth, is the source of that moral excellence on account of which we are accepted by God. It is perhaps only a different way of expressing the same idea to say that God, in the case of Abraham – and, therefore, of other men – accepts the pious state of mind involved in the exercise of faith or confidence in God, in lieu of perfect righteousness.

Romanists make faith mere assent; that is, faith does not justify as a virtue, nor as apprehending the offered righteousness of Christ. It is neither the formal nor the instrumental cause of justification; it is merely the predisposing or occasional cause. A man assents to the truth of Christianity and to the more special truth that the Roman Church is the divine institution for saving men. He therefore comes to the Roman Church and receives the sacrament of baptism, by which, *ex opere operato*, a habit of grace or spiritual life is infused into the soul, which is the formal cause of justification, that is, it renders the soul inherently just or holy. In this sense the sinner may be said to be justified by faith. This is the first justi-

All who profess to be Christians admit the doctrine of justification by faith. There are different views, however, as to the relation between faith and justification.

253

fication. After the man is thus rendered holy or regenerated, then the exercises of faith have real merit and enter into the ground of his second justification, by which he becomes entitled to eternal life. But here faith stands on a level with other Christian graces. It is not the only, nor the most important, ground of justification. It is in this view inferior to love, from which faith indeed derives all its virtue as a Christian grace. It is then *fides formata*, that is, faith of which love is the essence, the principle which gives it character.

Roman Catholic Doctrine

According to the Romish scheme:

(1) God is the efficient cause of justification, as it is by his power or supernatural grace that the soul is made just.

(2) Christ is the meritorious cause, as it is for his sake God grants this saving grace or influence of the Spirit to the children of men.

(3) Inherent righteousness is the formal cause, since thereby the soul is made really just or holy.

(4) Faith is merely the occasional and predisposing cause, as it leads the sinner to seek justification (regeneration) and disposes God to grant the blessing. In this aspect it has the merit of congruity only, not that of condignity.

(5) Baptism is the essential instrumental cause, as it is only through or by baptism that inherent righteousness is infused or justification is effected.

So much for the first justification. After this justification, which makes the sinner holy, then,

(6) Good works, all the fruits and exercises of the new life, have real merit and constitute the ground of the Christian's title to eternal life.

The language of the Council of Trent on this subject is as follows:

> The reasons for this justification are finally the glory of God and of Christ and eternal life; but also the compassionate God, who freely washes away and sanctifies, signifying and anointing by means of the Holy Spirit of promise.... Moreover, his own most beloved only begotten Son, our Lord Jesus Christ, who

According to Roman Catholic doctrine, baptism is the essential instrumental cause, as it is only through or by baptism that inherent righteousness is infused or justification is effected.

earned justification [that is, regeneration] for us with his own most sacred suffering on the wooden cross, because of his great love, whereby he loved us although we were hostile, and who gave all that was required to God the Father on our behalf. Likewise instrumental is the sacrament of baptism, which is a sacrament of faith, without which justification has never touched anyone. Finally, the only formal reason is the righteousness of God, not whereby he himself is righteous, but whereby he makes us righteous; namely, when we have been granted this by him, we are renewed in the spirit of our mind, and not only are we reputed to be perfect, but we are called, and are, truly perfect, receiving righteousness in ourselves, each man according to his own measure, which the Holy Spirit distributes severally just as he wishes, and according to the characteristic disposition and cooperation of each.[1]

Again, it is said: "For this righteousness is said to be ours, since we are justified through its cleaving to us; that same righteousness is God's, since it is poured upon us by God through Christ's merit."[2]

All this relates to the first justification, or regeneration, in which the soul passes from spiritual death to spiritual life. Of the second justification, which gives a title to eternal life, Bellarmin says, "The common idea of all Catholic principles

"The common idea of all Catholic principles maintains that good works of the truly righteous are in themselves merits, and merits not of any available reward but of eternal life itself."
– Cardinal Bellarmin

1. "Hujus justificationis causæ sunt, finalis quidem, gloria Dei et Christi, ac vita æterna: efficiens vero, misericors Deus, qui gratuito abluit et sanctificat, signans et ungens Spiritu promissionis sancto,… meritoria autem dilectissimus unigenitus suus, Dominus noster, Jesus Christus, qui, cum essemus inimici, propter nimiam caritatem, qua dilexit nos, sua sanctissima passione in ligno crucis nobis justificationem [*i.e.,* regeneration] meruit et pro nobis Deo Patri satisfecit: instrumentalis item, sacramentum baptismi, quod est sacramentum fidei, sine qua nulli unquam contigit justificatio: demum unica formalis causa est justitia Dei, non qua ipse justus est, sed qua nos justos facit: qua videlicet ab eo donati, renovamur spiritu mentis nostræ et non modo reputamur, sed vere justi nominamur, et sumus, justitiam in nobis recipientes, unusquisque suam secundum mensuram, quam Spiritus Sanctus partitur singulis prout vult, et secundum propriam cujusque dispositionem et cooperationem."

2. "Quæ enim justitia nostra dicitur, quia per eam nobis inhærentem justificamur; illa eadem Dei est, quia a Deo nobis infunditur per Christi meritum" (Session VI. cap. 7, 16; Streitwolf, *Libri Symbolici*, Göttingen, 1846, Volume 1, 24, 25, 32).

maintains that good works of the truly righteous are in themselves merits, and merits not of any available reward but of eternal life itself."[3]

The thirty-second canon of the Tridentine Council at this sixth session anathematizes anyone who teaches a different doctrine:

> If anyone says that the good works of a justified man thus are gifts of God, and so not also real merits of the justified man himself; or that the justified man himself does not truly deserve an increase in grace and eternal life because of his good works, which are done by him through God's grace and the merits of Jesus Christ, whose living part he is, if nevertheless he dies in a state of grace, [that he does not truly deserve] the effect, and even an increase in glory; it is anathema.[4]

It appears from all this that, according to the doctrine of the Church of Rome, faith has no special or direct connection with justification, and that "justification by faith" in that Church means something entirely different from what is intended by those words on the lips of Christians.

According to the doctrine of the Church of Rome, faith has no special or direct connection with justification, and that "justification by faith" in that Church means something entirely different from what is intended by those words on the lips of Christians.

Arminian Doctrine

According to the Remonstrants or Arminians, faith is the ground of justification. Under the Gospel, God accepts our imperfect obedience – including faith and the obedience springing from it – in place of the perfect obedience demanded by the law originally given to Adam. There is one passage in the Bible, or rather one form of expression that occurs in several places, which seems to favor this view of

---

[3] "Habet communis catholicorum omnium sententia, opera bona justorum vere, ac proprie esse merita, et merita non cujuscunque præmii sed ipsius vitæ æternæ" (*De Justificatione*, v. 1; *Disputationes*, Paris, 1608, 949a).

[4] "Si quis dixerit, hominis justificati bona opera ita esse dona Dei, ut non sint etiam bona ipsius justificati merita; aut ipsum justificatum bonis operibus, quæ ab eo per Dei gratiam et Jesu Christi meritum, cujus vivum membrum est, fiunt, non vere mereri augmentum gratiæ vitam æternam et ipsius vitæ æternæ, si tamen in gratia decesserit, consecutionem, atque etiam gloriæ augmentum; anathema sit."

the subject. In *Romans* 4:3, it is said, "Abraham believed God, and it was counted unto him for righteousness"; and again in verse 22 of that chapter and in *Galatians* 3:6. If this phrase be interpreted according to the analogy of such passages as *Romans* 2:26, "Shall not his uncircumcision be counted for circumcision?" it does mean that faith is taken or accepted for righteousness. The Bible, however, is the Word of God and therefore self-consistent. Consequently, if a passage admits of one interpretation inconsistent with the teaching of the Bible in other places, and of another interpretation consistent with that teaching, we are bound to accept the latter. This rule, simple and obvious as it is, is frequently violated, not only by those who deny the inspiration of the Scriptures, but even by men professing to recognize their infallible authority. They seem to regard it as a proof of independence to make each passage mean simply what its grammatical structure and logical connection indicate, without the least regard to the analogy of Scripture. This is unreasonable. In *Genesis* 15, we are told that Abraham lamented before the Lord that he was childless, and that one born in his house was to be his heir. And God said unto him,

> This shall not be your heir, but he that shall come forth out of your own bowels shall be your heir. And he brought him forth abroad and said, "Look now toward Heaven and tell the stars, if you be able to number them." And he said unto him, "So shall your seed be." And he believed in the Lord, and he counted it to him for righteousness.

Taking this passage by itself, it is inferred that the object of Abraham's faith was the promise of a numerous posterity. That Abraham's faith's being imputed to him for righteousness means anything more than when it is said that the zeal of Phinehas was imputed for righteousness (*Psalm* 106:31); or when in *Deuteronomy* 24:13 it is said that to return a poor man's pledge "shall be righteousness unto you before the Lord your God." No one supposes that one manifestation of zeal or one act of benevolence is taken for complete obedience to the law. All that the phrase "to impute for righteousness" by itself means, according to Old Testament usage, is to esteem as

If a passage admits of one interpretation inconsistent with the teaching of the Bible in other places, and of another interpretation consistent with that teaching, we are bound to accept the latter.

right, to approve. The zeal of Phinehas was right. Returning a poor man's pledge was right. These were acts which God approved. And so he approved of Abraham's faith. He gained the favor of God by believing.

Now while this is true, far more, as the apostle teaches, is true. He teaches, first, that the great promise made to Abraham (faith in which secured his justification) was not that his natural descendants should be as numerous as the stars of Heaven, but that in his seed all the nations of the Earth should be blessed; second, that the seed intended was not a multitude, but one person, and that that one person was Christ (*Galatians* 3:16); and third, that the blessing which the seed of Abraham was to secure for the world was redemption. "Christ has redeemed us from the curse of the law, being made a curse for us:… that the blessing of Abraham (that is, the promise made to Abraham) might come on" us. The promise made to Abraham therefore, was redemption through Christ. Hence those who are Christ's, the apostle teaches, are Abraham's seed and heirs of his promise. What, therefore, Abraham believed was that the seed of the woman, the Shiloh, the promised Redeemer of the world, was to be born of him. He believed in Christ as his Savior, as his righteousness and deliverer; and therefore it was that he was accepted as righteous – not for the merit of his faith, and not on the ground of faith, or by taking faith in lieu of righteousness – but because he received and rested on Christ alone for his salvation.

Unless such be the meaning of the apostle, it is hard to see how there is any coherence or force in his arguments. His object is to prove that men are justified, not by works, but gratuitously; nor for what they are or do, but for what is done for them. They are saved by a ransom, by a sacrifice. But it is absurd to say that trust in a ransom redeems or is taken in place of the ransom, or that faith in a sacrifice, and not the sacrifice itself, is the ground of acceptance. To prove that such is the Scriptural method of justification, Paul appeals to the case of Abraham. He was not justified for his works, but by faith in a Redeemer. He expected to be justified as ungodly (*Romans* 4:5). This, he tells us, is what we must do. We have

What, therefore, Abraham believed was that the seed of the woman, the Shiloh, the promised Redeemer of the world, was to be born of him. He believed in Christ as his Savior, as his righteousness and deliverer.

no righteousness of our own. We must take Christ for our wisdom, righteousness, sanctification, and redemption. In the immediately preceding chapter the apostle had said we are justified by faith in the blood of Christ as a propitiation for sin. For him to prove this from the fact that Abraham was justified on account of his confiding, trusting state of mind, which led him to believe that although a hundred years old he should be the father of a numerous posterity, would be a contradiction.

Besides, it is to be remembered not only that the Scriptures never say that we are justified "on account" of faith (διὰ πίστιν), but always "by," or "through" faith (διὰ or ἐκ πίστεως or πίστει) but also that it is not by faith as such; not by faith in God, nor in the Scriptures; and not by faith in a specific divine promise such as that made to Abraham of a numerous posterity, or of the possession of the land of Canaan; but only by faith in one particular promise, namely, that of salvation through Christ. It is, therefore, not on account of the state of mind of which faith is the evidence, nor of the good works which are its fruits, but only by faith as an act of trust in Christ, that we are justified. This of necessity supposes that he, and not our faith, is the ground of our justification. He, and not our faith, is the ground of our confidence. How can any Christian wish it to be otherwise? What comparison is there between the absolutely perfect and the infinitely meritorious righteousness of Christ and our own imperfect evangelical obedience as a ground of confidence and peace?

This doctrine of faith as the ground of our justification is, moreover, dishonoring the the Gospel. It supposes the Gospel to be less holy than the law. The law required perfect obedience; the Gospel is satisfied with imperfect obedience. And how imperfect and insufficient our best obedience is, the conscience of every believer certifies. If it does not satisfy us, how can it satisfy God?

The grand objection, however, to this Arminian doctrine as to the relation between faith and justification is that it is in direct contradiction to the plain and pervading teaching of the Word of God. The Bible teaches that we are not justified

The grand objection, however, to this Arminian doctrine as to the relation between faith and justification is that it is in direct contradiction to the plain and pervading teaching of the Word of God.

by works. This doctrine affirms that we are justified by works. The Bible teaches that we are justified by the blood of Christ – that it is for his obedience that the sentence of justification is passed on men. This doctrine affirms that God pronounces us righteous because of our own righteousness. The Bible from first to last teaches that the whole ground of our salvation or of our justification is objective: what Christ as our Redeemer, our ransom, our sacrifice, and our surety has done for us. This doctrine teaches us to look within to what we are and to what we do as the ground of our acceptance with God. It may safely be said that this is altogether unsatisfactory to the awakened conscience. The sinner cannot rely on anything in himself. He instinctively looks to Christ, to his work done for us as the ground of confidence and peace. This in the last resort is the hope of all believers, whatever their profession of justification may be. Whether Papist, Arminian, or Augustinian, they all cast their dying eyes on Christ: "As Moses lifted up the serpent in the wilderness, even so must the Son of man be lifted up – that whosoever believes in him should not perish, but have eternal life."

Protestant Doctrine

The common doctrine of Protestants on this subject is that faith is merely the instrumental cause of justification. It is the act of receiving and resting upon Christ and has no other relation to the end than any other act by which a proffered good is accepted. This is clearly the doctrine of Scripture:

(1) Because we are constantly said to be justified by, or through, faith.

(2) Because the faith which justifies is described as a looking, as a receiving, as a coming, as a fleeing for refuge, as a laying hold of, and as a calling upon.

(3) Because the ground to which our justification is referred, and that on which the sinner's trust is placed, is declared to be the blood, the death, the righteousness, the obedience of Christ.

(4) Because the fact that Christ is a ransom, a sacrifice – and as such effects our salvation – of necessity supposes that the

> The Bible from first to last teaches that the whole ground of our salvation or of our justification is objective: what Christ as our Redeemer, our ransom, our sacrifice, and our surety has done for us.

faith which interests us in the merit of his work is a simple act of trust.

(5) Because any other view of the case is inconsistent with the gratuitous nature of justification, with the honor of Christ, and with the comfort and confidence of the believer.

The faith which interests us in the merit of his work is a simple act of trust.

12

Objections to the Protestant Doctrine of Justification

It is said to lead to licentiousness

If good works are not necessary to justification, they are not necessary at all, goes the primary objection to the doctrine of justification by faith alone.

THE FIRST, most obvious, and most persistently urged objection against the doctrine of gratuitous justification through the imputation of the righteousness of Christ has already been incidentally considered. That objection is that the doctrine leads to license: that if good works are not necessary to justification, they are not necessary at all – that if God accepts the chief of sinners as readily as the most moral of men on the simple condition of faith in Christ, then what profit is there in circumcision? in Judaism? in being in the church? in being good in any form? Why not live in sin that grace may abound? This objection having been urged against the apostle, it needs no other answer than that which he himself gave it. That answer is found in the sixth and seventh chapters of his epistle to the Romans and is substantially as follows:

First: the objection involves a contradiction. To speak of salvation in sin is as great an absurdity as to speak of life in death. Salvation is deliverance from sin. How then can men be delivered from sin in order that they may live in it? Or, as Paul expresses it, "How shall we, who are dead to sin, live any longer therein?"

Second, the very act of faith which secures our justification secures also our sanctification. It cannot secure the one without securing also the other. This is not only the intention and the desire of the believer, but it is the ordinance of God – a necessary feature of the plan of salvation and secured by its nature. We take Christ as our Redeemer from sin, from its power as well as from its guilt. And the imputation of his righteousness consequent on faith secures the indwelling of the Holy Spirit as certainly, and for the very same reasons (the covenant stipulations), that it secures the pardon of our sins. And, therefore, if we are partakers of his death, we are also partakers of his life. If we die with him, we rise with him. If we are justified, we are sanctified. He, therefore, who lives in sin, proclaims himself an unbeliever. He has neither part nor lot in the redemption of him who came to save his people from their sins.

Third, our condition, the apostle says, is analogous to that of a slave, belonging first to one master, then to another. So long as he belonged to one man, he was not under the authority of another. But if freed from the one and made the slave of the other, then he comes under an influence which constrains obedience to the latter. So we were the slaves of sin, but now, freed from that hard master, we have become the servants of righteousness. For a believer, therefore, to live in sin is just as impossible as for the slave of one man to be at the same time the slave of another. We are indeed free, but not free to sin. We are free only from the bondage of the devil and introduced into the pure, exalted, and glorious liberty of the sons of God.

Fourth, the objection as made against the apostle and as constantly repeated since is urged in the interest of morality and of common sense. Reason itself, it is said, teaches that a man must be good before he can be restored to the favor of God; and if we teach that the number and heinousness of a man's sins are no barrier to his justification, and his good works are no reason why he should be justified rather than the chief of sinners, we upset the very foundations of morality. This is the wisdom of men. The wisdom of God, as revealed in the Scriptures, is very different. According to the

The imputation of Christ's righteousness consequent on faith secures the indwelling of the Holy Spirit as certainly, and for the very same reasons (the covenant stipulations), that it secures the pardon of our sins.

Bible the favor of God is the life of the soul. The light of his countenance is to rational creatures what the light of the Sun is to the Earth, the source of all that is beautiful and good. So long, therefore, as a soul is under his curse, there is no life-giving or life-sustaining intercourse between it and God. In this state it can only, as the apostle expresses it, "bring forth fruit unto death." As soon, however, as it exercises faith, it receives the imputation of the righteousness of Christ; God's justice is thereby satisfied, and the Spirit comes and takes up his dwelling in the believer as the source of all holy living. There can therefore be no holiness until there is reconciliation with God, and no reconciliation with God except through the righteousness imputed to us and received by faith alone. Then follow the indwelling of the Spirit, progressive sanctification, and all the fruits of holy living.

The intercession of Christ secures for those given to him by the Father the renewing of the Holy Ghost. The first act of the renewed heart is faith.

It may be said that this scheme involves an inconsistency. There can be no holiness until there is reconciliation, and no reconciliation until there is faith. But faith is a fruit of the Spirit, and an act of the renewed soul. Then there is and must be, after all, holy action before there is reconciliation. It might be enough to say in answer to this objection that logical order and chronological succession are different things, or that the order of nature and order of time are not to be confounded. Many things are contemporaneous and co-instantaneous which nevertheless stand in a certain logical and even causal relation to each other. Christ commanded the man with a withered arm to stretch forth his hand. He immediately obeyed, but not before he received strength. He called to Lazarus to come forth from the grave and he came forth. But this presupposes a restoration of life. So God commands the sinner to believe in Christ, and he thereupon receives him as his Savior, though this supposes supernatural power or grace.

Our Lord, however, gives another answer to this objection. He says, as recorded in *John* 17:9, "I pray not for the world, but for them which you have given me; for they are yours." The intercession of Christ secures for those given to him by the Father the renewing of the Holy Ghost. The first act of the renewed heart is faith; as the first act of a restored eye is to see. Whether this satisfies the understanding or not, it remains clear as the doctrine of the Bible that good works are the fruits and consequences of reconciliation with God through faith in our Lord Jesus Christ.

It is "inconsistent with the grace of the Gospel"

It is objected that the Protestant doctrine destroys the gratuitous nature of justification. If justice be satisfied, if all the demands of the law are met, there can, it is said, be no grace in the salvation of the sinner. If a man owes a debt and someone pays it for him, the creditor shows no grace in giving an acquittal. This objection is familiar, and so also is the answer.

The work of Christ is not of the nature of a commercial transaction. It is not analogous to a pecuniary satisfaction except in one point. It secures the deliverance of those for whom it is offered and by whom it is accepted. In the case of guilt the demand of justice is upon the person of the offender. He, and he alone, is bound to answer at the bar of justice. No one can take his place, unless with the consent of the representative of justice and of the substitute, as well as of the sinner himself. Among men, substitution in the case of crime and its penalty is rarely, if ever, admissible, because no man has the right over his own life or liberty. He cannot give them up at pleasure, and no human magistrate has the right to relieve the offender or to inflict the legal penalty on another. But Christ had power, that is, the right (ἐξουσία) to lay down his life and "power to take it again." And God, as absolute judge and sovereign, the Lord of the conscience and the proprietor of all his creatures, was at full liberty to accept a substitute for sinners. This is proved beyond contradiction by what God has actually done. Under the old dispensation every sacrifice appointed by the law was a substitute for him in whose behalf it was offered. In the clearest terms it was predicted that the Messiah was to be the substitute for his people – that the chastisement of their sins was to be laid on him, and that he was to make his soul an offering for sin. He was hailed as he entered on his ministry as the Lamb of

Under the old dispensation every sacrifice appointed by the law was a substitute for him in whose behalf it was offered. In the clearest terms it was predicted that the Messiah was to be the substitute for his people.

God who was to bear the sins of the world. He died, the just for the unjust. He redeemed us from the curse of the law by being made a curse for us. This is what is meant by being a substitute. To deny this is to deny the central idea of the Scriptural doctrine of the redemption. To explain it away is to absorb as with a sponge the lifeblood of the Gospel.

It is the glory, the power, and the preciousness of the Protestant doctrine that it makes the salvation of sinners a matter of grace from the beginning to the end. On the part of the eternal Father it was of grace, that is, of unmerited, mysterious, and immeasurable love that he provided a substitute for sinners, and that he spared not his own Son but freely gave him up for us all. It was a matter of grace – that is, of love to sinners, to the ungodly, to his enemies that the eternal Son of God became man, assumed the burden of our sins, fulfilled all righteousness, obeying and suffering even unto death, that we might not perish but have eternal life. It is of grace that the Spirit applies to men the redemption purchased by Christ, that he renews the heart, that he overcomes the opposition of sinners, making them willing in the day of his power; that he bears with all their ingratitude, disobedience, and resistance, and never leaves them until his work is consummated in glory. In all this the sinner is not treated according to his character and conduct. He has no claim to any one in this long catalogue of mercies. Everything to him is a matter of unmerited grace. Merited grace, indeed, is a solecism. And so is merited salvation in the case of sinners.

Grace does not cease to be grace because it is not exercised in violation of order, propriety, and justice. It is not the weak fondness of a doting parent. It is the love of a holy God who, in order to reveal that love and manifest the exceeding glory of that attribute when exercised towards the unworthy, did what was necessary to render its exercise consistent with the other perfections of the divine nature. It was indispensable that God should be just in justifying the ungodly, but he does not thereby cease to be gracious, inasmuch as it was he who provided the ransom by which

It is the glory, the power, and the preciousness of the Protestant doctrine that it makes the salvation of sinners a matter of grace from the beginning to the end.

the objects of his love are redeemed from the curse of the law and the power of sin.

"God cannot declare the unjust to be just"

Another standing objection to the Protestant doctrine has been so often met that nothing but its constant repetition justifies a repetition of the answer. It is said to be absurd that one man should be righteous with the righteousness of another – that for God to pronounce the unjust just is a contradiction. This is a mere play on words. It is, however, very serious play; for it is caricaturing truth.

It is indeed certain that the subjective, inherent quality of one person or thing cannot by imputation become the inherent characteristic of any other person or thing. Wax cannot become hard by the imputation of the hardness of a stone; nor can a brute become rational by the imputation of the intelligence of a man; nor the wicked become good by the imputation of the goodness of other men. But what has this to do with one man's assuming the responsibility of another man? If among men the bankrupt can become solvent by a rich man's assuming his responsibilities, then in the court of God may not the guilty become righteous by the Son of God's assuming their responsibilities? If he was made sin for us, why may we not be made the righteousness of God in him? The objection assumes that the word *just* or *righteous* in this connection expresses moral character; whereas in the Bible, when used in relation to this subject, it is always used in a judicial sense, that is, it expresses the relation of the person spoken of to justice. Δίκαιος is antithetical to ὑπόδικος. The man with regard to whom justice is unsatisfied is ὑπόδικος, "guilty." He with regard to whom justice is satisfied is δίκαιος, "righteous." To declare righteous, therefore, is to declare holy; and to impute righteousness is not to impute goodness, but simply to regard and pronounce those who receive the gift of Christ's righteousness free from condemnation and entitled to eternal life for his sake. Some philosophical theologians seem to think that there is real antagonism between love and justice in the divine nature, or that these attributes are

The objection assumes that the word just or righteous in this connection expresses moral character; whereas in the Bible, when used in relation to this subject, it is always used in a judicial sense, that is, it expresses the relation of the person spoken of to justice.

*He can be just
and yet justify,
love, sanctify, and
glorify the chief
of sinners; for
which all sinners
should render
him everlasting
thanksgiving and
praise.*

incompatible or inharmonious. This is not so in man; why then should it be so in God? The highest form of moral excellence includes these attributes as essential elements of its perfection. The Scriptures represent them as mysteriously blended in the salvation of man. The Gospel is a revelation to principalities and powers in Heaven of the πολυποίκιλος σοφία του Θεοῦ, because therein he shows that he can be just and yet justify, love, sanctify, and glorify the chief of sinners; for which all sinners should render him everlasting thanksgiving and praise.

13

Departures from the
Protestant Doctrine

Arminian Doctrine

Jacobus Arminius, a man of learning, talents, attractive accomplishments, and exemplary character, was born in Holland in 1560 and died professor in the University of Leyden in 1609, having filled the chair of theology since 1603. His departures from the Reformed doctrines in which he had been educated were far less serious than those of his successors, although involving them, apparently, by a logical necessity. His great difficulty was with the doctrine of predestination or the sovereignty of God in election. He could not, however, get rid of that doctrine without denying the entire inability of man to do what is spiritually good. He, therefore, taught that although mankind fell in Adam and are born in a state of sin and condemnation, and are of themselves entirely unable to turn from sin to holiness, yet they are able to cooperate with the grace of the Holy Spirit given to all men – especially to all who hear the Gospel – in sufficient measure to enable them to repent and believe and to persevere in holy living unto the end. But whether any man does thus repent and believe, or, having believed, perseveres in a holy life, depends on himself and not on God. The purpose of election, therefore, is not a purpose

Arminius' great difficulty was with the doctrine of predestination or the sovereignty of God in election. He could not, however, get rid of that doctrine without denying the entire inability of man to do what is spiritually good.

to save, and to that end to give faith and repentance to a definite number of individuals, but a purpose to save those who repent, believe, and persevere in faith until the end. The work of Christ has, therefore, an equal reference to all men. He made full satisfaction to God for the sins of all and every man, so that God can now consistently offer salvation to all men on the conditions laid down in the Gospel.

This is a self-consistent scheme. One part implies or necessitates the admission of the others. The above statement includes all the doctrines presented by the followers of Arminius after his death to the authorities in the form of a Remonstrance, as a justification of their views. Hence the Arminians were called Remonstrants. The document just mentioned contains the five points on which its authors and their associates differed from the Reformed faith. The first relates to predestination, which is explained as the purpose

> to save in Christ, because of Christ, and through Christ, those men who believe by the grace of the Holy Spirit, in his same Son, and who persevere in those things until the end, because of the obedience of faith, through the same grace; but otherwise to leave behind and to condemn those who are not converted and are faithless, in sin, and subject to wrath, according to the *Gospel of John* 3:36.[1]

The second relates to the work of Christ, as to which it is said,

> Therefore, Jesus Christ, the Savior of the world, died for each and every one, and so indeed, that through Christ's death he has obtained for all men reconciliation and remission of sins: Nevertheless, on this condition, that no one in fact have the benefit of that remission of sins except the faithful man, and this too is according to the *Gospel of John* 3:16, and *1 John* 2:2.[2]

"Jesus Christ, the Savior of the world, died for each and every one, and so indeed, that through Christ's death he has obtained for all men reconciliation and remission of sins: Nevertheless, on this condition, that no one in fact have the benefit of that remission of sins except the faithful man."

– The Arminian Remonstrants

---

1. "illos in Christo, propter Christum et per Christum servare, qui Spiritus Sancti gratia, in eundem ejus filium credunt, et in ea, fideique obedientia, per eandem gratiam in finem perseverant: contra vero eos, qui non convertentur et infideles, in peccato et iræ subjectos relinquere, et condemnare, secundum illud Evang. Joann. iii. 36."

2. "Proinde Jesum Christum mundi servatorem pro omnibus et singulis mortuum esse, atque ita quidem, ut omnibus per mortem Christi

The third, concerning the sinner's ability, declares,

> But a man does not have true faith from himself alone, nor from the strength of his free decision, because there is nothing good in a state of weakness and sin, because that truly is good, which healing faith can realize and create from itself. But it is necessary for him to be brought forth again in Christ by God through the Holy Spirit and renewed in his mind, his dispositions, or his will and all his faculties, so that he can understand, realize, desire, and accomplish any good. The *Gospel of John* 15:5.[3]

No Augustinian, whether Lutheran or Calvinist, can say more than that, or desire more to be said by others.

The fourth article, concerning grace, however, shows the point of departure:

> This grace of God is the beginning, the advancement, and the completion of every good man, and indeed so far that man himself having been reborn without this prerequisite, or by some accident, without the subsequent and cooperating grace, can neither realize, desire, nor perform anything good, nor can he resist any evil temptation; so far as all good works which we are able to devise must indeed be attributed to God's grace in Christ; but in fact that is how that grace works: It is not irresistible, for it is said of many men that they resist the Holy Spirit, *Acts* 7:51 and in many passages elsewhere.[4]

"All good works which we are able to devise must indeed be attributed to God's grace in Christ; but in fact that is how that grace works: It is not irresistible."

– The Arminian Remonstrants

---

reconciliationem et peccatorum remissionem impetravit: ea tamen conditione, ut nemo illa remissione peccatorum re ipsa fruatur, præter hominem fidelem, et hoc quoque secundum Evang. Joann. iii. 16, et 1 Joann. ii. 2."

3. "Hominem vero salutarem fidem a se ipso non habere, nec vi liberi sui arbitrii, quandoquidem in statu defectionis et peccati nihil boni, quandoquidem vere bonum est, quale quid est fides salutaris, ex se possit cogitare, vel facere: sed necessarium esse eum a Deo in Christo per Spiritum Sanctum regigni et renovari mente, affectibus, seu voluntate et omnibus facultatibus, ut aliquid boni possit intelligere, cogitare, velle et perficere. Ev. Joann. xv. 5."

4. "Hanc Dei gratiam esse initium, progressum ac perfectionem omnis boni, atque id eo quidem usque ut ipse homo regenitus absque hac præcendentia seu adventitia excitante, consequente et cooperante gratia, neque boni quid cogitare, velle, aut facere possit, neque etiam ulli malæ tentatione resistere; adeo quidem ut omnia bona opera, quæ excogitare

It was not to be expected, in a brief exposition of principles designed for the justification of those who hold them, as members of a Reformed or Calvinistic church, that doubtful terms should be explained. It is beyond controversy, however, and, it is believed, is not controverted, that *irresistible* is here used in the sense of certainly efficacious. The Holy Spirit operates on the hearts of all men. Some are thereby renewed and brought to faith and repentance; others are not. This difference, according to the Arminians, is not to be referred to the nature of the influence exerted, but to the fact that some yield to this grace and cooperate with it, while others reject and resist it.

The fifth article refers to the perseverance of the saints and is indefinite. It admits that the Spirit furnishes grace abundantly sufficient to enable the believer to persevere in holiness:

> But can it really be that those men themselves are not able, because of their own carelessness, to disregard that their beginning is in Christ, and to embrace the world at hand again, to desert that sacred doctrine that was once handed down to them, to suffer a shipwreck of conscience, to be lost from grace? Inwardly a penalty must be paid, according to the holy Scripture, before they can show that with full tranquility and πληροφορία of spirit.[5]

Of course no man who believed the doctrine could write thus, and this doubtful mode of expression was soon laid aside, and "falling from grace," in the common sense of the phrase, was admitted to be an Arminian doctrine.

It will be observed that the doctrine of justification is not embraced in the five points in the Remonstrance as presented to the authorities in Holland and as made the basis

It will be observed that the doctrine of justification is not embraced in the five points in the Remonstrance as presented to the authorities in Holland.

---

possumus, Dei gratiæ in Christo tribuenda sint; quod vero modum operationis illius gratiæ illa non irresistibilis; de multis enim dicitur eos Spiritui Sancto resistere, *Act.* vii. 51 et alibi multis locis."

5. "Sed an illi ipsi negligentia sua initium sui esse in Christo deserere non possint, et præsentem mundum iterum amplecti, a sancta doctrina ipsis semel tradita deficere, conscientiæ naufragium facere, a gratia excidere; penitus ex sacra Scriptura esset expendum, antequam illud cum plena animi tranquillitate et πληροφορία docere possent."

of the decisions of the Synod of Dort. The aberration of the Arminians, however, from the faith of the Reformed churches extended to all the doctrines connected with the plan of salvation. Arminius himself, at least, held far higher and more Scriptural views on original sin, inability, and the necessity of supernatural grace than those which have since become so prevalent even among the Reformed or Calvinistic churches themselves. In matters concerning the method of salvation, especially as to the nature of Christ's work and its application to the believer, they at first adhered closely to the language of the Reformed confessions. Thus they did not hesitate to say that Christ made full satisfaction for the sins of men; that he was a ransom, a sacrifice, a propitiation; that he made expiation for sin; that his righteousness or obedience is the ground of our acceptance with God; that the faith which saves is not mere assent to some random truth or pious confidence in God, but specifically faith in Christ as the Savior of men; and that justification is an act of God pronouncing the sinner just, or in which he pardons sin and accepts the sinner as righteous. All this is satisfactory to the ear. Language, however, admits of different interpretations; and it soon became apparent and avowed that the Remonstrants intended something very different from what the Reformed church meant to express by the same terms.

Language, however, admits of different interpretations; and it soon became apparent and avowed that the Remonstrants intended something very different from what the Reformed church meant to express by the same terms.

The Arminians said that Christ's work was a satisfaction to divine justice. But they did not mean by *satisfaction* either a *solutio*, a real value rendered for what was due; nor even an *acceptio*, taking one thing for another as an equivalent; but an *acceptilatio*, a gracious acceptance as a satisfaction of that which in its own nature was no equivalent, as though God should accept the life of a brute for that of a man, or faith for perfect obedience. Neither did the Remonstrants mean by *justice* the attribute which requires the righteous distribution of rewards and punishments, and which renders it necessary that the penalty of the law should be executed in case of transgression.

With regard to this latter point (the nature of justice) the language of Grotius, and of the great body of the

Remonstrant or Arminian theologians, is perfectly explicit. Grotius says:

> To inflict punishments, or to free someone from punishments whom you are able to punish, which the Scripture calls justification, does not exist except for a ruler, as such at first and by itself: as, say, in a father's family, in a king's state, in God's universe…. From which it follows, considering God here altogether as a ruler.[6]

Again,[7]

> The reason [why "a ruler is not permitted to relax such a law, unless some reason, if not necessary, then at least sufficient, is an additional factor"]…is, because the act of proposing or relaxing a law is not an act of unconditional power but an act of command, which ought to extend to the preservation of a good arrangement.[8]

> For all punishment has the common good as its purpose.[9]

> Prudence also urges a ruler to punishment for this purpose. Further, the reason for punishing is increased when some law is published that threatens punishment. For then the omission of punishment usually detracts somewhat from the authority of the law among the subjects.[10]

Here everything is purely governmental. It is not justice, in the proper and ordinary sense of the word, that is satisfied, but God's wise and benevolent regard to the interests of his

According to Grotius, it is not justice, in the proper and ordinary sense of the word, that is satisfied, but God's wise and benevolent regard to the interests of his moral government.

6. "Pœnas infligere, aut a pœnis aliquem liberare, quem punire possis, quod justificare vocat Scriptura, non est nisi rectoris, qua talis primo et per se: ut, puta, in familia patris; in republica regis, in universo Dei…. Unde sequitur, omnino hic Deum considerandum, ut rectorem" (*De Satisfactione Christi*, cap. 2; *Works*, London, 1697, Volume III, 306b [19-24]).

7. *De Satisfactione Christi*, cap. 5; 317b (35-41).

8. "Ratio [cur "rectori relaxare legem talem non liceat, nisi causa aliqua accedat, si non necessaria, certe sufficiens"]…est, quod actus ferendi aut relaxandi legem non sit actus absoluti dominii, sed actus imperii, qui tendere debeat ad boni ordinis conservationem" (*De Satisfactione Christi*, cap. 2; 307b [62, 63]).

9. "Pœna enim omnis propositum habet bonum commune."

10. "Prudentia quoque hoc nomine rectorem ad pœnam incitat. Augetur præterea causa puniendi, ubi lex aliqua publicata est, quæ pœnam minatur. Nam tunc omissio pœnæ ferme aliquid detrahit de legis authoritate apud subditos" (*De Satisfactione Christi*, cap. 5; 316b [9-13]).

moral government. This changes everything. If God's justice be not satisfied, guilt is not removed, sin is not expiated, conscience is not appeased – nor can the real authority and honor of the law be upheld.

As to the other point, the nature of the satisfaction rendered: It was not a real equivalent, which by its intrinsic value met the obligations of the sinner, but it was something graciously accepted as such. Although Grotius rejects the use of the word *acceptilatio*, and endeavors to show that it does not express his meaning, nevertheless, though he repudiates the word, he retains the idea. He says, "It is the nature of value that one moves another to concede a matter, or some right, such as impunity, by virtue of one's own valuation or worth."[11]

This amounts to the principle of Duns Scotus that a thing avails (is worth) for what God pleases to take it. Although Grotius does not carry out the principle to the length to which the Schoolmen carried it and say that God might have accepted the death of one man as a satisfaction for the sins of the world, or the blood of bulls or of goats as a real expiation, nevertheless he teaches that God graciously accepted *aliquid pro aliquo*, the death of Christ for the death for all the world, not because of its being a real equivalent in itself, but because as ruler, having the right to remit sin without any satisfaction, he saw that the interests of his government could thereby be promoted. Still more clearly is this idea expressed by Limborch:

> They err in this most of all, that they desire that the price of redemption in all respects ought to be equal to that unhappiness from which redemption is made; for the price of redemption is usually established according to the free assessment of the one who holds the prisoner, not, however, paid off according to the worth of the prisoner.... Thus the price which Christ has paid was paid according to the assessment of God the Father.[12]

If God's justice be not satisfied, guilt is not removed, sin is not expiated, conscience is not appeased – nor can the real authority and honor of the law be upheld.

11. " Ea est pretii natura, ut sui valore aut æstimatione alterum moveat ad concedendam rem, aut jus aliquod, puta impunitatem" (*De Satisfactione*, cap. 7; *Works*, London, 1679, Volume III, 328b [12-14]).

12. "In eo errant quam maxime, quod velint redemtionis pretium per omnia equivalens esse debere miseriæ illi, e qua redemtio fit: redemtionis

According to Grotius, Christ died as an example, *exemplum pœnæ*. The whole efficacy of his work was its moral impression on the universe. It was not an expiation or satisfaction for past sins, but a means of deterring from the commission of sin in the future. This, as Baur[13] and Strauss[14] remark, is the point in which the theory of Grotius and that of Socinus coincide. They both refer the efficacy of Christ's work to the moral impression which it makes on the minds of intelligent creatures. They refer that moral influence, indeed, to different causes, but moral impression is all the efficacy it has. Although the word *satisfaction* is retained by Grotius, the idea attached to it by the church is rejected.

The leading Remonstrant or Arminian theologians – Episcopius, Curcellæus, and Limborch – differ from Grotius in their mode of presenting this subject. Instead of regarding the work of Christ as an example of punishment designed to deter from the commission of sin, they adhere to the Scriptural mode of regarding him as a ransom and sacrifice. The difference, however, is more in form than in reality. They admit that Christ redeems us by giving himself as a ransom for many. But a ransom, as Currcellæus says, is not an equivalent; it is anything the holder of the captive sees fit to accept. It is admitted, also, that Christ gave himself as a sacrifice for our salvation; but a sacrifice is said not to be a satisfaction to justice, but simply the condition on which pardon is granted. Under the Old Testament, God pardoned sin on the occasion of the sacrifice of irrational animals; under the New Testament, on the occasion of the sacrifice of Christ. "Sacrifices," says Limborch, "are not payments of debts, nor full satisfactions for sins; but they permit the finishing spontaneous remission of sin." "The price of redemption is established only by the free estimation of him

The theory of Grotius and that of Socinus coincide. They both refer the efficacy of Christ's work to the moral impression which it makes on the minds of intelligent creatures.

pretium enim constitui solet pro libera æstimatione illius, qui captivum detinet, non autem solvi pro captivi merito…. Ita pretium, quod Christus persolvit, juxta Dei Patris æstimationem persolutum est" (*Theologia Christiana*, III, xxi, 8, Amsterdam, 1715, 262a).

13. *Die christliche Lehre von der Versöhnung*, II, i, 4, Tübingen, 1838, 429.
14. *Dogmatik*, Tübingen and Stuttgart, 1841, Volume II, 315.

who holds the captive."[15] We know, however, from Scripture that a sacrifice was not merely an arbitrarily appointed antecedent of gratuitous forgiveness; it was not simply an acknowledgment of guilt. We know also that the blood of bulls and of goats under the Old Testament could not take away sin; it availed only to the purifying of the flesh or the remission of ceremonial penalties. The only efficacy of the Old Testament sacrifices, so far as sin committed against God is concerned, was sacramental; that is, they signified, sealed, and applied the benefits of the only real and effectual expiation for sin to those who believed. As the victim symbolically bore the penalty due to the offender, so the eternal Son of God really bore our sins, really became a curse for us, and thus made a true and perfect satisfaction to God for our offenses.

As the Arminians denied that Christ's work was a real satisfaction for sin, they of necessity denied any real justification of the sinner. Justification with them is merely pardon.

As the Arminians denied that Christ's work was a real satisfaction for sin, they of necessity denied any real justification of the sinner. Justification with them is merely pardon. This is asserted by Grotius in the passage above cited; and even the Rev. Richard Watson, whose excellent system of theology, or *Theological Institutes*, is deservedly in high repute among the Wesleyan Methodists, not only over and over defines justification as pardon, but elaborately argues the question. "The first point," he says, "which we find established by the language of the New Testament is, that justification, the pardon and remission of sins, the non-imputation of sin, and the imputation of righteousness, are terms and phrases of the same import."[16] He then goes on to try to establish that position.

If therefore, pardon and justification are distinct things – the one the executive act of a ruler, the other a judicial act; the one setting aside the demands of justice, the other a declaration

15. "Sacrificia non sunt solutiones debitorum, neque plenariæ pro peccatis satisfactiones; sed illis peractis conceditur gratuita peccati remissio." "Redemtionis pretium constitui solet pro libera æstimatione illius, qui captivum detinet" (*Theologia Christiana*, III, xxi, 6, 8, *ut supra*, 261, 1, 262).

16. II, xxiii; New York, 1832, 426.

that justice is satisfied – then those who reduce justification to mere pardon deny the doctrine of justification as understood and professed by the Lutheran and Reformed churches. It of course is not intended that these Remonstrant or Arminian theologians do not hold what they call justification; nor is it denied that they at times, at least, express their doctrine in the very language of the confessions of the Protestant churches. Thus the Remonstrants say,

> Justification is an act of God, which God at times produces purely in his own mind, because nothing is changed, as to will or decree, because he wishes to remit sin and impute righteousness to him who believes; that is, because he wishes not to inflict the punishment which his sins deserve, and so to influence and treat the righteous.[17]

Nevertheless, they tell us that they mean by this only pardon. Protestants, when they say justification includes pardon "and" the imputation of righteousness, mean two distinct things by pardon and imputation of righteousness. The Remonstrants regard them as identical, and, therefore, can use the very language of Protestants while rejecting their doctrine. As everyone knows that when a criminal is pardoned by the executive and allowed to resume his rights of property and right of voting, he is not thereby justified; so every candid mind must admit that there is an immense difference between the Remonstrant or Arminian doctrine of justification and that held as the cardinal principle of the Reformation by both Lutherans and Reformed.

This difference becomes still more apparent when we consider what the Arminians make the ground of justification. As they deny that Christ made any real satisfaction to divine justice (as distinguished from benevolence), so they deny that

The Arminians can use the very language of Protestants while rejecting their doctrine…. There is an immense difference between the Arminian doctrine of justification and that held as the cardinal principle of the Reformation by both Lutherans and Reformed.

17. "Justificatio est actio Dei, quam Deus pure pute in sua ipsius mente efficit, quia nihil aliud est, quam volitio aut decretum, quo peccata remittere, et justitiam imputare aliquando vult iis, qui credunt, id est, quo vult pœnas peccatis eorum promeritas, iis non infligere, eosque tanquam justos tractare et premio afficere" (*Apologia pro Confessione Remonstrantium*, cap. 11, 12; Episcopii *Opera*, Rotterdam, 1665, Volume II, 166, a, of second set).

the righteousness of Christ is imputed to the believer as the ground of his justification. On this point, Limborch says,

> That itself, which is imputed to us, is not the righteousness of Christ; indeed Scripture nowhere teaches that the righteousness of Christ is imputed to us, but only faith is imputed to us as righteousness and indeed because of Christ.[18]

And Curcellæus says,

> Not one Scripture teaches that the righteousness of Christ is imputed to us. And it is absurd. Indeed no one in himself unrighteous can be formally righteous with the righteousness that belongs to another, any more than an Ethiopian is white because of a whiteness that belongs to another.[19]

As the righteousness of Christ is not imputed to the believer, the ground of his justification – that which is accepted as righteousness – is faith and its fruits, or faith and evangelical obedience. On this subject Limborch says that under the new covenant God demands

> the obedience of faith, that is, not rigid and equal obedience from all, just as the law demands; but only as much as faith, that is, a certain conviction about divine promises, can produce in each man. In that God also overlooks our imperfections and faults, only with a sincere spirit may we concentrate on the observation of his commands and immediately be eager to make progress in those same commands.[20]

According to the Arminians, as the righteousness of Christ is not imputed to the believer, the ground of his justification – that which is accepted as righteousness – is faith and its fruits, or faith and evangelical obedience.

18. "Hæc autem, quæ nobis imputatur, non est Christi justitia; nusquam enim Scriptura docet, Christi justitiam nobis imputari; sed tantum fidem nobis imputari in justitiam, et quidem propter Christum" (*Theologia Christiana*, VI, iv, 18, *ut supra*, 703a).

19. "Nullibi docet Scriptura justitiam Christi nobis imputari. Et id absurdum est. Nemo enim in se injustus aliena justitia potest esse formaliter justus, no magis, quam aliena albedine Æthiops esse albus" (*Relig. Christ. Inst.* 7, 9, 6).

20. "obedientiam fidei, hoc est, non rigidam et omnibus æqualem prout exigebat lex; sed tantam, quantam fides, id est, certa de divinis promissionibus persuasio, in unoquoque efficere potest; in qua etiam Deus multas imperfectiones et lapsus condonat, modo animo sincero præceptorum ipsius observationi incumbamus, et continuo in eadem proficere studeamus" (*Theologia Christiana*, VI, iv, 37, *ut supra*, 706a).

And again, "God does not judge that the righteousness of men is perfect; no, he judges that it is imperfect, but he freely accepts that righteousness, which he judges imperfect, as if it were perfect."[21]

He, therefore, thus defines justification,

> It is a favorable valuation, or rather acceptance of our imperfect righteousness (which, if God wished to act inflexibly with us, could by no means stand in God's judgment) as perfect, because of Jesus Christ.[22]

The same view is presented when he speaks of faith in its relation to justification. Faith is said to be imputed for righteousness; but Limborch says, "It must be known that when we say that we are justified by means of faith, we do not exclude works that faith demands, just as a fruitful mother brings forth; but we include them."[23]

Again,

> Faith is a condition in us and required of us, so that we may obtain justification. And so it is such an act, which although having been seen is by no means perfect in itself, but failing in many things, nevertheless is accepted as full and complete by God, because of his favorable and very unrestrained will, and because of which God graciously wishes to attribute to man remission of sins and the reward of eternal life.[24]

"It must be known that when we say that we are justified by means of faith, we do not exclude works that faith demands, just as a fruitful mother brings forth; but we include them."
– Limborch

---

21. "Deus non judicat hominum justitiam esse perfectam, imo eam judicat esse imperfectam; sed justitiam, quam imperfectam judicat, gratiose accipit ac si perfecta esset" (*Theologia Christiana,* VI, iv, 41; 706b, 707a).

22. "Est gratiosa æstimatio, seu potius acceptatio justitiæ nostræ imperfectæ (quæ si Deus rigide nobiscum agere vellet, in judicio Dei nequaquam consistere posset) pro perfecta, propter Jesus Christum" (*Theologia Christiana,* VI, iv, 18; 703, 1).

23. " Sciendum, quando dicimus, nos fide justificari, nos non excludere opera, quæ fides exigit et tanquam fœcunda mater producit; sed ea includere" (*Theologia Christiana,* VI, iv, 32; 705b).

24. "Fides est conditio in nobis et a nobis requisita, ut justificationem consequamur. Est itaque talis actus, qui, licet in se spectatus perfectus nequaquam sit, sed in multis deficiens, tamen a Deo gratiosa et liberrima voluntate pro pleno et perfecto acceptatur et propter quem Deus homini gratiose remissionem peccatorum et vitæ æternæ præmium conferre vult" (*Theologia Christiana,* VI, iv, 31; 705a).

Fletcher says:

> With respect to the Christless law of paradisaical obedience, we entirely disclaim sinless perfection.
>
> We shall not be judged by that law, but by a law adapted to our present state and circumstances, a milder law, called the law of Christ.
>
> Our Heavenly Father never expects of us, in our debilitated state, the obedience of immortal Adam in paradise.[25]

Dr. Peck says, "The standard of character set up in the Gospel must be such as is practicable by man, fallen as he is. Coming up to this standard is what we call Christian perfection."[26]

Under the covenant of works as made with Adam, perfect obedience was the condition of acceptance with God and of eternal life; under the Gospel, for Christ's sake, imperfect, or evangelical obedience, is the ground of justification, that is, it is that (*propter quam*) on account of which God graciously grants us the remission of sin and the reward of eternal life.

Summary

We have then the three great systems. First, that of the Romanists which teaches that on account of the work of Christ God grants, through Christian baptism, an infusion of divine grace by which all sin is purged from the soul and all ground for the infliction of the penalty is removed and the sinner rendered inherently just or holy. This is the first justification. Then in virtue of the new principle of spiritual life thus imparted, the baptized or regenerated are enabled to perform good works, which are really meritorious and on account of which they are admitted to Heaven.

Second, the Arminian theory, that on account of what Christ has done, God is pleased to grant sufficient grace to all men and to accept the imperfect obedience which the believer is thus enabled to render in lieu of the perfect

"The standard of character set up in the Gospel must be such as is practicable by man, fallen as he is. Coming up to this standard is what we call Christian perfection."
– Peck

25. *Last Check to Antinomianism*, Section i; *Works*, New York, 1833, Volume II, 493-494.

26. *Christian Perfection*, New York, 1843, 294.

obedience required under the covenant made with Adam; and on account of that imperfect obedience, eternal life is graciously bestowed.

Third, the Protestant doctrine that Christ, as the representative and substitute of sinners or of his people, takes their place under the law; and in their name and in their behalf fulfils all righteousness, thereby making a real, perfect, and infinitely meritorious satisfaction to the law and justice of God. This righteousness is imputed, or set to the account of the believer, who is thereupon and on that account freely pardoned and pronounced righteous in the sight of God and entitled not only to the remission of sin but also to eternal life. Being united to Christ by faith, the believer becomes partaker of his life, so that it is not he that lives but Christ that lives in him; and the life which the believer now lives in the flesh is by faith in the Son of God who loved him and gave himself for him.

Comparison of the Different Doctrines

The first remark which suggests itself on the comparison of these several schemes is that the relation between the believer and Christ is far more close, peculiar, and constant on the Protestant scheme than on any other. He is dependent on him every hour – for the imputation of his righteousness, for the supplies of the Spirit of life, and for his care, guidance, and intercession. He must look to him continually, and continually exercise faith in him as an everpresent Savior in order to live. According to the other schemes, Christ has merely made the salvation of all men possible. There his work ended. According to Romanists, he has made it possible that God should give sanctifying grace in baptism; according to the Arminians, he has rendered it possible for him to give sufficient grace to all men whereby to sanctify and save themselves. We are well aware that this is theory; that the true people of God, whether Romanists or Remonstrants, do not look on Christ thus as a Savior afar off.[27] They doubtless have the same exercises

> *According to the other schemes, Christ has merely made the salvation of all men possible. There his work ended. According to Romanists, he has made it possible that God should give sanctifying grace in baptism; according to the Arminians, he has rendered it possible for him to give sufficient grace to all men whereby to sanctify and save themselves.*

27. That is, despite their church membership they do not believe Romanist or Arminian doctrine. – *Editor*

toward him that their fellow believers have; nevertheless, such is the doctrine. The doctrine places a great gulf between the soul and Christ.

Second, it hardly admits of question that the Protestant view conforms to the Scriptural mode of presenting the plan of salvation. Christ in the Bible is declared to be the head of his people, their representative; they were in him in such a sense that they died in him; they are raised with him and sit with him in heavenly places. They were in him as the race was in Adam, and as branches are in the vine. They individually receive the sprinkling of that blood which cleanses from all sin. They are constituted righteous by his obedience. As he was made sin for them, so are they made the righteousness of God in him. He is not an example of punishment as Grotius represents, a mere governmental device, but a sacrifice substituted for us on whose head every believer must lay his hand and to whom he must transfer the burden of his sins.

Third, what is included indeed in the above, but is so important and decisive as to require distinct and repeated mention: All schemes, other than the Protestant, refer the proximate ground of our acceptance with God to our own subjective character. It is because of our own goodness that we are regarded and treated as righteous. Conscience demands, the Scriptures reveal, and the believer instinctively seeks something better than that. His own goodness is badness. It cannot satisfy his own bleared vision; how then can it appear before the eyes of God? It matters not how the Romanist may exalt his "inward habits of grace" or how the Arminian may sublimate his evangelical obedience to perfection; neither can satisfy either the conscience or God.

Fourth, the Protestant doctrine is the only one on which the devout soul can live. This has been urged before when speaking of the work of Christ. It is fair to appeal from theology to hymnology. It is enough to say on this point that Lutheran and Reformed Christians can find nowhere, out of the Bible, more clear, definite, soul-satisfying expression of their doctrinal views upon this subject than are to be found in

All schemes, other than the Protestant, refer the proximate ground of our acceptance with God to our own subjective character.

many of the hymns of the Latin and Arminian churches. As a single example may be cited the following stanzas from John Wesley's "Hymns and Spiritual Songs":

> Join, Earth and Heaven to bless
> The Lord our Righteousness.
> The mystery of redemption this,
> This the Savior's strange design –
> Man's offence was counted his,
> Ours his righteousness divine.
>
> In him complete we shine;
> His death, his life, is mine;
> Fully am I justified;
> Free from sin, and more than free,
> Guiltless, since for me he died;
> Righteous, since he lived for me.

In him complete we shine; his death, his life, is mine; fully am I justified; free from sin, and more than free, guiltless, since for me he died; righteous, since he lived for me.

Scripture Index

Index

Foxe, John 102, 103
free decision 271
friends 114, 125
fruit 220
fulfillment 12
full surrender 11
future 136

Galatia 145
Galatians 160, 208
Galilee 93
Gentiles 48, 145, 147, 153, 157, 160, 175, 178, 197, 217, 219, 236-237, 238
Gethsemane 37, 83, 93
gifts 132, 249
glory 42, 51-54, 65, 93-94, 96-98, 110, 116, 177, 201, 254, 266
God 19, 22, 27, 39, 42-44, 49, 60, 77, 81, 87-88, 112, 132, 155-156, 167, 173, 183-184, 214; acceptance with 17, 149, 151, 157-159, 171-172, 176, 185, 187-190, 195, 209, 215, 220-222, 228, 230, 234, 239-240, 256, 260, 262, 280-281, 283; approval of 258; benevolence of 213; cause of justification 254; character of 201; covenant with Adam 215; curse of 67, 251, 264; dealings with elect 65, 70; dealings with man 25-26; exaltation of Christ 51; faith in 259; Father 18, 20, 23, 34, 37, 38, 40, 42, 47-49, 51, 61-62, 68, 72, 82, 94-93, 98, 113, 122, 162, 179, 227, 229, 232, 243, 252, 255, 266, 275, 281; favor of 35; forgiveness from 56; gifts of 62, 256; glory of 177, 179, 254; grace of 2, 10, 67, 111, 146, 160, 162, 271; holiness of 28, 176; Holy

Spirit 11, 16, 20, 40, 50-51, 54, 60, 76, 80, 90, 103, 118-119, 123, 125-126, 129, 131, 135, 142-143, 158, 160, 167-168, 171, 182-183, 197, 214, 220, 243-244, 249-250, 254-255, 263-264, 266, 269, 270-272, 282; image of 172; immutability of 23; Jehovah 19, 32, 37, 45-46, 59, 62-63, 67, 71, 80, 252; joy in 15; Judge 18, 28, 37, 56, 71, 229, 265; judgment of 196, 209; judicial demands of 75; justice of 67, 107, 176, 180, 191, 193, 197, 199-211, 204, 208, 210, 234, 264, 282; justification before 76; justification by 67; kindness of 178; law of 10, 21, 73, 107, 150, 153-154, 189-190, 191, 227; love for 69, 217; love of 29, 46, 50, 56, 62, 74, 84, 113-114, 117, 122, 124, 129, 132, 135, 176-178, 180, 203, 205, 235; mercy of 71, 102-103, 107, 179; merit before 142; nearness to 136; peace of 16; peace with 106-107, 115-116, 201, 204; power of 162, 171, 176, 197, 235-236; praise of 203; promise of 108, 251; quickening of 169; reconciliation with 29, 104, 161, 163, 207, 220, 238, 243; redemption to 52; remembrance of 114; revelation of 243; righteousness of 13, 22, 62, 64-78, 117, 163, 175, 217, 224, 236-237, 241, 245, 255, 267, 283; righteousness before 143; salvation from 57; salvation of 242; satisfaction to 270; Savior 32; Son of God 20, 162, 168, 170-173, 182, 195, 202, 220, 243, 247, 252, 266-

The Crisis of Our Time

HISTORIANS have christened the thirteenth century the Age of Faith and termed the eighteenth century the Age of Reason. The present age has been called many things: the Atomic Age, the Age of Inflation, the Age of the Tyrant, the Age of Aquarius; but it deserves one name more than the others: the Age of Irrationalism. Contemporary secular intellectuals are anti-intellectual. Contemporary philosophers are anti-philosophy. Contemporary theologians are anti-theology.

In past centuries, secular philosophers have generally believed that knowledge is possible to man. Consequently they expended a great deal of thought and effort trying to justify knowledge. In the twentieth century, however, the optimism of the secular philosophers all but disappeared. They despaired of knowledge.

Like their secular counterparts, the great theologians and doctors of the church taught that knowledge is possible to man. Yet the theologians of the present age also repudiated that belief. They too despaired of knowledge. This radical skepticism has penetrated our entire culture, from television to music to literature. *The Christian at the beginning of the twenty-first century is confronted with an overwhelming cultural consensus – sometimes stated explicitly but most often implicitly: Man does not and cannot know anything truly.*

What does this have to do with Christianity? Simply this: If man can know nothing truly, man can truly know nothing. We cannot know that the Bible is the Word of God, that Christ died for his people, or that Christ is alive today at the right hand of the Father. Unless knowledge is possible, Christianity is nonsensical, for it claims to be knowledge. What is at stake at the beginning of the twenty-first century is not simply a single doctrine, such as the virgin birth, or the existence of Hell, as important as those doctrines may be, but the whole of Christianity itself. If knowledge is not possible to man, it is worse than silly to argue points of doctrine – it is insane.

The irrationalism of the present age is so thoroughgoing and pervasive that even the Remnant – the segment of the professing church that remains faithful – has accepted much of it, frequently without even being aware of what it is accepting. In some religious circles this irrationalism has become synonymous with piety and humility, and those who oppose it are denounced as rationalists, as though to be logical were a sin. Our contemporary anti-theologians make a contradiction and call it a Mystery. The faithful ask for truth and are given Paradox and Antinomy. If any balk at swallowing the absurdities of the anti-theologians who teach in the seminaries or have graduated from the seminaries, they are frequently marked as heretics or schismatics who seek to act independently of God.

There is no greater threat facing the church of Christ at this moment than the irrationalism that now controls our entire culture. Totalitarianism, guilty of tens of millions of murders – including those of millions of Christians – is to be feared, but not nearly so much as the idea that we do not and cannot know the literal truth. Hedonism, the popular philosophy of America, is not to be feared so much as the belief that logic – that "mere human logic," to use the religious irrationalists' own phrase – is futile. The attacks on truth, on knowledge, on propositional revelation, on the intellect, on words, and on logic are renewed daily. But note well: The misologists – the haters of logic – use logic to demonstrate the futility of using logic. The anti-intellectuals construct intricate intellectual arguments to prove the insufficiency of the intellect. Those who deny the competence of words to express thought use words to express their thoughts. The proponents of poetry, myth, metaphor, and analogy argue for their theories by using literal prose, whose competence – even whose possibility – they deny. The anti-theologians use the revealed Word of God to show that there can be no revealed Word of God – or that if there could, it would remain impenetrable darkness and Mystery to our finite minds.

Nonsense Has Come

Is it any wonder that the world is grasping at straws – the straws of experientialism, mysticism, and drugs? After all, if people are told that the Bible contains insoluble mysteries, then is not a flight into mysticism to be expected? On what grounds can it be condemned? Certainly not on logical grounds or Biblical grounds, if logic is futile and the Bible unknowable. Moreover, if it cannot be condemned on logical or Biblical grounds, it cannot be condemned at all. If people are going to have a religion of the mysterious, they will not adopt Christianity: They will have a genuine mystery religion. The popularity of mysticism, drugs, and religious experience is the logical consequence of the irrationalism of the present age. There can and will be no Christian reformation – and no restoration of a free society – unless and until the irrationalism of the age is totally repudiated by Christians.

The Church Defenseless

Yet how shall they do it? The official spokesmen for Christianity have been fatally infected with irrationalism. The seminaries, which annually train thousands of men to teach millions of Christians, are the finishing schools of irrationalism, completing the job begun by the government schools and colleges. Most of the pulpits of the conservative churches (we are not speaking of the obviously apostate churches) are occupied by graduates of the anti-theological schools. These products of modern anti-theological education, when asked to give a reason for the hope that is in them, can generally respond with only the intellectual analogue of a shrug – a mumble about Mystery. They have not grasped – and therefore cannot teach those for whom they are responsible – the first truth: "And you shall know the truth." Many, in fact, explicitly contradict Christ, saying that, at best, we possess only "pointers" to the truth, or something "similar" to the truth, a mere analogy. Is the impotence of the Christian church a puzzle? Is the fascination with Pentecostalism, faith healing, Eastern Orthodoxy, and Roman Catholicism – all sensate and anti-intellectual religions – among members of Christian churches an enigma? Not when one understands the pious nonsense that is purveyed in the name of God in the religious colleges and seminaries.

The Trinity Foundation

The creators of The Trinity Foundation firmly believe that theology is too important to be left to the licensed theologians – the graduates of the schools of theology. They have created The Trinity Foundation for the express purpose of teaching believers all that the Scriptures contain – not warmed over, baptized, Antichristian philosophies. Each member of the board of directors of The Trinity Foundation has signed this oath: "I believe that the Bible alone and the Bible in its entirety is the Word of God and, therefore, inerrant in the autographs. I believe that the system of truth presented in the Bible is best summarized in the *Westminster Confession of Faith*. So help me God."

The ministry of The Trinity Foundation is the presentation of the system of truth taught in Scripture as clearly and as completely as possible. We do not regard obscurity as a virtue, nor confusion as a sign of spirituality. Confusion, like all error, is sin, and teaching that confusion is all that Christians can hope for is doubly sin.

The presentation of the truth of Scripture necessarily involves the rejection of error. The Foundation has exposed and will continue to expose the irrationalism of the present age, whether its current spokesman be an existentialist philosopher or a professed Reformed theologian. We oppose anti-intellectualism, whether it be espoused by a Neo-orthodox theologian or a fundamentalist evangelist. We reject misology, whether it be on the lips of a Neo-evangelical or those of a Roman Catholic Charismatic. We repudiate agnosticism, whether it be secular or religious. To each error we bring the brilliant light of Scripture, proving all things, and holding fast to that which is true.

The Primacy of Theory

The ministry of The Trinity Foundation is not a "practical" ministry. If you are a pastor, we will not enlighten you on how to organize an ecumenical prayer meeting in your community or how to double church attendance in a year. If you are a homemaker, you will have to read elsewhere to find out how to become a total woman. If you are a businessman, we will not tell you how to develop a social conscience. The professing church is drowning in such "practical" advice.

The Trinity Foundation is unapologetically theoretical in its outlook, believing that theory without practice is dead, and that practice without theory is blind. The trouble with the professing church is not primarily in its practice, but in its theory. Churchgoers and teachers do not know, and many do not even care to know, the doctrines of Scripture. Doctrine is intellectual, and churchgoers and teachers are generally anti-intellectual. Doctrine is ivory tower philosophy, and they scorn ivory towers. The ivory tower, however, is the control tower of a civilization. It is a fundamental, theoretical mistake of the "practical" men to think that they can be merely practical, for practice is always the practice of some theory. The relationship between theory and practice is the relationship between cause and effect. If a person believes correct theory, his practice will tend to be correct. The practice of contemporary Christians is immoral because it is the practice of false theories. It is a major theoretical mistake of the "practical" men to think that they can ignore the ivory towers of the philosophers and theologians as irrelevant to their lives. Every action that "practical" men take is governed by the thinking that has occurred in some ivory tower – whether that tower be the

British Museum; the Academy; a home in Basel, Switzerland; or a tent in Israel.

In Understanding Be Men

It is the first duty of the Christian to understand correct theory – correct doctrine – and thereby implement correct practice. This order – first theory, then practice – is both logical and Biblical. It is, for example, exhibited in Paul's *Epistle to the Romans,* in which he spends the first eleven chapters expounding theory and the last five discussing practice. The contemporary teachers of Christians have not only reversed the Biblical order, they have inverted the Pauline emphasis on theory and practice. The virtually complete failure of the teachers of the professing church to instruct believers in correct doctrine is the cause of the misconduct and spiritual and cultural impotence of Christians. The church's lack of power is the result of its lack of truth. The *Gospel* is the power of God, not religious experiences or personal relationships. The church has no power because it has abandoned the Gospel, the good news, for a religion of experientialism. Twentieth-first-century American churchgoers are children carried about by every wind of doctrine, not knowing what they believe, or even if they believe anything for certain.

The chief purpose of The Trinity Foundation is to counteract the irrationalism of the age and to expose the errors of the teachers of the church. Our emphasis – on the Bible as the sole source of knowledge, on the primacy of truth, on the supreme importance of correct doctrine, and on the necessity for systematic and logical thinking – is almost unique in Christendom. To the extent that the church survives – and she will survive and flourish – it will be because of her increasing acceptance of these basic ideas and their logical implications.

We believe that The Trinity Foundation is filling a vacuum in Christendom. We are saying that Christianity is intellectually defensible – that, in fact, it is the only intellectually defensible system of thought. We are saying that God has made the wisdom of this world – whether that wisdom be called science, religion, philosophy, or common sense – foolishness. We are appealing to all Christians who have not conceded defeat in the intellectual battle with the world to join us in our efforts to raise a standard to which all men of sound mind can repair.

The love of truth, of God's Word, has all but disappeared in our time. We are committed to and pray for a great instauration. But though we may not see this reformation in our lifetimes, we believe it is our duty to present the whole counsel of God, because Christ has commanded it. The results of our teaching are in God's hands, not ours. Whatever those results, his Word is never taught in vain, but always accomplishes the result that he intended it to accomplish. Professor Gordon H. Clark has stated our view well:

> There have been times in the history of God's people, for example, in the days of Jeremiah, when refreshing grace and widespread revival were not to be expected: The time was one of chastisement. If this twentieth century is of a similar nature, individual Christians here and there can find comfort and strength in a study of God's Word. But if God has decreed happier days for us, and if we may expect a world-shaking and genuine spiritual awakening, then it is the author's belief that a zeal for souls, however necessary, is not the sufficient condition. Have there not been devout saints in every age, numerous enough to carry on a revival? Twelve such persons are plenty. What distinguishes the arid ages from the period of the Reformation, when nations were moved as they had not been since Paul preached in Ephesus, Corinth, and Rome, is the latter's fullness of knowledge of God's Word. To echo an early Reformation thought, when the ploughman and the garage attendant know the Bible as well as the theologian does, and know it better than some contemporary theologians, then the desired awakening shall have already occurred.

In addition to publishing books, the Foundation publishes a monthly newsletter, *The Trinity Review*. Subscriptions to *The Review* are free to U.S. addresses; please write to the address on the order form to become a subscriber. If you would like further information or would like to support our work, please let us know.

The Trinity Foundation is a non-profit foundation, tax exempt under section 501 (c)(3) of the Internal Revenue Code of 1954. You can help us disseminate the Word of God through your tax-deductible contributions to the Foundation.

JOHN W. ROBBINS

Intellectual Ammunition

T HE Trinity Foundation is committed to bringing every philosophical and theological thought captive to Christ. The books listed below are designed to accomplish that goal. They are written with two subordinate purposes: (1) to demolish all non-Christian claims to knowledge; and (2) to build a system of truth based upon the Bible alone.

Philosophy

Ancient Philosophy
Gordon H. Clark   Trade paperback $24.95
This book covers the thousand years from the Pre-Socratics to Plotinus. It represents some of the early work of Dr. Clark – the work that made his academic reputation. It is an excellent college text.

Behaviorism and Christianity
Gordon H. Clark   Trade paperback $5.95
Behaviorism is a critique of both secular and religious behaviorists. It includes chapters on John Watson, Edgar S. Singer, Jr., Gilbert Ryle, B. F. Skinner, and Donald MacKay. Clark's refutation of behaviorism and his argument for a Christian doctrine of man are unanswerable.

Christ and Civilization
John W. Robbins   Trade paperback $3.95

Civilization as we know it is a result of the widespread proclamation and belief of the Gospel of justification by faith alone in the sixteenth century. Christ foretold this result in the Sermon on the Mount: "Seek first the Kingdom of God and his righteousness, and all these things will be added to you."

This brief overview of the history of western civilization makes it clear that our cultural debt is to the Gospel, not to Greece and Rome.

Christian Philosophy   Hardback $29.95
Gordon H. Clark   Trade paperback $21.95

This book, Volume 4 in *The Works of Gordon Haddon Clark*, combines three of his most important works in philosophy: *Three Types of Religious Philosophy*; *Religion, Reason and Revelation*; and *An Introduction to Christian Philosophy*. Together they constitute Dr. Clark's principal statement of his Christian philosophy.

A Christian Philosophy of Education   Hardback $18.95
Gordon H. Clark   Trade paperback $12.95

The first edition of this book was published in 1946. It sparked the contemporary interest in Christian schools. In the 1970s, Dr. Clark thoroughly revised and updated it, and it is needed now more than ever. Its chapters include: The Need for a World-View; The Christian World-View; The Alternative to Christian Theism; Neutrality; Ethics; The Christian Philosophy of Education; Academic Matters; and Kindergarten to University. Three appendices are included: The Relationship of Public Education to Christianity; A Protestant World-View; and Art and the Gospel.

A Christian View of Men and Things Hardback $29.95
Gordon H. Clark Trade paperback $18.95

No other book achieves what *A Christian View* does: the presentation of Christianity as it applies to history, politics, ethics, science, religion, and epistemology. Dr. Clark's command of both worldly philosophy and Scripture is evident on every page, and the result is a breathtaking and invigorating challenge to the wisdom of this world. This is Volume 1 in *The Works of Gordon Haddon Clark.*

Clark Speaks from the Grave
Gordon H. Clark Trade paperback $3.95

Dr. Clark chides some of his critics for their failure to defend Christianity competently. *Clark Speaks* is a stimulating and illuminating discussion of the errors of contemporary apologists.

Ecclesiastical Megalomania: The Economic and Political Thought of the Roman Catholic Church
John W. Robbins Hardback $29.95

This detailed and thorough analysis and critique of the social teaching of the Roman Church-State is the only such book available by a Christian economist and political philosopher. The book's conclusions reveal the Roman Church-State to be an advocate of its own brand of faith-based fascism. *Ecclesiastical Megalomania* includes the complete text of the *Donation of Constantine* and Lorenzo Valla's exposé of the hoax.

Education, Christianity, and the State
J. Gresham Machen Trade paperback $10.95

Machen was one of the foremost educators, theologians, and defenders of Christianity in the twentieth century. The author of several scholarly books, Machen saw clearly that if Christianity is to survive and flourish, a system of Christian schools must be established. This collection of essays and speeches captures his thoughts on education over nearly three decades.

Essays on Ethics and Politics
Gordon H. Clark   Trade paperback $10.95
   Dr. Clark's essays, written over the course of five decades, are a major statement of Christian ethics.

Gordon H. Clark: Personal Recollections
John W. Robbins, editor   Trade paperback $6.95
   Friends of Dr. Clark have written their recollections of the man. Contributors include family members, colleagues, students, and friends such as Harold Lindsell, Carl Henry, Ronald Nash, and Anna Marie Hager.

Historiography: Secular and Religious
Gordon H. Clark   Trade paperback $13.95
   In this masterful work, Dr. Clark applies his philosophy to the writing of history, examining all the major schools of historiography.

An Introduction to Christian Philosophy
Gordon H. Clark
   See *Christian Philosophy.*

Language and Theology
Gordon H. Clark   Trade paperback $9.95
   There were two main currents in twentieth-century philosophy – Language Philosophy and Existentialism. Both were hostile to Christianity. Dr. Clark disposes of Language Philosophy in this brilliant critique of Bertrand Russell, Ludwig Wittgenstein, Rudolf Carnap, A. J. Ayer, Langdon Gilkey, and many others.

Logic
Gordon H. Clark   Hardback $16.95
   Written as a textbook for Christian schools, *Logic* is another unique book from Dr. Clark's pen. His presen-

tation of the laws of thought, which must be followed if Scripture is to be understood correctly, and which are found in Scripture itself, is both clear and thorough. *Logic* is an indispensable book for the thinking Christian.

Lord God of Truth, Concerning the Teacher
Gordon H. Clark and
Aurelius Augustine   Trade paperback $7.95
   This essay by Dr. Clark summarizes many of the most telling arguments against empiricism and defends the Biblical teaching that we know God and truth immediately. The dialogue by Augustine is a refutation of empirical language philosophy.

The Philosophy of Science and Belief in God
Gordon H. Clark   Trade paperback $8.95
   In opposing the contemporary idolatry of science, Dr. Clark analyzes three major aspects of science: the problem of motion, Newtonian science, and modern theories of physics. His conclusion is that science, while it may be useful, is always false; and he demonstrates its falsity in numerous ways. Since science is always false, it can offer no alternative to the Bible and Christianity.

Religion, Reason and Revelation
Gordon H. Clark   Trade paperback $10.95
   One of Dr. Clark's apologetical masterpieces, *Religion, Reason and Revelation* has been praised for the clarity of its thought and language. It includes these chapters: Is Christianity a Religion? Faith and Reason; Inspiration and Language; Revelation and Morality; and God and Evil. It is must reading for all serious Christians.
   See also *Christian Philosophy*.

The Scripturalism of Gordon H. Clark
W. Gary Crampton   Trade paperback $9.95
   Dr. Crampton has written an introduction to the philosophy of Gordon H. Clark that is helpful to both

beginners and advanced students of theology. This book includes a bibliography of Dr. Clark's works.

Thales to Dewey: A History of Philosophy   Hardback $29.95
Gordon H. Clark   Trade paperback $21.95
   This is the best one-volume history of philosophy in print. This is Volume 3 in *The Works of Gordon Haddon Clark.*

Three Types of Religious Philosophy
Gordon H. Clark
   See *Christian Philosophy.*

William James and John Dewey
Gordon H. Clark   Trade paperback $8.95
   William James and John Dewey are two of the most influential philosophers America has produced. Their philosophies of instrumentalism and pragmatism are hostile to Christianity, and Dr. Clark demolishes their arguments.

Without A Prayer: Ayn Rand and the Close of Her System
John W. Robbins   Hardback $27.95
   Ayn Rand has been a best-selling author since 1957. *Without A Prayer* discusses Objectivism's epistemology, theology, ethics, and politics in detail. Appendices include analyses of books by Leonard Peikoff and David Kelley, as well as several essays on Christianity and philosophy.

Theology

Against the Churches: The Trinity Review 1989-1998
John W. Robbins, editor   Oversize hardback $39.95
   This is the second volume of essays from *The Trinity Review*, covering its second ten years, 1989-1998. This volume, like the first, is fully indexed and is very useful in research and in the classroom. Authors include: Gordon

Clark, John Robbins, Charles Hodge, J. C. Ryle, Horatius Bonar, and Robert L. Dabney.

Against the World: The Trinity Review 1978-1988
John W. Robbins, editor   Oversize hardback $34.95
   This is a clothbound collection of the essays published in *The Trinity Review* from 1978 to 1988, 70 in all. It is a valuable source of information and arguments explaining and defending Christianity.

The Atonement
Gordon H. Clark   Trade paperback $8.95
   In *The Atonement,* Dr. Clark discusses the covenants, the virgin birth and incarnation, federal headship and representation, the relationship between God's sovereignty and justice, and much more. He analyzes traditional views of the atonement and criticizes them in the light of Scripture alone.

The Biblical Doctrine of Man
Gordon H. Clark   Trade paperback $6.95
   Is man soul and body or soul, spirit, and body? What is the image of God? Is Adam's sin imputed to his children? Is evolution true? Are men totally depraved? What is the heart? These are some of the questions discussed and answered from Scripture in this book.

By Scripture Alone
W. Gary Crampton   Trade paperback $12.95
   This is a clear and thorough explanation of the Scriptural doctrine of Scripture and a refutation of the recent Romanist attack on Scripture as the Word of God.

Can the Orthodox Presbyterian Church Be Saved?
John W. Robbins   Trade paperback $3.95
   This small book, which demonstrates the central errors of OPC history and theology since the 1940s, is an alarm to awaken members of the OPC from their slumbers.

The Changing of the Guard

Mark W. Karlberg   Trade paperback $3.95

    This essay is a critical discussion of Westminster Seminary's anti-Reformational and un-Biblical teaching on the doctrine of justification. Dr. Karlberg exposes the doctrine of justification by faith and works – not *sola fide* – taught at Westminster Seminary for the past 25 years, by Professors Norman Shepherd, Richard Gaffin, John Frame, and others.

Christianity and Neo-Liberalism: The Spiritual Crisis in the Orthodox Presbyterian Church and Beyond

Paul M. Elliott   Trade paperback $19.95

    This massively-documented book details the influence Westminster Theological Seminary has had on the Orthodox Presbyterian Church and other churches and organizations. It is both a work of theological analysis and a call to action.

The Church Effeminate

John W. Robbins, editor   Hardback $29.95

    This is a collection of 39 essays by the best theologians of the church on the doctrine of the church: Martin Luther, John Calvin, Benjamin Warfield, Gordon Clark, J. C. Ryle, and many more. The essays cover the structure, function, and purpose of the church.

The Clark-Van Til Controversy

Herman Hoeksema   Trade paperback $9.95

    This collection of essays by the founder of the Protestant Reformed Churches – essays written at the time of the Clark-Van Til controversy in the 1940s – is one of the best commentaries on those events in print.

A Companion to The Current Justification Controversy

John W. Robbins   Trade paperback $9.95

    This book includes documentary source material not available in *The Current Justification Controversy*, an essay tracing the origins and continuation of this controversy throughout American Presbyterian churches, and an essay on the New Perspective on Paul by Robert L. Reymond.

Cornelius Van Til: The Man and The Myth
John W. Robbins   Trade paperback $2.45
　　The actual teachings of this eminent Philadelphia theologian have been obscured by the myths that surround him. This book penetrates those myths and criticizes Van Til's surprisingly unorthodox views of God and the Bible.

The Current Justification Controversy
O. Palmer Robertson   Trade paperback $9.95
　　From 1975 to 1982 a controversy over justification raged within Westminster Theological Seminary and the Philadelphia Presbytery of the Orthodox Presbyterian Church. As a member of the faculties of both Westminster and Covenant Seminaries during this period, O. Palmer Robertson was an important participant in this controversy. This is his account of the controversy, vital background for understanding the defection from the Gospel that is now widespread in Presbyterian churches.

The Everlasting Righteousness
Horatius Bonar   Trade paperback $8.95
　　Originally published in 1874, the language of Bonar's masterpiece on justification by faith alone has been updated and Americanized for easy reading and clear understanding. This is one of the best books ever written on justification.
　　See also *Not What My Hands Have Done*.

Faith and Saving Faith
Gordon H. Clark
　　See *What Is Saving Faith?*

God and Evil: The Problem Solved
Gordon H. Clark   Trade paperback $5.95
   This volume is Chapter 5 of *Religion, Reason and Revelation,* in which Dr. Clark presents his solution to the problem of evil.

God-Breathed: The Divine Inspiration of the Bible
Louis Gaussen   Trade paperback $16.95
   Gaussen, a nineteenth-century Swiss Reformed pastor, comments on hundreds of passages in which the Bible claims to be the Word of God. This is a massive defense of the doctrine of the plenary and verbal inspiration of Scripture.

God's Hammer: The Bible and Its Critics
Gordon H. Clark   Trade paperback $10.95
   The starting point of Christianity, the doctrine on which all other doctrines depend, is "The Bible alone, and the Bible in its entirety, is the Word of God written, and, therefore, inerrant in the autographs." Over the centuries the opponents of Christianity, with Satanic shrewdness, have concentrated their attacks on the truthfulness and completeness of the Bible. In the twentieth century the attack was not so much in the fields of history and archaeology as in philosophy. Dr. Clark's brilliant defense of the complete truthfulness of the Bible is captured in this collection of eleven major essays.

The Holy Spirit
Gordon H. Clark   Trade paperback $8.95
   This discussion of the third person of the Trinity is both concise and exact. Dr. Clark includes chapters on the work of the Spirit, sanctification, and Pentecostalism.

The Incarnation
Gordon H. Clark   Trade paperback $8.95
   Who is Christ? The attack on the doctrine of the Incarnation in the nineteenth and twentieth centuries was

vigorous, but the orthodox response was lame. Dr. Clark reconstructs the doctrine of the Incarnation, building and improving upon the Chalcedonian definition.

The Johannine Logos
Gordon H. Clark   Trade paperback $5.95
 Dr. Clark analyzes the relationship between Christ, who is the truth, and the Bible. He explains why John used the same word to refer to both Christ and his teaching. Chapters deal with the Prologue to John's Gospel; *Logos* and *Rheemata*; Truth; and Saving Faith.
 See also *What Is Saving Faith?*

Justification by Faith Alone
Charles Hodge   Trade paperback $10.95
 Charles Hodge of Princeton Seminary was the best American theologian of the nineteenth century. Here, for the first time, are his two major essays on justification in one volume. This book is essential in defending the faith.
 See also *Not What My Hands Have Done.*

Karl Barth's Theological Method
Gordon H. Clark   Trade paperback $18.95
 Karl Barth's Theological Method is perhaps the best critique of the Neo-orthodox theologian Karl Barth ever written. Dr. Clark discusses Barth's view of revelation, language, and Scripture, focusing on his method of writing theology, rather than presenting a comprehensive analysis of the details of Barth's theology.

Logical Criticisms of Textual Criticism
Gordon H. Clark   Trade paperback $3.25
 Dr. Clark's acute mind enables him to demonstrate the inconsistencies, assumptions, and flights of fancy that characterize the science of New Testament criticism.
 See also *Commentaries on Paul's Letters.*

Not Reformed at All:
Medievalsim in "Reformed" Churches
John Robbins and Sean Gerety   Trade paperback $9.95
    This book is a response to and refutation of Douglas
Wilson's book *"Reformed" Is Not Enough: Recovering the Ob-jectivity of the Covenant.* Wilson, one of the leading figures
in the Neolegalist movement in Reformed and Presbyte-
rian circles, attacked covenant theology and proposed a
"visible, photographable" covenant which one enters by
ritual baptism, making one a Christian. That salvation can
be lost by one's own lack of performance or by action of
authorized representatives of the church. This refutation
of Wilson is a defense of the Covenant of Grace.

Not What My Hands Have Done
Charles Hodge, Horatius Bonar   Trade paperback $16.95
    This is the combined edition of *Justification by Faith
Alone* (by Hodge) and *The Everlasting Righteousness* (by
Bonar). Combined, these books offer both an introduc-
tion to and an in-depth discussion of the central doctrine
of Christianity, justification by faith alone.

Predestination
Gordon H. Clark   Trade paperback $10.95
    Dr. Clark thoroughly discusses one of the most contro-
versial and pervasive doctrines of the Bible: that God is,
quite literally, Almighty. Free will, the origin of evil, God's
omniscience, creation, and the new birth are all presented
within a Scriptural framework. The objections of those
who do not believe in Almighty God are considered and
refuted. This edition also contains the text of the booklet,
Predestination in the Old Testament.

Sanctification
Gordon H. Clark   Trade paperback $8.95
    In this book Dr. Clark discusses historical theories of
sanctification, the sacraments, and the Biblical doctrine
of sanctification.

Study Guide to the Westminster Confession

W. Gary Crampton   Oversize paperback $10.95

This *Study Guide* can be used by individuals or classes. It contains a paragraph-by-paragraph summary of the *Westminster Confession,* and questions for the student to answer. Space for answers is provided. The *Guide* will be most beneficial when used in conjunction with Dr. Clark's *What Do Presbyterians Believe?*

A Theology of the Holy Spirit

Frederick Dale Bruner   Trade paperback $16.95

First published in 1970, this book has been hailed by reviewers as "thorough," "fair," "comprehensive," "devastating," "the most significant book on the Holy Spirit," and "scholarly." Gordon Clark described this book in his own book *The Holy Spirit* as "a masterly and exceedingly well researched exposition of Pentecostalism. The documentation is superb, as is also his penetrating analysis of their non-scriptural and sometimes contradictory conclusions." Unfortunately, the book is marred by the author's sacramentarianism.

The Trinity

Gordon H. Clark   Trade paperback $8.95

Apart from the doctrine of Scripture, no teaching of the Bible is more fundamental than the doctrine of God. Dr. Clark's defense of the orthodox doctrine of the Trinity is a principal portion of his systematic theology. There are chapters on the Deity of Christ; Augustine; the Incomprehensibility of God; Bavinck and Van Til; and the Holy Spirit; among others.

What Calvin Says

W. Gary Crampton   Trade paperback $10.95

This is a clear, readable, and thorough introduction to the theology of John Calvin.

What Do Presbyterians Believe?
Gordon H. Clark   Trade paperback $10.95
    This classic is the best commentary on the *Westminster Confession of Faith* ever written.

What Is Saving Faith?
Gordon H. Clark   Trade paperback $12.95
    This is the combined edition of *Faith and Saving Faith* and *The Johannine Logos.* The views of the Roman Catholic Church, John Calvin, Thomas Manton, John Owen, Charles Hodge, and B. B. Warfield are discussed in this book. Is the object of faith a person or a proposition? Is faith more than belief? Is belief thinking with assent, as Augustine said? In a world chaotic with differing views of faith, Dr. Clark clearly explains the Biblical view of faith and saving faith.

    In *The Johannine Logos*, Dr. Clark analyzes the relationship between Christ, who is the truth, and the Bible. He explains why John used the same word to refer to both Christ and his teaching. Chapters deal with the Prologue to John's Gospel; *Logos* and *Rheemata;* Truth; and Saving Faith.

Clark's Commentaries on the New Testament

Colossians	Trade paperback	$6.95
Commentaries on Paul's Letters		
(*Colossians, Ephesians, 1 and 2*		
Thessalonians, Logical Criticisms	Hardback	$29.95
of Textual Criticism)	Trade paperback	$21.95
First Corinthians	Trade paperback	$10.95
First John	Trade paperback	$10.95
New Heavens, New Earth		
(*First* and *Second Peter*)	Trade paperback	$10.95
The Pastoral Epistles	Hardback	$29.95
(*1 and 2 Timothy* and *Titus*)	Trade paperback	$14.95
Philippians	Trade paperback	$9.95

All of Clark's commentaries are expository, not technical, and are written for the Christian layman. His purpose is to explain the text clearly and accurately so that the Word of God will be thoroughly known by every Christian.

The Trinity Library

We will send you one copy of each of the books listed above for $500 (retail value $800), postpaid to any address in the U.S. You may also order the books you want individually on the order form on the next page. Because some of the books are in short supply, we must reserve the right to substitute others of equal or greater value in The Trinity Library. This special offer expires October 31, 2008.

Order Form

NAME   _____

ADDRESS   _____

_____

TELEPHONE _____

E-MAIL   _____

Please:

❏ add my name to the mailing list for The Trinity Review. I understand that there is no charge for single copies of The Review sent to a U. S. address.

❏ accept my tax deductible contribution of $ _____ .

❏ send me _____ copies of *Not What My Hands Have Done*. I enclose as payment U. S. $ _____ .

❏ send me the Trinity Library. I enclose U. S. $500 as full payment.

❏ send me the following books. I enclose full payment in the amount of $_____ for them.

_____

_____

_____

_____

The Trinity Foundation
Post Office Box 68
Unicoi, Tennessee 37692
Website: http://www.trinityfoundation.org/
United States of America

Shipping: Please add $6.00 for the first book, and 50 cents for each additional book. For foreign orders, please add $1.00 for each additional book.